# Comfort

# Comfort

*An Atlas for the Body and Soul*

$\infty$

# Brett C. Hoover

RIVERHEAD BOOKS

*New York*

**RIVERHEAD BOOKS**
**Published by the Penguin Group**
**Penguin Group (USA) Inc.**
**375 Hudson Street, New York, New York 10014, USA**
Penguin Group (Canada), 90 Eglinton Avenue East, Suite 700, Toronto, Ontario M4P 2Y3, Canada
(a division of Pearson Penguin Canada Inc.)
Penguin Books Ltd., 80 Strand, London WC2R 0RL, England
Penguin Group Ireland, 25 St. Stephen's Green, Dublin 2, Ireland (a division of Penguin Books Ltd.)
Penguin Group (Australia), 250 Camberwell Road, Camberwell, Victoria 3124, Australia
(a division of Pearson Australia Group Pty. Ltd.)
Penguin Books India Pvt. Ltd., 11 Community Centre, Panchsheel Park, New Delhi—110 017, India
Penguin Group (NZ), 67 Apollo Drive, Rosedale, Auckland 0632, New Zealand
(a division of Pearson New Zealand Ltd.)
Penguin Books (South Africa) (Pty.) Ltd., 24 Sturdee Avenue, Rosebank, Johannesburg 2196,
South Africa

Penguin Books Ltd., Registered Offices: 80 Strand, London WC2R 0RL, England

While the author has made every effort to provide accurate telephone numbers and Internet addresses at the time of publication, neither the author nor the publisher assumes any responsibility for errors, or for changes that occur after publication. Further, the publisher does not have any control over and does not assume any responsibility for author or third-party websites or their content.

Scripture quotations are from New Revised Standard Version Bible: Catholic Edition, copyright © 1989, 1993 National Council of the Churches of Christ in the United States of America. Used by permission. All rights reserved.

Scripture quotations marked (NIV) are taken from the Holy Bible, New International Version®, NIV®. Copyright © 1973, 1978, 1984 by Biblica, Inc.™ Used by permission of Zondervan. All rights reserved worldwide. www.zondervan.com

Excerpt from the Rite of Confirmation (Second Edition) © 1975, International Commission on English in the Liturgy Corporation. All rights reserved.

*The Far Side* © cartoons by Gary Larson.

First Riverhead trade paperback edition: November 2011

Library of Congress Cataloging-in-Publication Data

Hoover, Brett C., date.
  Comfort: an atlas for the body and soul / Brett C. Hoover.
    p. cm.
  ISBN 978-1-59448-548-0
  1. Contentment.   2. Quality of life.   3. Senses and sensation.   4. Satisfaction.
5. Peace of mind.   I. Title.
  BJ1533.C7 H66       2011       2011005454
  128.4—dc22

PRINTED IN THE UNITED STATES OF AMERICA

10   9   8   7   6   5   4   3   2   1

# Acknowledgments

My gratitude goes first to Tony Marchini, who, in his quiet, behind-the-scenes way, cleared a path for this book. He led me to Joy Harris, my agent, who took a chance on something she felt people needed to hear. Then there was editor Jake Morrissey, who with great patience and humor helped turned this chaos into creation. Gratefully I acknowledge the generosity of people who made valuable contributions along the way:

My parents, Jim and Karen; my sister, Tiffany; her husband, Denis; my brother, Blair, and his wife, Tina; my nephew, Chase; my beloved friends James and Azita; good priest friends Ken and Gilbert; and a host of others whose advice and stories appear in these pages.

Azita's kind and humorous nurse friends Carol and Heather, with whom I discussed comfort for hours in a San Francisco bar.

Tiffany's enthusiastic students and coworkers, who gathered at a fitness club in Walnut Creek, California.

My friend Ike's buddies, who gathered to talk to me at his home in Northern California.

Tracey Smith of the British downshifting movement.

The extremely smart women of Tuesday Afternoon Theology at the university parish in Berkeley, California, who gave feedback on the book.

I thank you all. I dedicate the words that follow to Monica, who probably would never expect it.

# Contents

# Part Two: Complicating Comfort

# Part Three: Way Beyond Easy Street: Real-Life Comforts

# Part One

# The Roots of Comfort

*But . . . to plant an orchard, to enlarge a dwelling, to
be always making life more comfortable and
convenient, to avoid trouble, and to satisfy the smallest
want without effort and almost without cost. These
are small objects, but the soul clings to them.*

—Alexis de Tocqueville

# Chapter One

# The Human Story of Comfort

*For everything there is a season,*
*and a time for every matter under heaven.*

—Ecclesiastes 3:1, NRSV

## In the Beginning

In the beginning, there was comfort.

You and I and everyone we know started life suspended in the warmth of a mother's womb. For most of us, it was a homeostatic Jacuzzi paradise, everything safe and peaceful. Nourishment and oxygen arrived dependably via umbilical cord. We hovered in the cozy amniotic waters, balanced, temperature-controlled, cushioned by a mother's flesh against the bumps and scrapes of the outside world. No bright lights, all loud ambient noise filtered down. Nothing hurt; nothing made us afraid. Primordial comfort.

It could not last, and the hour arrived when the complicated world made its claim on us. Birth came as an interruption. We emerged to a difficult world through that messy, painful, joyful, conehead-producing event.

That, to a large extent, is the human story of comfort: stretches of tranquillity interrupted by periods of struggle. Rest and run, play and work, weekend and workday, celebration and crisis—our lives are built on such cycles. We ride back and forth from comfort to discomfort, even from those very first moments. We learn that life is both beloved ease and uncomfortable challenge, often in succession, sometimes shifting without warning. Always both.

We wish it were not so.

I was raised in the suburbs of Southern California. To Americans, suburbs function as the archetypal symbol of comfort, a middle-class nirvana for shelter and security. This was the way I experienced them in the 1970s. In 1971, when I was but a toddler, my parents packed up their worldly goods from a two-bedroom apartment and bought a house in a relatively recent development on the improbably named Flintstone Lane. A short, wide street in the middle of a large suburban housing tract, Flintstone Lane had a womblike quality to it. Major traffic was confined to other, major thoroughfares outside the housing tract. The suburb itself got chronically rated as one of the safest cities of its size in the country. While I lived there, pleasant single-family homes all seemed to produce children near my age. Especially in those years before my siblings and I began school, everything felt idyllic and cozy. We would slip through the gap in the grape-stake fence to play with the kids next door; the neighborhood boys would set up ever-higher bicycle ramps on the street in front of our houses; the girls invented secret clubs; we built forts of blankets and pillows; my younger brother and I engaged in gargantuan construction projects of LEGOs. Each night ended with my folks switching on Walter Cronkite, who summarized the day's events, telling us, "And that's the way it is," reassuring us with his grandfatherly face and voice.

In my earliest years I looked upon such coziness and security as normal. But even then I saw signs that safety and comfort had limits. My father told us stories of how he had grown up poor in the Midwest, and how his father drank too much. Our county suddenly fielded thousands of refugees from a war in Southeast Asia that ended before I could fathom what had happened. The baffling, complicated world slowly penetrated our sheltered existence despite the social and economic fortifications the suburbs provided. At six I went to Catholic school and found myself lined up at recess with the other boys to play kickball, presided over by bullying monitors from the older grades. I was engulfed in the strict hierarchy of boys, a world of athletic and fighting braggadocio I did not understand. Blacktop mockery, recess wrestling matches, and forced participation in sports became part of my world, and—sheltered child that I was—I marveled at how uncomfortable that world could get.

Experience marks and teaches us. In the end, I learned as much from these struggles as from the cozy foundation. As I look back now, that combination of comfort and discomfort, side by side from the beginning, seems eminently normal, a perfectly adequate lesson in how the universe does business. It's what everyone needs to know. But back then I did not want to believe that at all.

Even as adults, during comfortable times, we forget how normal it is to have both comfort *and* discomfort in our lives. Optimism takes hold of us. We imagine that carefree days could last. We could somehow protect ourselves from the disasters and problems that afflict *other* people (with secret suspicions that they have brought it on themselves). The real shock of recognition comes when the normality of *discomfort* intrudes upon that cozy little world, when we suddenly uncover a quotidian world of distress or unease hiding in our midst. Once I attended a memorial service in New York City for the husband of an elderly woman who lived in my neighborhood. They had been married many decades, and I reflected on how comfortable two people must grow with each other over the years and what an example such a commitment is to younger people like me. As the evening wore on, I approached the woman and very softly and solemnly offered my condolences. She took one look at me, frowned, and said, "Son of a bitch, I never loved him. I'm glad he's dead."

It's so easy for discomfort to come across like someone else's problem rather than part of the real human story of comfort. This is why we need to know the truth about comfort *and* discomfort, about both the human *need* for comfort and the human value of the challenges and ordeals that occur in its absence.

## Catholic Comfort

I am by profession a priest, privileged to have spent years listening to and learning from the ordinary struggles of many good people. I trained for that work spending several years studying my own spiritual tradition, gaining a good background in other faith traditions, developing a general sense of the human processes of psychological and spiritual growth. Later I attempted to prove my mettle as an interdisciplinary scholar, pursuing a Ph.D. in theology and culture.

Being a religious person has helped me understand life's journey of comfort and discomfort, a traveling back and forth from a smooth and easy street to the potholed boulevard of challenge. No doubt being Jewish or Protestant or Muslim could have proven just as effective in this (an Iranian-American friend informs me, for instance, that Muslim guilt can be formidable), but Catholicism did it for me. I am, in the memorable phrase of one acquaintance, a "Catholic geek." In Catholic elementary school I was an altar boy, a teacher's pet, and a member of the children's choir at church. I even played Noah in the seventh-grade choir pageant. Then there was Catholic high school, in my case a big upwardly mobile coed college-prep affair. I sang in the choir there, too, attended mass at lunch, sweated my way through regular confessions, felt guilty about many ridiculously human things, and thought about being a priest. All this made for what I would call a fairly high "CQ," Catholic quotient, especially for someone of my post–Vatican II, post-Latin-mass generation. Last I checked, my generation's chance of showing up at weekly mass was less than half that of my grandparents' generation. Yet I have to say, my happiest memories of high school were sharing retreats and masses with my fellow choir mates—that peculiarly intense sense of teenage community best captured for me when everyone was hugging their way through the sign of peace.

Still, after high school I was pretty sure my life had been a little too comfortably Catholic, and I left home and went off to a University of California campus where I didn't know a soul, this one known far and wide as a "party school." Arriving there in the mid-1980s, I might as well have been arriving in Beijing;

my roommate hauled into our room a bong, a strange device whose precise use in smoking marijuana had to be explained to me. I loosened up a bit, widening my social circle, getting acquainted with cheap beer and late-night pizza runs (along with new observations about the mechanics of drug paraphernalia). Church and priesthood fell way down among my priorities. Yet after a year or two of this college partying scene, I grew confused and bored. Was this all there was?

Once again I found myself drawn to the old Catholic locales, in this case the university parish. Sandwiched between fraternity houses a few blocks off campus, the church was a boxy brown functional building from the 1960s. But the droll exterior concealed a breathtaking dynamism within. Over the next few years I encountered people who would become lifelong friends. It became like a second home to us, as we ordered pizza from the lobby, studied (sort of), laughed, and occasionally fell in love. Administering the parish were the Paulist Fathers, who were unlike any priests I had met before. Seldom found in clerical uniform, these down-to-earth Paulists confounded our expectations again and again—eschewing religious language for the common idiom, asking us to add our feedback at the end of sermons, quoting Monty Python, descending from the church ceiling at fund-raisers dressed as Batman to present a pair of bat-symbol-encrested boxer shorts to the bishop (really). I was enchanted. If these spiritually focused, wise, sailor-mouthed fellows with their creative antics could be priests, maybe I could do the priest thing after all.

Still I resisted. Celibacy was a problem. I liked dating. Raised on romantic comedies like most other Americans, I expected the story of my youth to happily conclude in love. Nevertheless, the question of vocation and career, of what in the world I would *do* with my life, persistently nagged at me. Lifelong idealism kept at me like a toddler pulling at my sleeve. Ultimately the inner Catholic geek won out. When it came down to it, I could not seriously imagine myself doing anything else besides being a priest. I spent a couple of restless years working for a Christian college and then for the Muscular Dystrophy Association, but neither moved my heart. In the end I moved to the East Coast to enter the Paulist novitiate in New Jersey, followed by seminary studies in Washington, D.C. Six years later I was ordained a Paulist priest.

What does all this have to do with comfort? All those years of "Catholic immersion" taught me that Catholic spirituality carries an innate ambiguity about the world of comfort. On the one hand, if comfort means enjoying and appreciating the pleasures of this world, of sight and taste and hearing and touch, then it's difficult to conceive of a more sensual approach to religion than Catholicism. Catholics are always eating, drinking, celebrating feast and saints' days, blessing ourselves, fingering rosaries, looking at our art and statues and images. There has even developed a modern, touchy-feely version of this, where liberal-minded Catholics burn the home incense, sing along with the guitars, and hug their friends on retreat and during mass. Irish wakes, New Orleans Mardi Gras, Brazilian Carnaval, and Mexican piñata-whacking are all at their root Catholic religious customs. A former Internet executive from Rio de Janeiro described the very Catholic nation of Brazil this way: "They have this idea that, well, God wanted it to be this way, so I'll make the best out of it. Dance, drink, and watch soccer." For Catholics it seems perfectly normal to think of a big celebratory meal as something given by God, "which we are about to receive from thy bounty," according to the traditional Catholic grace before meals in

English. Throughout my childhood I heard stories from my grandmother about having to sneak out of her teetotaling Methodist sister's house to go get an emergency dry sherry. When Grandmother later became a Catholic, she seemed genuinely relieved to take on a religion where having an occasional drink and taking trips to Las Vegas were not morally frowned upon. For better and for worse, Catholicism has a reputation as a partying sort of faith.

Oddly, though, coupled with this Catholic friendliness toward sensual comforts comes an equal and opposite suspicion and *discomfort* with them, especially if they involve (egad!) sex and the body. Our philosophical hangover from the ancient Greeks is that the soul is the real me and the body is a suspicious prison of awkward passions. I am spiritually charged with jailbreak. The ultimate destination, after all, is supposed to be the next world. Thus, Catholics famously spend our confessional time rapping about sexual faults, in thought or in deed, alone or with others, real or imagined.

## Meditations on Life Being a Bitch

I have a friend who is a priest in his early fifties. He's a tall man with curly salt-and-pepper hair and has been a priest going on two decades. Well traveled and visionary, he's an extraordinary storyteller, appreciative of good food, bad movies, and has a booming laugh. Raised in a small town by devout parents, he's a former park ranger and law enforcement officer. Now he's gone on to pastor complex churches where tensions can flare. In other words, he's a guy perpetually in need of a vacation.

Vacation he does, but periodically my friend also gets away

for a few days of spiritual retreat. He loves the time away to read and be silent, to breathe deeply, muse about his life and its latest direction. As the urban distractions disappear, gentle quiet takes possession of him. He begins to appreciate simple things around him. By the second or third day he is grounded, back to center, enjoying an unusual sense of clarity. It is then, as anyone familiar with retreats knows, that the inner demons begin to crowd around a person—fears, obsessions, old conflicts, spiritual and moral dilemmas. Without the customary diversions, all the unpleasant dramas of the mind and heart reemerge. Nasty little challenges creep in to destroy that lovely sense of comfort. Fortunately, my friend is experienced enough in such matters to know that this is not necessarily bad news. Working through these fears, conflicts, and challenges in good time is the whole point. The odd combination of peace and angst that such retreats bring does a person good in the long run. The net effect is growth. Off he goes again and again on retreat.

While on one of his assignments, he would sometimes get away for his retreats to a lovely New England retreat house efficiently yet unobtrusively run by a small group of nuns. One summer when he arrived, one particular sister, tall and earnest, welcomed him and was most determinedly hospitable. She gave him the most comprehensive tour of the place he had ever received. She showered upon him little bits of local history and described in great detail the spiritual resources available. My friend was growing weary—and hungry for his silence—when she finally ushered him to his quarters and proclaimed, "If there is anything at all we can do to make your stay more comfortable, please let us know."

Mouth before mind, my friend retorted, "Thank you, Sister, but I didn't come here to be comfortable."

Why such a blunt rejoinder? Certainly there is nothing wrong with being comfortable, even on retreat. Is this another manifestation of that famous Catholic ambivalence about comfort? I am not so sure. My priest friend told me this story some time ago, and I find that, as the years go by, his words to the good sister come back to me more and more often. I am no ascetic—to me, a really good banana split or dining by the ocean with friends is a spiritual experience comparable or more likely superior to multiple rosaries or fasting. Still, I know from experience, as probably most everyone reading this does, that my friend was on to something. There are life lessons comfort simply cannot teach us. In fact, it gets in the way.

## Leaving the Comfort Zone

I made two different journeys to the heartland of Mexico in my teens and twenties. I was seventeen the first time, finally away without parental supervision. I went with a friend a few years older, and it seemed like the perfect escape—he spoke Spanish and, as it turned out, had a bit of money to burn. The peso was sinking; a few dollars went a long way. We sought the good life, smoked and drank, staying in a gargantuan purple-and-yellow hotel equipped with American cable television, purified water, bilingual signs, and a paper-accepting septic system. The place was a virtual importation of the north. We could have had no more comfortable existence while still in an unfamiliar place.

Not all remained perfect. Montezuma arrived with his revenge, but I recovered quickly enough. After that we frequented American restaurants to compensate, becoming regulars at a Denny's near Chapultepec Park, and we strove to prove my friend's theory that sufficient cocktails could defend us against all hostile microbes. Even the spectacular pyramids of Teotihuacán could not disturb our ease with their evocation of a world two millennia past. The familiar arrived there in the form of a man at the peak of the Pyramid of the Moon selling Coca-Cola. Still, by the end of this tour, on our eighth day in Mexico City, my appetite for the surreal and unfamiliar was fading. We secured an early flight home. Stateside, I ran to Carl's Jr. for a fast-food hamburger.

In 1995 I came back, this time to Guadalajara to spend the summer improving my own Spanish. Guadalajara is a small colonial capital that in the twentieth century morphed into a metropolis. That summer I ran into gastrointestinal distress as well, but American comforts were less plentiful. I lived with a family that did not speak English, and there was no Denny's to be seen. I nevertheless resolved to take on the daily grind of appropriating a foreign language and its world.

My guru each weekday was a teacher and nun originally from Mexico City. A political scientist by training, she had spent decades living and working in the United States until her father's illness called her back. Once he passed away, she converted the house she inherited into a new school of Spanish language and Mexican culture for North Americans. The project had succeeded, probably largely due to my teacher's near-magical ability to see the two cultures at once. Thus she confided to me the nuances of Mexican culture along with those of Spanish grammar. I was treated to lessons and stories of etiquette and politics, of determined hospitality and family loyalty. She spoke honestly of economic desperation and what perpetuated it in a resource-rich country—election irregularities, backdoor deals, the irredeemable dishonesty of the police. Some days we'd skip out of class entirely, climb into her trusty Volkswagen, and drive to places like Tlaquepaque, an arts-and-crafts capital. Or we would visit an under-constructed school in a poor neighborhood and the home of a family she knew. There I met a young mother who hosted American college students. At one time, only one room of her hodgepodge house had a roof, but on account of the powerful and generous traditions of Mexican hospitality, she was bound to offer it to her guests. Throughout all of this, I learned the national sense of humor—ironic sarcasm in the face of absurdity and insecurity.

I learned one other thing as well. Some of the people I met in Guadalajara had virtually nothing. There were mothers and their children living in plywood shacks, day laborers waiting in vain for work, dirty children vending chewing gum on the streets. Even many middle-class professionals I encountered seemed no more than a paycheck or two ahead of poverty. That whole summer the economy was sick, and prospects remained bleak. Yet I never knew my neighbors' passion for life to falter. They went on eating and drinking, chatting and telling stories. In the United States, economic security means everything, and a future without it sounds utterly hopeless. These folks went on eagerly from day to day, despite the insecurity of tomorrow. Their tenacity and zest for life taught me a powerful and practical lesson in hope.

Looking back to my first trip at seventeen, I think of it now as a failed adventure. I *wanted* an adventure—something new, excitement, the unknown—but I constantly retreated from it to be reassured by the familiar. Back and forth, back and forth. It was the inexperience and hesitancy of a sheltered adolescent, but the pattern is human and familiar enough to all of us. We advance and retreat our way through life, wanting to move forward but more often doubling back to our bases of comfort. In each instance it seems logical. After immersion in an unfamiliar environment, I want comfort, the familiar. So I go back or at least stall. In each individual instance the cost seems negligible. Yet things add up. Individual acts become habits. All the retreating and stalling impede the forward movement of life. I learn very slowly. A friend once asked me what I would change if I could go back and be seventeen years old again. I answered without hesitation: "I was too cautious, too addicted to comfort. I would take more chances."

When I want to remind myself of the costs of constant stalls and retreats to comfort, I recall how, in the Bible, the Israelites escape from slavery in Egypt. Out in the desert, they find themselves hungry and yearning for the security and comfort of their life in slavery. They repeatedly stop and complain to Moses and then drag themselves back onto the road to the land of milk and honey. Thanks to this and other diversions, their trip took forty years. Or I think of Odysseus of Greek mythology. Eager to return home to Ithaca, he nevertheless spends ten years at sea stayed by complaints from his men, the lure of sirens and the nymph Calypso, a charmed interlude on Circe's island, and other ill-begotten adventures. Closer to our own reality, I think of many stories of psychotherapy I have heard. People admit that despite the epiphanies that spur them forward, fear and discomfort return to restrain progress. It's just easier to stay where you are than to move forward.

On that first journey to Mexico I learned very little about Mexico, or about cultural diversity, or even about *me*. I had a good time, but clinging to what was familiar was too time-consuming to allow for much growth or learning. The second trip was different, challenging. Forced by circumstances out of my "comfort zone," I paid extra attention to the world around me, and the experience stretched me. At the end I was glad to return home, but in the meantime I understood I had received a gift—the view from the other side. A close-up view of somebody else's reality. And I was stronger. The experience, as they say in Spanish, *vale la pena*—literally, was worth the hardship.

## The Arc of Comfort

Different spiritual traditions teach what my trips to Mexico taught me—and what my friend was trying to say to the sister at the retreat house. Very often life's challenges rather than its easy comforts drive our spiritual growth. The famous journeys of spiritual growth in world history occurred not when someone got comfortable but on account of what made that person *uncomfortable.* The Bhagavad Gita of the Hindus gives us the tale of Arjuna the archer, who, distraught by the awful tragedy of fratricidal war, prostrates himself before Krishna and begins his journey to wisdom. The biblical patriarch Abraham became ancestor to great nations and three religions, but none of it would have taken place had he not left his familiar life in Ur and made the hard journey to Canaan. The Renaissance saint Catherine of Siena renounced the comfortable married life her family had prepared for her, enduring strict ascetical discipline, the plague, and her family's retaliations so that she might go on to become a legendary mystic, visionary, and spiritual adviser to royalty and popes. A more contemporary tale is that of Malcolm Shabazz, also known as Malcolm X, who discovered spiritual life after his reckless youth sent him to prison. Later, infighting within the Nation of Islam drove him to a more expansive and inclusive Muslim faith. Those familiar with Buddhist lore will remember that it was Gautama's inadvertent and disconcerting exposure to the sick, the old, a monk, and the dead that set him on a spiritual quest that would change the history of Asia.

In the lives of these spiritual giants, crises and upsets led them to see things *differently*. Difficult experiences smashed their comfortable old expectations about life. They were forced to unlearn the conventions of their early life and let their spiritual imaginations wander. Horizons widened; new worlds opened up. They found that others wanted to listen to what they had learned. For some, repeated struggles yielded wisdom they never imagined uncovering. This is why, in the classics of spirituality from around the world, indeed in all great stories, the protagonists don't live comfortable lives. They contend with suffering, with hypocrisy, with baffling eventualities and constant opposition, all in the course of a life adventure that awakens them within and without. In this way they come to great wisdom.

This is all the first half of what you might call the arc of comfort. Everyone starts this journey from the same base—a very human desire to enjoy and preserve a comfortable life, to preserve and hold tight to ease, and to the security and stability that we remember as being so important to us as children. But life enters in with its problems and challenges, even suffering. What do we do? How do we respond? Often that is exactly what defines us as people. Avoiding difficulties and holding tenaciously on to the comforts at hand provide no lasting answer to the problem. Facing discomfort and loss, engaging the adventure of life and learning from it, these provide more substantial answers. There is satisfaction in wisdom, in having loved people and accomplished things, in having not wasted all our time with caution and escape. This is the spiritual path of the ancients.

But the arc of comfort has another side to it. Not everything was a struggle and a drag for the personalities of religion and myth. They also had a good time, often in circumstances considered somewhat scandalous by their contemporaries. Take Jesus for example. Perhaps no one has been invoked more consistently to break up a good party or prevent folks from savoring life's pleasures. And true, he did have a remarkably short and difficult life. But the stories of him in the Christian Bible are only occasionally dark and brooding. More often he is enjoying food and wine, breaking bread with his friends and with both sinners and saints. He draws people into conversation, waxes ironic and sarcastic, and leaps mysteriously into a good, controversial story. If the religious records are to be believed, his critics thought him a drunk and a gluttonous pig.

Others also knew a lot about the other side of the arc of comfort. Sufi Jelaluddin Rumi writes in his Persian *rubai* poems about the travails but also the deep pleasures of love. Ascetical Saint Catherine is nevertheless known for her cheerfulness and having erupted into laughter at her moment of greatest enlightenment. The biblical King David struggled endlessly for his people and at times for his life, but he celebrated with relish and even danced wildly before the sacred Ark of the Covenant, the symbol of God's presence in the world. The sixteenth-century Italian priest Saint Philip Neri founded an unconventional new religious order that received not infrequent harassment from fellow clergy and at one point nonstop objections from the pope's right-hand man. Yet Philip was famously enthusiastic and humorous despite (or perhaps because of) it all, walking around Rome in outlandish clothing with half his beard shaven, playing practical jokes as a form of spiritual direction. Even the reputedly depressed Abraham Lincoln, slogging his way through the Civil War, through political opposition, struggling with his own psychological demons and those of his family, always came back to that famous witty storytelling that had his constituents rolling in the aisles. His deep laughter came from the heart. Some say he could hardly keep from breaking out into a wide grin even as he attempted to sit absolutely still for a photograph.

# Chapter Two

# The Anatomy of Comfort

*Cure sometimes, treat often, comfort always.*

—Hippocrates

## Faces of Comfort

Comfort looks and feels different, depending on your perspective. The late cartoonist Charles Schulz of *Peanuts* fame felt that a puppy did the trick (and many dog owners would no doubt agree), but for the non–animal lover that might sound more like a walking slobbery mess. Talking to a former denizen of the West Coast punk-rock scene who also spent time living homeless on the streets, I learned that comfort for her has a lot to do with celebrating her now-happy life with her young daughter. On the other end of the lifestyle spectrum, an elderly gas-station attendant in a small town in eastern Arizona similarly said that comfortable was time with his wife and kids. For a thirtysomething Scottish immigrant working in San Francisco, comfort had to do with unwinding from her physically and emotionally demanding work: "I sit in the bath [with] a glass of wine . . . I usually do that every night. The worse the day, the longer the soak." Another San Franciscan, a ninety-two-year-old who spent a good chunk of her life traveling, first while she worked for the military as a civilian and then on her own, said comfort was being surrounded by all your old things, everything that reminded you of the people and places you had known. A sixtysomething attorney from the suburbs told me that comfort amounted to the happy memories themselves.

Comfort looks and feels different for everyone, rooted in unique life experiences. Most of us could trace a lot of it back to our parents. No doubt my own rather unsentimental notions about comfort come straight from my folks. When queried about comfort, my father claimed it was not a puppy but a vodka and tonic (just one), delivered to his table by a solicitous waitperson or bartender. Vodka and tonic is his favorite drink, and he still looks on food and drink delivered to his table as a surprising luxury. My dad is now retired, but he grew up poor. When I was young, he often held down a couple of jobs at a time to finance the ever-increasing cost of raising a family in Southern California. My father also says that losing himself in a good book is near the top of his comfort list. He has the mental escape of a good story in mind, I think, the relaxation of immersion in another world. But my mom thinks there is more to it. She says he means to make up for lost reading hours from all those years when he never had time.

As for my mom, my father calls the chair and ottoman where she perches in their family room the "control center." Within a radius of my mom's reach lie the telephone, the remote control for the television, the latest novel she's reading, and, most important, the sleeping figure of her cat. You see her there, and you realize that indeed she has all that she needs to let go of her worries. For my mom (who has also been busy all her life), the cat is the key to the experience. This creature, thick-furred, porcelain white, and fat-proud, stretches out on the ottoman and the neck of the couch and sleeps or purrs. She has a tiny little meow. Whenever we teased my mother about her attachment to cats over the years, she always claimed that the cats never gave her a hard time or talked back. I have my own theories. The Scottish writer and veterinarian James Herriot called cats "connoisseurs of comfort." Their lazy contentment with the world and simple need for attention breed calm, send the message that all is well, that there is no reason to worry. The message apparently has tangible benefits. In the past decade a multitude of studies have indicated that people with pets indicate more satisfaction with their lives, higher levels of happiness, even greater longevity. Nursing homes and assisted living facilities now routinely bring in furry animals as an extra comfort for their residents. My now-deceased grandmother had Alzheimer's disease, and even in her deepest dementia, calendars and picture books with fuzzy friends never failed to bring a smile to her face.

I suppose it's because I am a priest, but I picture my mom with the cats and I cannot help thinking of Jesus instructing his followers in the gospels, "I tell you, do not worry about your life." When they were beside themselves with anxiety about daily cares, he referenced nature to get them to mellow out. "Look at the birds of the air; they neither sow nor reap nor gather into barns, and yet your heavenly Father feeds them. Are you not of more value than they? And can any of you by worrying add a single hour to your span of life? . . . Therefore do not worry, saying, 'What will we eat?' or 'What will we drink?' or 'What will we wear?'" (Matthew 6:25–27, 31; NRSV). Animals do seem to demonstrate the pointlessness of worrying. I wonder what Jesus thought about cats.

Experience and background may give us different ideas about what everyday comfort is, but a lot of those involve what we call "creature comforts"—cozy surroundings, a cool breeze, good food. This explains the aforementioned Scot's bath with a glass of wine and my mom's comfy chair and ottoman. Of course, even here people have their different approaches. For my sister, a fitness instructor who works her body pretty hard, half an hour with the massage therapist is salvation. One middle-aged man I know can't get enough of the steam room at the gym. It leaves him feeling cleansed and relaxed. When I asked a young 7-Eleven clerk in Albuquerque, New Mexico, about comfort, she giggled and admitted it meant being home in her bed. (A nurse I met proclaimed her bed her "retreat.") Bright fluorescent lights give me a headache, so I long for soft lamplight. Certain family members need the television going to fall asleep. Many people have a time—morning or night—when they *have to have* their shower or bath. Most of us rejoice in these creature comforts, and we gladly accept whatever we are offered. Several years ago my family stole away for a couple of days after Christmas to San Diego, and my parents kindly splurged for the hotel rooms. They were nicer than I had expected, each equipped with a glass patio door leading to a flower-laden courtyard, an overfluffed queen-size bed, cable television, and a big bathtub. To a single seminarian accustomed to his narrow twin bed and drippy, temperature-fluctuating shower on the second floor of a gloomy fortresslike building, this was darn close to paradise.

Nevertheless, I do not want to somehow communicate that Catholic seminaries today resemble medieval monasteries, strict and ascetical, absent all creature comforts. We had all the usual American comforts—television, air-conditioning, decent food. In fact, when a Catholic seminary building I lived in got renovated in the 1980s, a small exercise room was added, a nod to the growing awareness of physical health as a part of spiritual health. But, almost on the sly, a tiny Jacuzzi was slipped into the locker room. The legend goes that a visiting Franciscan friar was among those who gathered for the inaugural soak. Accustomed to more spartan quarters, he waxed ironic about the traditional Catholic religious vows of poverty, chastity, and obedience: "Wow, if this is holy poverty, bring on holy chastity!"

## Comfort 101

We may all be creatures of comfort, but what *is* comfort anyway? How would you "get to the bottom" of it if you were talking to the proverbial Martian anthropologist, or at least to someone who had never experienced it?

One of the remarkable details about comfort is that many people agree on its basics. A patent agent from the San Francisco suburbs got right to the point when I asked him about it: "There's physical comfort and then there's emotional comfort." A group of nurses, the experts on comfort, said the same thing, and they wanted me to know that you cannot have one without the other. Understanding that was crucial to patient care. Apparently that was clear to the author of the Book of Job in the Bible as well, for Job vividly expresses how little creature comforts will mean to him while he remains tormented in his heart and mind: "When

I say, 'My bed will comfort me, my couch will ease my complaint,' then you scare me with dreams and terrify me with visions, so that I would choose strangling and death rather than this body" (Job 7:13–15, NRSV). In a more humorous take on these matters, Mark Twain, writing about the great outdoors, declares how well what we would call "comfort food" aids the enjoyment of sublime scenery:

> It was a comfort in those succeeding days to sit up and contemplate the majestic panorama of mountains and valleys spread out below us and eat ham and hard boiled eggs while our spiritual natures reveled alternately in rainbows, thunderstorms, and peerless sunsets. Nothing helps scenery like ham and eggs.

Comfort, it seems, is always part physical and part emotional experience. Yet, according to the nurse experts, it is even more complicated than that. One of them said:

> It's both physical and emotional, and for some people it's very spiritual, so it's not just one thing. Are they comforted? Is their anxiety addressed or not? They're worried about their family members, how they are going to react to the news [of their illness] and stuff.

Comfort, they all agreed, was not only physical and emotional, it was also a relational affair. If their patients were to find comfort, the nurses had to attend to their physical needs, their emotional states, and even to the impact of illness on their family members who came visiting. Cultural expectations also matter— the nurses I talked to were white American, Persian, and Scottish and they had patients from all over the world in a diverse urban area.

To me, these reflections capture the gist of what I have heard and read about comfort. They also confirm what I know from my own experience.

Leaving home is an American rite of passage—stepping out into the unfamiliar world on one's own. For me it began with the emotionally disorienting experience of moving to a large anonymous university about three hours from home where I knew not one single person. After graduation, like a good postmodern nomad, I kept going. I moved to the San Francisco Bay Area, where several friends were living at the time. Then, at age twenty-three, I picked up my worldly belongings and joined the Paulist Fathers, spending the next thirteen years living on the East Coast, with intermittent short stays in Minnesota, Texas, Mexico, the Dominican Republic, and back in California.

That initial move to the East Coast meant new work, a new set of friends and acquaintances, but it also involved a striking change in the physical environment. The world not only felt different to me, it looked different. Southern California, after all, has a mostly arid climate and seasonal temperatures. We live by the fiction of four seasons, but in reality we have two—wet and a slightly shorter dry season. The rains come most intensely in December and January, and it rarely rains a single drop from May to October. The hills remain green and lush in the winter but go yellow brown during the summer. Forests are tall but sparse. Mountains are large and imposing. The sky is often untroubled by clouds, and the sunlight is almost palpable. Cities spread out like blankets through the canyons and valleys, criss-crossed by the ubiquitous freeways.

On the East Coast, on the other hand, there are four proper seasons. The color scheme is reversed—yellow and brown in the winter, green and lush in the summer. Precipitation comes all year round—rain, thundershowers, mist, fog, sleet, snow. Leaves change colors in the autumn. The forests that remain outside the cities are dense and deciduous, and the mid-Atlantic Appalachians underneath them have been pounded down by nature over the millennia, barely more than hills by West Coast standards. In the cities, the buildings seem to lie closer together and to be more vertical. The skies are often cloudy, the light diffuse. There are an infinite number of different types of highways and different forms of transportation. Initially I looked and felt like an alien in this environment. It took time to grow accustomed to it. Especially when I got to New York City, I walked around with shoulders tensed, vaguely on guard.

As the months and then years in the East piled up, I physically relaxed. I grew accustomed to these things and more. I began to like the seasonal fluctuations in cold and heat—I anticipated them in my body each time I opened the front door. As I moved from New Jersey to Washington, D.C., to New York City, I began to know the Eastern physical surroundings as my own. At first, moving to New York City felt like the biggest shock of all, navigating the crowded terrain of Manhattan. Walking on the streets, down among the canyons of midtown, slammed into subway cars, I felt that physical tension. Why was everyone standing so close to me? It passed. I grew to love New York. By the time my years there were ending, I was surely as relaxed shoehorned into a subway train as any other New Yorker. I was *comfortable*, at home.

Physical comfort is key in life—warmth, softness, relaxation, a full stomach, human touch. We know that our coveted "comfort food" is a matter of our physical sense of taste, while creature comforts remain a matter of what feels good on the back, the neck, the head, what takes a load off the feet, what feels soft against the skin. The ancient Greek philosopher Epicurus and his disciples agreed. Believing the mind was a physical organ (lodged in the chest, incidentally) intimately connected with the body, they felt the important human thing was to enjoy in a limited way basic physical comforts—food, wine, a warm and dry place to sleep. On the other hand, and against all stereotypes about "Epicureans," Epicurus believed that stoking the desire for wealth, fame, and other unnecessary pleasures destroys us. Although British utilitarian philosophers like Jeremy Bentham and John Stuart Mill knew a bit more about physiology than the ancient Greeks, they still believed in the maximization of human comforts and pleasures (but for the largest number of people) as the most important thing in life.

But you don't have to be a Greek or British philosopher to know that physical comfort is crucial. My little nephew knows it. The week after Christmas one year he came to my house for dinner while my parents, his grandparents, were visiting. At the time he was about a year and a half and going through that particular stage of insecurity about persons unknown to him, "stranger danger," exacerbated since his parents were enjoying a weekend on their own. In our parish-house living room, I scooped him up to introduce him to one of my housemates, an elderly priest with a kind smile. He immediately wrapped his arms around my neck and dug his little face into my shoulder, refusing to come out as long as my eightysomething housemate stood there. In the face of the unfamiliar and (to him) frightening, he nestled into my arms to feel warm and safe. He did the same thing one afternoon when I picked him up out of his crib while he cried from a night terror that had awakened him from an afternoon nap. And, of course, I'd seen him do this many more times with his mom and dad. Comfort for my nephew on some primary level was warmth and physical closeness. And he knew this on some level, always wanted to make sure it was available to him. Whenever his mother or father would leave the room, he used to walk around calling out for them.

In the late 1950s, psychologist Harry Harlow and his colleagues stumbled onto evidence of this connection between comfort and touch. Originally, they hadn't aimed to study comfort at all; instead, they were studying learning in monkeys. But an epidemic broke out in Dr. Harlow's laboratory, and he had to isolate the infant monkeys from the adults to save their lives. Eventually he started noticing among the young primates what in humans we might term "antisocial" behavior—they were withdrawn, not going about playing their usual monkey games. He found that baby monkeys, like their human cousins, don't do so well without their mothers.

Further experiments ensued. Results from the most famous of these were published in the journal *Science* in 1959. The experiment involved infant rhesus monkeys in cages having to choose between a "mother" made of wire and a "mother" made of terry cloth. (A note to animal lovers: It is extremely unlikely that a university ethics committee would allow this experiment to go on today.) In any case, in a good many of the trials, despite the fact that the wire mothers actually had the formula milk, the baby rhesus spent his or her time clinging to the terrycloth mother. This was particularly true when little scary objects were inserted into the cages. Up to that point, psychologists had assumed that mother-child attachments—in monkeys or human beings—had a lot to do with who *feeds* the child. The person with the bottle would be the one the child cried for. The experiment showed that hugging and holding and comforting actually trumped everything else.

We are not monkeys, but we know there's something to all this hugging and holding. People pick up crying babies by instinct and it's nearly as difficult for a parent as it is for a child when the time comes to let them cry. A middle-aged educator and counselor I knew, who had no children of her own, used to frequent a ward for premature babies as a volunteer. She would come by just to hold these undercomforted children. When I visited an orphanage in Managua, Nicaragua, the first thing that happened upon my group's arrival there was that the youngest children began to reach out their arms, asking to be picked up and held. The regular nurses, kind as they were, simply didn't have enough arms to go around. The folks from our group were only too happy to oblige. In fact, this melted the hearts of some of those least familiar with and most intimidated by child care. In the end, two of the women on my trip ended up adopting children from the orphanage.

Comfort, at its root, is a bodily thing, carnal, physical.

## Comfort Physiology

Ironically, it is precisely when we examine this *bodily* aspect of comfort in a more thorough and scientific manner—when we look at what you might call the "physiology of comfort"—that its emotional elements emerge. The physiology of comfort has not been high on research wish lists, but we do know scattered things about the role of comfort and discomfort in respiration, circulation, digestion, the muscular and skeletal systems, and general body temperature (what is sometimes called "thermal comfort"). Most of this medical and physiological research treats specific discomforts, everything from altitude sickness to causes of reduced blood flow to arthritis. Some research does look at how the body deals with ambient temperature, humidity, and other environmental factors affecting a person's physical comfort. Commercial interest in ergonomics has also spurred study of the sort of chairs and airplane cabins that facilitate comfort and reduce medical difficulties. Beyond all of these specifics, however, we find a comfort physiology gleaned from discoveries about emotions and the human brain.

Emotions, biologically speaking, are a particular kind of response to sensory input. What physically happens in an emotional reaction is that the senses detect something and emotions are evoked in the brain as a response. The psychological word for emotions, *affect*, is not incidental—emotions literally affect us as a result of what we sense. Your ex-husband appears in the doorway; you feel morose. The ball goes in the basket and the crowd jumps up; you feel excited. Evidence suggests evolution built emotions in us as a kind of lead-in to action. Sometimes this is easily seen, other times less so. Anger, for example, pushes blood to the hands and increases heart rate and adrenaline, as if preparing the body for defense. Anatomically speaking, the sensory data are going to a part of the brain called the thalamus, which in turn distributes (perhaps regulating as it goes) sensory information to the appropriate place in the higher brain or cerebrum. It is the cerebrum's job to interpret, organize, and precipitate action. Interestingly enough, however, the thalamus also has a small neural pathway to the amygdala, often thought of as the "seat of passion" in the brain. According to psychologist Daniel Goleman—best known for his books on emotional intelligence—this gives the brain a "neural tripwire" for the sake of emergencies, which is why sometimes we passionately and suddenly react to trauma and emergencies, real or imagined, before we actually consciously know what we are doing. The amygdala instigates various "fight-or-flight" responses in the body, while the toning down of those responses takes place in the left prefrontal lobe of the cerebrum (the area of the brain long associated with cheerfulness, affection, and a laid-back demeanor). Together they form a kind of system or circuit. One is the alarm, while the other is the post-alarm "all clear."

Though scientists have not gone this route, it is reasonable to speculate that comfort may be related to the "all clear." When I asked Dr. Goleman, the emotional intelligence guy, he agreed it made sense. Comfort, after all, has everything to do with the good feelings that soothe us. Or, according to the astute but nontechnical observation of my mother, "Comfort is whatever helps you to feel better when you feel like shit."

## The Feel of Comfort

Comfort is certainly about how we feel—but only certain kinds of feelings. Negative feelings do not suggest comfort (unless you count the complex pleasure—the infamous schadenfreude—people take in the misfortunes of others). Nor do all positive feelings. If my team makes a basket, that excitement has little to do with comfort, unless my team has been consistently performing poorly up to then. Thus comfort-oriented feelings not only have a positive connotation to them, but they almost always seem to emerge in relationship to previous or anticipated negative feelings, to discomfort. A patent agent from San Francisco spoke about "safe" social gatherings where he felt comfortable and did not worry about what he said. He contrasted these gatherings with those he has experienced that were characterized by awkward tensions, silent disagreements, and even open yelling matches. One woman, a married attorney with a plethora of hobbies, suggested to me that comfort is "the absence of anxiety." A psychotherapist told me she thought people sought out comfort to escape loneliness. It seems fair to say that comfort nearly always functions as a contrast experience. If we did not experience uneasiness, pain, insecurity, and distress, there would be no need for it at all. Nursing theory backs me up on this. Katharine Kolcaba, a professor in the College of Nursing at the University of Akron in Ohio, has become an expert on the subject. She claims that human beings have a need for the absence of, relief from, or to "rise above" discomfort—in all areas of their lives, from the physical to the spiritual and cultural. To her, comfort is both an experience and the resulting state that strengthens a person through words and actions that address those needs.

I had my first migraine headache when I was about eleven years old. I remember parts of this clearly, stumbling into the kitchen of the house where my parents used to live, downing a couple of aspirins, my head pounding. Nauseated as well, I wondered if there might be some way I could lop my head off temporarily and then reattach it later. The aspirin did me no good, but some hours later the nausea suddenly became more intense until I thought I might vomit. Standing in the bathroom over the toilet,

I felt a wave of heat and nausea spread over my head and torso; the headache began to subside. I remember uttering grateful prayers to God, feeling tremendously relieved.

My parents and I mentioned it to the pediatrician and the allergist. Neither had any advice. "It must be your allergies to dust or to the cat." Later physicians suggested tension. My last year in college I began to get the headaches frequently, sometimes every day, not knowing then how the fluorescent lights at my job affected me. Not until I was twenty-six did an ears, nose, and throat specialist correctly diagnose the headaches. By that time there were much better medicines for migraines, even ones to treat the decapitation-fantasy-producing symptoms. The neurologist I consulted immediately offered me sumatriptan shots (I eventually switched to pills). The first time I used one, I was frightened by the weird, face-tingling side effects, but the immediate impact on my headache was unmistakable. Within a half hour it was gone. I could not believe it. It was relief; it was peace; it was magic. I got accustomed to the fact, over the next months and years, that I did not have to live with frequent and terrible pain.

Occasionally the old routine returns. A few years back, one hit me at a daylong meeting in Washington, D.C. At that time I was working in New York on a ministry project of outreach to Catholics in their twenties and thirties, a new spirituality Web site called BustedHalo.com (it still exists). The meeting in Washington was initiated by a Catholic bishop to brainstorm about ministering to younger adult Catholics. It was the type of meeting that initially offers hope of change but then proves frustrating because it is so hard to get church leaders to commit real time and resources to the cause.

Some psychiatrists believe that stressful situations, especially those without any obvious remedy, can trigger migraines in those prone to them. About a quarter of the way through the meeting, a migraine set in, mild at first but persistent. I rummaged through my rucksack for the pill I knew would bring relief, but I had left my medication at home in New York. Meanwhile, frustrating discussions ensued, and the meeting room's fluorescent lights aggravated my headache with their brightness and imperceptible blinking. By the end of the meeting my head was throbbing, and the aspirin provided by the local staff had made no difference. In twenty minutes I was on a train back to New York. Placing a sweater over my head and lying down on the seat, I began to sweat, tremble, and become nauseated. The trip took three and a half hours. Three subway stops away from Penn Station in Manhattan, I was home and I quickly downed the medicine. It took no more than a half hour to kick in. As it did, I felt this incredible sense of relief, long delayed. This was comfort. I lay down to sleep, exhausted.

Feeling comfortable, of course, means more than just feeling relief. In fact, the oldest and most traditional cluster of meanings for the word *comfort*—found in medieval English writings from as far back as the thirteenth century—surround consolation, what we receive from others in a time of crisis or grief. In the Bible it says, "Blessed are those who mourn; they shall be comforted" (Matthew 5:4; NIV translation). Consolation does not mean relief. It may help someone deeply, but it cannot make the pain or the crisis go away. But then that is not really the point.

When I was a teenager my mom rightly chided me for not attending the funeral of a classmate's father, telling me then what most of us have discovered along the path of life. Even in the fog of grief people remember and appreciate those who come to a mother or father's funeral. Being surrounded by familiar faces in that dark hour provides a special kind of comfort. It convinces us that we are not alone in an intense isolating moment. When my grandfather died a few months after my thirtieth birthday, my friend Gilbert flew down for the funeral even though he had to return home that same evening (other priests from my religious order showed up as well—I remember each one). His presence all that day was a great comfort to me and to my family.

The comfort of consolation certainly has a strong physical component, expressed in touch and the simple presence of others (what can be said?). But it also works its magic more subtly, on a level more emotional and symbolic. Thus people remember odd details in times of grief, things with unexpected emotional resonance—the way someone smiled, who was standing there when there were tears, the food that arrived when it was absolutely impossible to cook for oneself. When I appeared at the traditional Dominican novena-rosary prayers for a deceased woman in a parish where I worked, I watched the smile on the widower's face when he saw that I had arrived in my clerical collar—an outward sign that "*el cura está.*" The priest was there—this was right and good. After the rosary, I observed him walking around, looking with satisfaction at his neighbors and fellow church members eating and talking. Everything and everyone had come together to honor his wife that night.

Another time I heard from a teacher and actress how, amid grief and depression, the sight of an odd little yappy dog in a park gave her an emotional lift. This kind of dog usually drove her crazy, but somehow in her gloomy depression its relentless vitality and absurd little orneriness brought her a smile, ironic humor, even consolation.

．　．　．

On a more everyday level, probably most of us associate comfort with that feeling of security that comes with familiarity. Much of life means grappling with the new, the strange, the unfamiliar— learning a new job, navigating new places, parents trying to understand the rules of their children's very different world. It is only natural to want a "comfort zone" around us—familiar household objects, food, habits, places, people—to help us face the onslaught.

Extremes of unfamiliarity reinforce the point. People gone to war hold tenaciously to photographs of their loved ones. Refugees and exiles talk exquisitely of back home—the food, seasonal weather, family parties. The more alien the circumstances, the more important these details become. A priest friend of mine on sabbatical in Ghana in West Africa somehow unearthed a box of Frosted Flakes cereal and dug into it with animal lust. As life presents us with the murky sea of the novel and uncomfortable, touching base with what we know well feels ever calming. As a result, *comfortable* has come to serve as almost a synonym for *familiar*—the comfortable old house, our comfortable old vacation spot, my favorite comfy chair.

## Comfort Food and the Mission of Meatloaf

During my second year serving as a parish priest in Manhattan, a group of us got together for a kind of post-Lent celebratory dinner. At a family-style Italian restaurant on the Upper West Side, we had a delightful evening of laughter and conversation. At some point that evening, while we were sipping wine and awaiting coffee or dessert, the conversation wandered to the topic of comfort food. Three of us, we discovered, had family roots in the Midwest, and we had more or less identical conceptions of what comfort food ought to be. A cross section of that menu: meatloaf, mashed potatoes, green-bean casserole, the ever-popular macaroni and cheese, pork chops, stewed tomatoes, baked potatoes with sour cream, and of course, hamburgers, hot dogs, french fries, and potato chips. By now you may be reacting as did one of my friends at the table that night. A Chinese-American from San Diego, he was horrified by the heavy carnivorous, cholesterol-laden assault. Another friend, Bostonian son of college professors, patron of herbalists, held that he understood the cultural need for meat-and-potatoes but was not drawn to the menu himself. Everyone agreed that comfort food has a lot to do with familiarity and your upbringing (a Texan I know defines comfort food as "what your grandmother made"). We concluded with an in-depth discussion of dessert (since it was about to arrive). There was a kind of class war between strawberry shortcake and tiramisu, with ice cream as the populist conscientious objector. Finally someone raised the question that drew an unusual reaction in Manhattan—silence. The question: What if every meal were made of our menu of comfort foods?

In the silence, each of us, schooled in his or her own tradition of comfort food, mentally flipped this hypothetical burger over and over. Speaking to juvenile notions about justice and taste, it grabbed us on a very primitive level. We of the Midwestern-rooted crowd immediately understood the cost—expanding waistlines and the frequent visitor program at the local hospital's cardiac care unit. Health concerns aside, the idea finally sputtered on the issues of excess and repetition. As an adult you know endless comfort food will ultimately make you sick and bored. In the end the vote was no.

I guess childish wishes aside, most of us instinctively understand that any fantasy of constant comfort would blow a hole in the purpose of comfort. You don't want comfort all the time— you wouldn't appreciate it. Don't we reserve comfort food for those days when we're sick, angry, stressed out, depressed, or on vacation? At the University of California at San Francisco they actually did a physiological study of rats that made a positive link between stress and their desire for "rat comfort food." We humans know that the "carrot of comfort" can inspire a person to plow through a trying day, to tackle a difficult project, to deal with an unhappy situation. However, if comfort (or comfort food) was along every path, why would anyone keep walking? If my basest culinary instincts were constantly heeded, if my most childish food fantasies were sated every night, what point would there be in having them? If comfort is the daily bread, it will cease to comfort. Specific to comfort food, the food will lose its pedestrian originality, and I will have to either develop new comfort tastes (almost a contradiction) or submit to a culinary depression.

I know what you're thinking. You've read books like *Fast Food Nation* or seen documentaries like *Super Size Me.* It happens. In the amazing first-world culture of choice in North America, Japan, Europe, and in wealthy neighborhoods across developing-world cities, so many options are instantly and easily available, it is entirely conceivable that the 24/7 comfort-food scenario could be the reality for not a few people. It is not impossible to imagine that this could be part cause of the current American epidemic of obesity. In fact, the UCSF scientists working with "rat comfort food" theorize that, while comfort food is a body's functional response to stress situations, habitual use of it, perhaps sparked by chronic stress, leads to obesity. The irony is that such "comfort binges" may actually *prevent* us from enjoying the comforts of life. If comfort is by nature a temporary pleasantness warding off the normal discomforts that attend life, a kind of rest stop amid the challenges and worries of this world, an extended stay at the Hotel Comfort only gets in the way. Things long at rest tend to stay at rest. The enjoyment of travel disappears, both the adventure and the eventual taking it easy. Put simply, if you permanently stop moving, you don't really know what it means to rest.

## Comfort Connections

When in early 1944 Bing Crosby recorded the already popular song "I'll Be Seeing You," his handsome baritone evoked bittersweet comfort for so many people that the song reached number one and stayed there for four weeks. Certainly the soft nostalgia of Sammy Fain's tune played a part in this. So did a certain comfortable *familiarity*, both in the "old familiar places" of Irving Kahal's lyrics and in the familiar voice of Bing Crosby himself, by that time a megastar of film and records. But did familiarity and tickling the heartstrings alone make the song an enduring hit? To understand, you have to reach back in time (even before "I'll Be Seeing You" became Liberace's theme song). The tune—initially part of a 1938 Broadway musical—was recorded in February of 1944, when millions of people were separated from those they loved by war and the deprivations and suffering it brought. Addressing this all-too-common tragedy, the song spoke of a lover who had not forgotten his love, who amid separation saw her everywhere he went, who spoke of happy things that seemed ever so remote from the difficult present. In other words, the song brought comfort to the shared distress of almost an entire generation, providing a temporary escape for imagination and heart and instilling hope in the possibility of enduring love. Each time someone heard the familiar words of the song, the whole thing worked not only because of the way it affected *that particular person*, but because he or she knew it was true for so many others. It captured what a whole generation felt, probably without anyone from that "silent generation" saying so much as a word about it.

My point is that comfort, while certainly a physical and emotional matter, is a *social* matter as well. As much as we may hate to admit it, part of how we know what things mean to us comes from what things mean to the other people in our lives. Part of how we feel about what happens to us in life is a product of how the people around us feel. I like having old family photographs around, and I inherit this from my mother, who taught me to appreciate them. My brother-in-law finds comfort in remembering the dead through humor (something that makes some people feel *un*comfortable). He learned that tactic from the Irish-American side of his family and is now passing it on to my sister, who is sometimes surprised to hear her own response to inquiries about the whereabouts of her husband's (deceased) parents. "They have a small place underground. Why?"

All human beings go through life accompanied and influenced by significant others. We are social creatures. How we see and interpret comfort cannot but be affected by our interactions with others, both as individuals and in groups. I would imagine that most of us trace our ideas about consolation in times of grief back to our earliest family experiences of death and mourning.

Our notions about creature comforts probably stem either from a desire to re-create our childhood home situation or to forever put the struggles of that past behind us. What we seek in terms of comfort food, vacations, the way we use medicines to relieve symptoms, all these things are influenced by people from our past and then negotiated with the people in our present. What kind of religious experience you feel comfortable with (or if any religion at all brings you comfort) probably has roots in the faith you knew (or rejected) in your family growing up, yet adjusted for the circumstances of the people who form your family and community today.

More dramatic evidence of the social nature of comfort comes from nurses. The group of nurses I mentioned earlier emphasized to me that paying attention to visiting families is frequently as important a part of their patient care as any other. Patients get concerned about their families, families about the patient. Unless *everybody* feels comforted in some kind of way, nobody gets comforted. One nurse who worked in an oncology unit even suggested that sometimes *all* you can do for someone is comfort the family. She confessed to "fluffing up the pillows" and straightening sheets for comatose or heavily sedated dying patients, just to let the family know that the patient's needs are being attended to, in order, as she put, "to reassure them that we are there." Of course, these nurses also saw the downside of the social nature of comfort. More than once they had seen a patient's comfort *interrupted* by a grief-stricken or testy family member. One nurse remembered asking the patient pointedly for *her* views on some aspect of her illness to counteract the visible discomfort wrought by her patronizing husband. Another spoke of family members suddenly making disruptive demands to compensate for guilt over not having been there all along. I guess, like all things involving more than one human being, comfort gets complicated.

## Cultured Comfort

If we can say that comfort is a social matter, is it also a cultural matter? Does where people grow up and the way they are socialized impact the way they think about and even *feel* comfort? Some years ago I was walking down a street in Mexico City with a seminarian I know in California. He grew up in Mexico, and we began comparing notes on the way things like rhythms of life, architecture, color, and street etiquette immediately affected our basic sense of ease. Without a doubt he felt right at home while I needed time to relax into it. I asked a cultural anthropologist I know what he thought about culture and comfort. Like a good teacher, he answered my question with another question (such that the answer became obvious). "Do you think comfort might look different for a white American teenager in Los Angeles and a Guatemalan farmworker in South Carolina?" Well, of course I did. He suggested a drop in the local swimming hole might be a great treat to a farmworker, but comfort for a Southern California teenager? Not so much. Maybe a trip to the movies or playing a computer game with friends. He reminded me how for a lot of British and Irish men the "local," that is, the local pub, remains a central "comfort space." Move to any of several East Asian countries, and it is the local tearoom. Then there are generational variations. Two Koreans in their early thirties told me that teahouses were not really for them. The anthropologist did note that across a lot of cultures, home provides comfort for people. But even there significant differences creep up. What part of the home do people congregate in? Latin Americans might tend to relax around the kitchen or dining room, around the food areas. North Americans may feel most comfortable wherever the TV is present. Even within a country, there might exist "cultural-comfort" differences among people of different classes. For example, in North Atlantic countries, in working-class homes, the living room is a comfortable place for talking and relaxing, but in middle-class and upper-class homes, the living room is a more formal place for entertaining. The "comfort zone" moves to a den or family room.

Not only anthropologists have something to say about the cultural relativity of comfort. A sixtysomething attorney I met who now lives in the suburbs in the United States but grew up in England talked to me about how her British upbringing affected her sense of comfort and security. The Labour government of her childhood, in a postwar frenzy of social responsibility, had seen to it that ordinary people got a panoply of free services, everything from free milk and cod liver oil to visiting nurses for new mothers and home care for the elderly. As the English-born attorney put it:

> When you grow up in that kind of society, you have this feeling of security, you grow up feeling that you are not going to end up under a bridge, that society as a whole will take care of you. I think in this country nobody ever had that . . . so how much money you have as an individual becomes more important.

As she saw it, wherever you lived as an adult, growing up in an environment of basic guarantees meant a certain kind of built-in comfort, a base sense of security. She felt that Americans, growing up without it, have greater needs for financial security. Money thus becomes important as a means for finding comfort—a topic for another chapter.

I talked with the group of nurses about culture and comfort as well. They work in a diverse city environment, and two are immigrants to the United States. One came from Iran, though she has lived in the United States now for twenty years or more. Her response to the discussion about cultural differences in comfort was that she "dreaded" serving as a nurse for fellow Persians. We looked at her in surprise. She said that they make strong demands: "When the person is sick, that means they can't do anything. That's the time they have to be attended to and waited on, and they're the queen bee . . . That's comfort for them. Especially the attention. That normally they may not get." Another nurse said a Chinese-American friend of hers said the same thing in her experience nursing Chinese patients. We all agreed that in cultures where family and community needs usually outweigh those of the individual, being sick is your one and only time to shine. Attention is comfort. It feels like a great luxury. In American culture, though, where individuals habitually compete for attention in school or in their work, comfort more often looks like relaxing or even being left alone. In a hospital setting, it might revolve around being reassured that you really are in control of your life.

Comfort, it seems, is vitally connected to culture. Certainly there are universal comforts: everyone likes to be warm. Yet what constitutes a comfortable "room temperature" varies. A friend from Cuzco, Peru, in the Andes Mountains, is always opening windows, no matter how cold it gets. While I was growing up in Southern California, people frequently pulled out down jackets in the winter, even though the temperature almost never fell below forty-five degrees Fahrenheit. Beyond temperature, other comfort variations occur across cultures. In most parts of Asia, people consider squatting a comfortable position, yet most Americans could not handle it for more than a few minutes. Anthropologist Louis Luzbetak wrote about how, in some mission schools in Asia and Africa, children found desks so uncomfortable that they would write squatting on the floor.

A lot of what constitutes "cultural comfort" also emerges from social rules people observe without thinking. A Mexican-American acquaintance once asked me incredulously why I preferred to communicate with him via e-mail. To him, face-to-face or voice-to-voice communication is always preferable, always more comfortable. To me, it is a matter of what is most efficient at the time. Guadalupe Valdés, a professor of education and Spanish at Stanford, writes about how in her fieldwork among Mexican immigrants in the American Southwest, she avoided asking that chain of "get-acquainted" questions that white Americans generally ask, as she knew from her own background that this was considered forward and impolite among Mexicans and would make people uncomfortable. In New York City, it irritates many people when others do not "get to the point" in conversation—they see it as inefficient and possibly a sign of manipulation. Thus, these different sets of cultural "rules" give us a great variety of ways of looking at comfort—a comfort cornucopia.

## Say the Word (Etymology)

Having come this far, we can say a few things of substance about comfort. It begins with our senses—warmth, softness, familiar sights, sounds, tastes. Even at that elementary physical level, however, physiology tells us that comfort is connected to our emotions, especially certain complex positive emotions—relief, consolation, security. A lot of it seems to involve the familiar, which stokes some of the emotions mentioned. Both physically and emotionally, comfort cannot exist without its shadow—it is a response to discomfort and distress, according to nursing studies, either as a reprieve or cessation of that experience, as a way of managing to avoid it in the first place, or as somehow overcoming or transcending it. Comfort also has a social and cultural component—we cannot understand it without reference to the other people in our lives, both individuals and groups.

Can we then "close the book" on comfort? Do we really fully understand it?

A short history of the word illustrates the perils of drawing too many fast conclusions about this complicated word. At one time, *comfort* had a pretty narrow range of meaning. It meant thoughtfulness or care, especially in difficult times. Often the connotation was spiritual. According to the historian John R. Gillis, the Victorian-era middle class pushed this definition of comfort beyond spiritual consolation and "mutual aid" to more direct physical and domestic concerns. *Comfortable* could be used in terms of hospitality—if your guests had sufficient blankets or a glass of water when they needed it. Still the word had not become what we think of as *comfort* today. An eightysomething priest recalled about the 1930s, "I can't remember that comfort as a *lifestyle* was a part of life back then."

Yet somewhere along the line the uses of *comfort* multiplied. We now put on comfortable clothes, search for comfortable solutions, shovel down comfort food, demand comfortable office furniture, long for financial comfort, and hope desperately for comfortable means of travel (please, God, just a little more leg-room and not that middle seat). In less tangible matters, people speak of the desire for friends "with whom I feel comfortable," and many wish for "spiritual comfort" in moments of doubt and chaos. Comfort is not only our lifestyle; it is an all-purpose descriptor, an approved way of evaluating almost anything in the world. Comfort feels, at times, like everything.

The etymology of the word actually comes from the Old French verb *conforter*, which also meant "to comfort." Like a lot of French words in English, it likely came to Britain with the Norman Conquest in 1066—when the defeated Anglo-Saxon peoples weren't feeling very comfortable. The linguistic trail runs back to the end of the fourth century, where the root word appears frequently in the Vulgate, Saint Jerome's Latin translation of the Bible. It combines the intensifying prefix *con-* and *fortis*, Latin for "strong." It meant "to strengthen," and its use in Latin was all about strength. The word in English retained that sense of "strengthening" for a long time, though it has now disappeared. The only signs of it in modern speech remain in technical legal terms like "aid and comfort" given by an accomplice after a crime. In contrast, the most common contemporary uses of *comfortable*, according to *The Oxford English Dictionary*, surround providing "tranquil enjoyment" or being "free from pain and trouble." If *to strengthen* was "the birth of comfort," the word has journeyed a long way. In our day, protein shakes or Wheaties are considered food to strengthen a person; but meatloaf and macaroni (or shrimp paste or tamales) are comfort food. Comfort has clearly transmogrified over the years.

I mention all this not to throw a wet blanket over the previous reflections on comfort. All that I said surely lies at the root of comfort, but the etymology thrusts this notion of *strength* before us. Our previous discussion of comfort as an emotional response made it sound like comfort always comes to an end more or less right away. The whole notion of comfort as a "rest stop," in fact, would not work if comfort lingered on and on. Yet in the first chapter, I described an "arc of comfort." Some comforts flee from us relatively quickly (television shows, meatloaf), but others (contentment, delight in our friends) appear to go the distance. How could that be? Comfort, like an onion, seems to have more and more layers as we peel.

That may make us impatient for *the* precise definition. But this elusiveness might prove a positive development. Certain kinds of science are all about very precise definitions. Other kinds of science, such as the cosmology or quantum branch of physics, hope for such precision but accept that they must live without it. In spirituality, my field, people may pretend to render precise definitions of God and the meaning of everything, but the harder we work at it, the more such things appear to evade us. In Christian theology, medieval theologians like Thomas Aquinas spoke of the "principle of analogy." He meant that you can talk about God and the ultimate mysteries of life by striking up analogies to human experience, but you must be aware that ultimately such descriptions will come up short. We do and do not know what we are talking about. With comfort, of course, we are not talking about an ultimate mystery, but there is a quality of mystery to it. Comfort remains complex and hard to get a hold of. We may need to look at it from a number of angles before it all begins to make sense.

# Chapter Three

# American Comfort

*After all, I long to be in America again . . .*
*if I can go home to return no more to Europe,*
*it seems to me that I shall ever enjoy more peace of*
*mind, and even physical comfort than I can meet*
*with in any portion of the world beside.*

—JOHN JAMES AUDUBON

## A Case Study

After all this exploration of the inner workings of comfort, it might help to take a look at comfort out there in the world. After all, you don't have to know all the inner mechanics of comfort to know what you like. But comfort remains notoriously relative. After you spend two weeks camping, a dumpy motel room feels like Shangri-la, but once you are back home, you long for something cozier to quench your comfort thirst. Standards of comfort diverge so wildly, we might reasonably wonder what sort of "case study in comfort" could give us any sense of perspective. My strategy is to pick a large target, to take a panoramic snapshot—comfort in the United States.

In New York I worked as a priest in a midtown parish for three years, and I spent a great deal of my time with the Latino immigrant community. When I arrived, one of the longtime members of the community had just returned from Central America with his family. Just a year or so before, they had moved back after years in the United States. The long civil war had ended. Politely I asked about their time in Central America. The man did not go into detail, but he did tell me that he had decided to come back for the children's sake. He told me, "Well, *padre, aquí la vida es más conveniente, ¿no?*" Life is just more convenient here.

The word *conveniente* has a bit more resonance in Spanish than in English—it can mean "suitable," "proper." That something fits. Yet it retains also that sense of comfortable or convenient.

Complicated circumstances draw immigrants to the United States, but the quest for comfort certainly factors into the equation—especially for the vast number of people who come from circumstances of near misery. Such has it always been—from landless Irish fleeing the potato famine in the 1840s to rural Latin Americans today whose subsistence farming has become redundant by changes in the global economy. People have always come (sometimes reluctantly) in order to make a living they could not make at home. Yet even as they experienced poverty and discrimination in the United States, most still lived more comfortably than they would have at home. Especially today, the difference in standards of living can be vast. This is not lost on people back in the so-called old country. A Pew Hispanic Center survey in Mexico some years ago found that across social classes, 46 percent of people said they would go to live and work in the United States if they had the means; three-quarters of that 46 percent added, even if that meant coming here illegally. When the Kennedy School of Government and National Public Radio surveyed immigrants already in the United States around the same time, a majority did not believe their adopted country performed better morally and socially than their home countries—most did not feel living in the United States was particularly good for the strength of the family, safety from crime, their moral values, or for ethnic and racial relations. A majority did believe, however, that this country brought other things not found back home, things one could easily associate with comfort—more economic opportunities and a better deal for poor people.

It used to be said that the world believes that American streets are paved in gold. But the metaphor is off. One can find ostentatious wealth in the United States, but you have to go looking for it. Every neighborhood is not Rodeo Drive in Beverly Hills. Moreover, such extremes of wealth exist in nearly every nation on earth. Chinese folk do not brave the ocean passage nor do Mexicans cross the Arizona desert in search of fabulous wealth. They come in search of a better standard of living, and the chance to send money home so that their families might enjoy one as well. The world does not really believe American streets to be paved in gold, but they know that they are paved. In a lot of American neighborhoods (not all), potholes get repaired, streetlamps stay lit, signs accurately identify the avenues and lanes. Once I spent a month in the Dominican Republic improving my Spanish, and I loved every day of it. Yet I admit that by the end, I began thinking of the hot water and the reliable electricity at home. Then there was the time I ran into a priest from the Philippines who had come to work in the United States for a spell. I asked him why he had come. He told me it was to *rest*.

Apparently life is just more comfortable here.

## Comfort by the Numbers

Even for something as seemingly subjective as comfort, something approaching "comfort statistics" does exist. They lie in surveys, economic reports, and census figures. They do not offer any kind of list of "comfort facts" so much as make up a kind of portrait of comfort in the country. To start off, they suggest there is a "comfort gap" between the United States and another major center of the wealthier countries, Europe. People in the United States, on average, have more appliances, spend more, and have homes nearly twice the size of Europeans. They own many more cars than Europeans or Japanese. Per capita private consumption in the United States is higher than in Luxembourg, the richest country in Europe, and much higher than the European Union on average.

Consider a more internal portrait. There are approximately 112 million households in the United States. The average new house in 2009, at 2,438 square feet, was more than three times the size of the average house in 1950 (750 square feet). Families are also smaller; each person in a house in the '00s had more than four times as much space as people did in 1950. Ninety-nine percent of households have some form of hot water, almost 99 percent have some form of home heating, almost 100 percent a refrigerator, around 99 percent an oven and a stove, 84 percent have some form of air-conditioning, 83 percent a washer, 79 percent a dryer, 88 percent microwave ovens, 58 percent a dishwasher. Ninety-one percent have a car available and telephone service of some kind.

That seems like pretty good comfort saturation in terms of what offers both physical comfort and convenience. The story in the sphere of what we might call "comforts for the brain"— mental and emotional comforts—is just as favorable. As of the mid-'00s, 98.7 percent of Americans had a color television in their home (27 percent large screen), 80 percent having VCRs and/or DVD players (not to mention DVR service). Seventy-nine percent of households had cable or satellite television, and 31 percent had TV gaming systems. This is according to a national survey of energy consumption. The same survey reported that 68 percent of American households had computers. By 2007, 85 percent of American adults had access to the Internet somewhere in their world.

Financial comfort in the United States is considerably more complicated. Again, we look much more comfortable than Europeans. Make the European Union a state, and its per capita gross domestic product ranks with the poorest U.S. states—Mississippi and Arkansas—this even minus the poorer countries of Eastern Europe. And the Census Bureau reported that the median income of Americans reached its highest point in history in 1999. Recent statistics show a large number of people below the federal poverty line (14.3 percent), and there is a huge gap between rich and poor. Research suggests it isn't as easy to move up the social ladder as it used to be.

# Before Comfort

It wasn't always so comfortable from sea to shining sea. Picture yourself living in the largest city of the newly independent United States, Philadelphia, at the time of George Washington's presidency. Even living in the city makes you something of an oddball, for the vast majority of the country's population makes a living by farming. Unless you have some inherited source of wealth (which is unusual), you scrape by for a living on a trade. Your house is always crowded with people—apprentices, visiting family, elderly boarders. There is no running water, and the toilet is outside. All heat for the house comes from a poorly ventilated fireplace. Thus, sleeping, eating, and work all take place in that one main room, which is functional and not really decorated. Everyone remembers outbreaks of cholera and typhoid in recent memory—the wealthy fled the city and many people who couldn't afford to flee died. Infant mortality and the death of women in childbirth are ever present, so much so that pregnancy is as much a cause for fear as for celebration.

Or picture yourself living in a small town after the Civil War. Now you have a stove heating one or more rooms in the house but still no plumbing inside. There is limited decor and fewer people coming and going. Childhood diseases remain not only a nuisance but a life-threatening danger, and almost everyone does not receive proper nutrition. As a result, by the time they reach fifty, nearly everyone suffers from some sort of chronic health problem from back pain to heart and lung disease. (One of six of the 80 percent of American men aged sixteen to nineteen who enlisted in the Union Army in 1861 was rejected on account of health problems.) And people generally work—exposed to the elements in the fields or at backbreaking household chores or the physically demanding trades—until they die. Only the very old get to retire, and rarely does anyone live that long.

For our ancestors life was short, uncomfortable, and often painful. They did not expect anything different. Social historians like Merritt Ierley remind us that home comforts in Western countries were very low. People still heated their homes with a fireplace. In 1850, 22 percent of white children and 34 percent of black children died in infancy. Within the nineteenth century some conveniences like gaslight, furnaces, and indoor bathrooms found their way into rich households, but most people never saw or enjoyed such comforts, even though Americans probably already enjoyed by the 1860s the highest standard of living in the world. Simpler technologies like running water (in the cities) and the "Franklin" heating stoves (named after founding father Benjamin Franklin) did become available to average Americans as the nineteenth century progressed. In terms of health and nutrition, food remained an expensive commodity until the twentieth century, and the wide availability of antibiotics and childhood vaccines that would make the vital difference in health would have to wait until the 1940s and '50s. In other words, for most people life remained an uncomfortable and plain functional experience right into the early 1900s.

## A Map of the Comfortable Home

Both technology and social changes brought an end to this world "before comfort" and ushered in the kind of homes that we inhabit today. The main contribution of technology was the production of inexpensive power and running water, gradually delivered right to people's homes. This made a host of convenient and hygienic improvements possible—indoor bathrooms and kitchens, gas and electric appliances. Over time, a radical change took place in what could be done at home and how much labor it required.

Even as power and water made their entrance into American homes, other forces, more social and cultural than technological, affected the notion of comfort. Social historian John Gillis relates this to the rise of a middle class and of the first suburbs in the Victorian era, both in England and the United States. No longer a place for work, separated from both insular village life and the invasive nature of urban life, people's homes began to serve as a refuge for their families. They became emotional shelter, relief for men after work in the world, protection for women and children. It became a woman's (long and difficult) work to create and preserve the home—the *home-maker*. People began to look at their homes as private and sacred. Those who came visiting did so formally. House decorations and pets were of sentimental importance. No longer did the house serve exclusively practical needs, but people thought of it as their emerging center for emotional comfort.

As the Victorian period wound down and the twentieth century began, the emotional and technological pieces came together. American homes had the means, the power, and the water to get more physically comfortable, and they did so quickly. Between 1900 and 1940 central heating was perfected. The incandescent lightbulb made for more and brighter work and play after dark. The old water closet became the complete bathroom, as toilet, bathtub (an émigré from the kitchen), sink, and eventually shower came indoors and nestled in the same room. The last development in environmental comfort was air-conditioning, much more recent in origin. When it did come after World War II, it raised whole new cities out of the swamps and deserts of the South and Southwest.

Kitchens became more comfortable as old wood-fire stoves gave way to gas and electric ranges, eliminating those monotonous trips to replenish the wood (or later coal) and the huge storage spaces required for fuel. Iceboxes gave way to refrigerators in the 1930s and '40s; suddenly there was no need to replenish ice either and less need for daily shopping. Freezers came after World War II, and even meat could be bought long in advance. Dishwashers were one of the last appliances to penetrate the market, gradually shortening that particular task, and the last major appliance to arrive in the kitchen was the microwave oven, child of that World War II invention radar, present in commercial kitchens early on, but not in most homes until their size and price shrank simultaneously in the 1970s. The final curtain came down on the "old-world house" when the most dreaded of household tasks got mechanized—the laundry. Electric washing machines checked into middle-class garages, kitchens, and utility rooms after World War II, and dryers followed.

Something else happened as well. In the 1950s, more people began to own homes than ever before. The federal government of the United States essentially began to subsidize the purchasing of middle-class homes and the development of suburbs. The interstate highway and other highway construction systems, built ostensibly for national defense reasons, facilitated the movement of much of the middle class and working class out of the cities. The Federal Housing Administration and the GI Bill allowed for much lower down payments on houses than had previously been the custom (5 to 10 percent as opposed to half). Veterans got a particularly good deal, sometimes having to put only a dollar down to buy a house. The government made it easy for savings and loans to offer longer-term mortgages. Unfortunately, because of racial discrimination in the world of real estate and government policies neglecting urban areas, these developments tended to benefit only whites and the growing middle class. In any case, by the 1950s, middle-class American homes were now independently owned, looked upon as a refuge from the world, and full of the latest household conveniences.

## Is Everybody Comfy?

The movement to provide more and more household conveniences has largely stabilized. We have gone from ever-new appliances to refinement of the old ones—energy-efficient dishwashers, compact washer-dryers, room-by-room climate control. Yet, now that the dust from the installation of the dryer has cleared, it might be worth asking if everyone benefited from all the creature comforts. Is everyone in the U.S.A. living at least a little more comfortably?

If you had spent your entire life in a rural village in Nicaragua or in a squatters' camp on the outskirts of Nairobi, you would immediately be impressed with the comforts even poorer Americans frequently enjoy. A recent study showed that only 2 percent of poor Tanzanians in rural areas have electricity. Eleven percent of Panamanians in poor rural areas have television. As I noted earlier, this compares with nearly all American households that have these things and more. Once I took a visitor from the Philippines on a walking tour of some of the poorer neighborhoods near where I lived in New York City. Walking through a scrappy housing project, she told me it looked like middle-class apartments in Manila, though the metal bars on the windows made her nervous.

Obviously there *are* people in the United States who lack basic comforts and conveniences—homeless people, farmworkers, indigenous people living on reservations (contrary to stereotype, casinos haven't solved everything), and the poorest folk in Appalachia. Two and a half million people in the United States live in areas without any phone service. Poorer Americans are obviously the most likely to have their electricity and heat shut off during seasonal extremes, either due to bills they cannot afford or to substandard local infrastructure that overloads and breaks down.

Query a little further, however, and you get a sense of what remains out of reach across poor America. Things abundant in the middle and upper classes—cable TV, computers, digital video recording, central air-conditioning—are cost-prohibitive to the poor. Even schools, churches, and businesses in poor areas frequently lack some or all of these types of conveniences. Not that you do not find occasional contradictions. A poor widow gets her cable TV paid for by her upwardly mobile son. Teenagers from urban housing projects get afterschool jobs and then pay-as-you-go cell phones to talk with their friends. The rapid "planned obsolescence" of kitchen appliances and CD and DVD players sends half-functioning versions from five to ten years ago to the Salvation Army and then to the houses of the poor.

And then there is the digital divide. This is easier to assess since the government has attempted to measure it. Although access to computers through schools and public libraries has extended high technology to poorer folk and their children, computer and Internet use is still strongly restricted by income and education. In fact, as the dot-com boom overtook the stock market in the 1990s, the digital divide widened, as computer and Internet use soared in certain quarters and limped in others. Single-parent households, the rural poor, and African-Americans and Latinos have been among the least likely to have a computer or Internet access. When I worked in a Catholic parish split between middle-class whites and Latino immigrants, almost all of the former and none of the latter had Internet addresses.

Thus, children do not grow up in worlds of equal technological access, but are split into two groups based on income, education, and on race (with white and Asian children in one group and black and Latino children in the other). Not everyone has been reaping the benefits of quick word processing, software skills, and rapid-fire e-mail exchanges. The supposedly democratic world of the Internet turns out to be only slightly more egalitarian than early American voting rights (you had to be white, male, and have property to qualify). True, time seems to be shrinking the divide.

A true examination of the "comfort divide," however, has to go beyond counting conveniences and computers. There are other factors that make life more or less comfortable. Take time as an example. Immigrants working double or triple service jobs, attorneys at high-priced New York law firms, working single mothers, and upwardly mobile junior executives do not have it. This obviously cuts into their ability to relax, spend time with family and friends, prepare for the future, learn new skills, or enjoy leisure activities (though the lawyers and execs have more choice in the matter). In a more concrete vein, look at health care. Libertarians routinely point out that most people in the United States can get emergency medical care even if they cannot pay—government hospitals are obliged to serve them. For our purposes here, however, it is worth noting that a significant "comfort gap" exists between the over 16 million Americans—including children— who have no health coverage at all (plus the additional unknown millions who have insufficient coverage) and others up the economic ladder who do. Those lacking it get more worry, pain, and bankruptcies, while they receive less clear information, preventive care, and prenatal care. The Institute of Medicine (of the National Academy of Sciences) estimated that eighteen thousand people a year die unnecessarily because of their lack of health insurance.

Other factors more difficult to nail down also affect the comfort level of Americans along the lines of income, education, culture, and race. The more educated you are, the better skills you have appropriated in the type of time management and planning for the future that helps one succeed in North American society. The more poverty in your neighborhood, the more likely you are to have to deal in a proximate or direct way with major life disruptions like crime, gangs, street violence, poverty-induced mobility, alcoholism, drug addiction, single parenthood, a lack of neighborhood services. If you are not white in the United States, you may have to spend time and energy battling stereotyping, housing discrimination, racial profiling, and just general prejudice. Unemployment hit African-Americans and Latinos harder during the Great Recession, and studies show that blacks and Latinos have tended to get steeper rates on their home loans than whites with similar qualifications. Recent immigrants will have their comfort reduced by all the stresses of finding their way in a complex and vastly different cultural environment.

.    .    .

In short, though comfort is *generally* more widespread in the United States today, and even though even some poor folk enjoy a slice of it, everyone is *not* comfortable. Perhaps to expect that it could be so is unrealistic, and yet one of the particular dangers of comfort itself is that it can dull us to and distract us from the moral challenges we would rather not face. Like seeing clearly who is comfortable and who is not, how it got that way, and what we can do to change it.

# Part Two

# Complicating Comfort

*For there is but an inch of difference between a
cushioned chamber and a padded cell.*

—G. K. Chesterton

# Chapter Four

# When Comfort Goes Bad

*A certain degree of physical harmony and comfort*
*is necessary, but above a certain level it*
*becomes a hindrance instead of a help.*

—MOHANDAS GANDHI

## When Comfort Goes Bad

A favorite cartoon from Gary Larson's *The Far Side* places a mundane-looking man in a suit walking down a street while, unbeknownst to him, just around the corner in an alley, a circus clown hides waiting to launch a cream pie at him. The clown has a clearly malicious look on his face. The caption reads: "When clowns go bad."

It may seem just as absurd to talk about comfort going bad. Like the proverbial circus clown, comfort's whole purpose is to make us feel better. There is always the "all things in moderation" argument, suggesting that too much of any good thing—including comfort—will prove bad for us, but I generally hold with Mae West, who thought that "too much of a good thing can be wonderful." Moderation makes sense when there is reason for it—water conservation in the desert, limiting gasoline use on account of global warming, watching carbohydrates to control diabetes—but do you hear anyone proclaiming the merits of moderation in generosity, affection for one's children, or eating vegetables?

If comfort can indeed go bad, there has to be more to it, something beyond just the thought that enough is enough.

## Orgasmic Rats, Anesthetized People

In a legendary set of experiments in the 1950s, Caltech psychologist James Olds inserted a stimulating electrode in the "pleasure center" of a rat's brain and connected it to a lever so the rat itself could control the flow of stimulation. Predictably, the rat got into the spirit of the thing, pressing the lever as many as six thousand times an hour, refusing food and drink, focusing only on that lever. It was as if the continual sense of pleasure had drowned out hunger, thirst, or any feeling at all. Maybe this experiment doesn't surprise some of us. I had one college roommate who got high so often he disappeared from school after a year, the months of smoking dope apparently zapping his motivation. The numbing effects of drug addiction, of course, are well known. People neglect their houses, their children, and their health. Though Pink Floyd band members David Gilmour and Roger Waters did not write the rock-and-roll song "Comfortably Numb" about heroin use, the song from the band's album *The Wall* has become for many an anthem about the paralysis and loss of feeling associated with the use of that narcotic. Many people find its evocations of reality somewhere out there at a distance, of a person unable to connect or communicate, a perfect rendition of the experience. It is odd, in a way, that a substance many people take precisely for comfort under strain, *to help them feel better*, in the end interferes with their ability to feel anything at all.

This does not happen to every person who experiments with drugs. Nor do you need to take drugs to get numbed to life.

A lot of what we assume offers comfort also anesthetizes—food shoveled down so quickly as to give our taste buds no time to enjoy it, climate control so eternally present that we forget the feel of fresh air, womblike automobiles that keep us moving from place to place without seeing or interacting with anyone. For those who can afford it, the anesthetics include the absurdity of five-star resorts so self-contained you never risk actual exposure to the people or culture of the place you visit. And we have distracting electronic entertainment so constantly available one need never bother stopping to do the heavy mental lifting of reflection, worry, critique. Comfort takes on a life of its own. These things keep us from feeling what we need to feel to be active and engaged. We live, but we are not alive. We keep moving, but we have stopped caring why. What we do, who we are, even sometimes how we feel about other people takes on an automatic quality. If Karl Marx were writing for our more secularized society today, perhaps he would say that comfort is the opiate of the masses, rather than religion.

Without a doubt addiction can addle a person into numbness, but can creature comforts really have this kind of effect? There seems a hint of exaggeration to all this talk of comfort-induced numbness. Certainly they cannot literally deaden our senses the way drugs can, yet material comforts do have the power over time to rob us of a certain sensitivity, to leave us oblivious regarding whatever is going on beyond our little comfort zone. Most of us hardly notice the numbing effect until some gesture, dramatic event, or well-timed commentary draws attention to it. I knew a woman living in New York City who was scraping by but saved up enough to travel to the country where she grew up to visit her mother, who is fairly well off. My friend wanted to communicate to her mother the difficult times she had been experiencing in New York and how homesick she had been feeling, but her mom, psychically caught up in her comfortable lifestyle and new (younger) boyfriend, couldn't seem to attend to her daughter's story. Every attempt my friend made was met with, at best, a blank look. One evening the daughter discovered a statue of the infant Jesus guarding the entrance to one of her mother's wardrobe closets. Around the neck of the statue was a necklace with a diamond cross on the end. It seemed like just the combination emblem of faith and of home that would make her feel safe and connected back in New York. She asked if her mother could grant her this one favor and offer it to her as a gift. Her mother, however, thought it "bad luck to take it away from Jesus." At that moment it was as if my friend's eyes were opened, and she saw her own mother's numbness to her. Her mom had almost no awareness of life beyond her own carefully guarded circle of comfort.

Beyond the idiosyncrasies of family interactions and interpersonal crises, events in public life and even more adeptly in popular culture serve to kindle awareness of the numbing effects of material comforts. Many years ago, the ever-controversial comic strip *Doonesbury* by Garry Trudeau featured a mock-ethical

dilemma for its main character, advertising guy Mike Doonesbury. Trudeau had Mike assigned a tobacco-company account.
Sitting in the office talking to a coworker, he mulls over the ethics of promoting cigarettes. Is it right to help sell a product that
costs millions of people their lives? Then his ethical musings take
a sudden turn—his family needs a new washer and dryer. The
coworker endorses the washer and dryer. Trudeau's comic genius
here is showing how material comforts make it easy for us to
sell out.

The scene, of course, is absurd. Most of us, faced with accepting a job at odds with our value system, would either reject it
outright or attempt some kind of extended and complex ratio-
nalization. In cases like Mike Doonesbury's, I hear people justify
their choices by invoking the sanctity of the free market, by
drawing attention to the free will of those who choose to smoke
in the first place, by claiming that their actions don't have much
impact anyway. But no one really stands smiling at the watercooler and weighs the deaths of millions of people against the
need for a washer and dryer. Trudeau, however, seems to want
us to consider that ethically in such circumstances we may be
doing just that. Our comfort-driven lifestyle so numbs us that
we block out the consequences of our actions, develop an amne-
sia around compassion or moral duty. A smoker dying of lung
cancer seems very far away when I'm sitting watching TV. In a
typical middle-class family home, each child may sit in his or her
own bedroom occupied with computer games; the car stands
ready to go for errands to the store; everything is fine. Nothing
beyond that world seems to matter much at all.

# Bullied by Ease

So does comfort subtly work its magic on us, gradually numbing our powers to respond. But comfort has more than one way to beguile us. We are creatures of comfort, and what we powerfully crave we also greatly fear to lose.

During my last semester in college, I interviewed with the Peace Corps. It was the kind of thing I had always wanted to do, to travel and do volunteer work, to learn a different language, to learn what life was like from someone else's perspective. But after the first interview, I dropped out of the screening process. Later a lot of people asked me why. Apparently it seemed to them just like the sort of thing an idealistic young man like me would do. My answer had to do with ibuprofen. I was downing the stuff with alarming frequency at the time (medically dangerous to your stomach and liver, by the way) to treat my as-yet-undiagnosed migraine headaches. I told everyone that I couldn't go to Africa (the probable destination for a teacher of English in the Peace Corps in those days) because I could not imagine ready access to a stock of Advil. A few fellow idealists looked at me oddly when I said this, but the amazing thing is how many people—fellow students, friends, teachers—thought it a satisfactory answer. No Advil, no Africa. No one could find fault with me for being afraid to give up that or any other familiar comfort. Comfort is the all-purpose reasonable excuse.

It happens to most everyone who has lived in the United States, I find. We get used to a certain lifestyle and its accompanying comforts, limited though they may be. The prospect of losing even small conveniences begins to look like a serious problem, even if from an objective perspective we might admit that some of them are actually rather trivial or superficial. After all, many people live contentedly without a dishwasher or a big-screen TV. (It is much more challenging to live without friends or education, for example.) In my work as a priest, I have long observed how people get seduced by comfort when it comes to their work. Many admit to me they have little interest in what they do; but the pay or the simple fact that they know what to expect every day keeps them doing it. At times, such comforts keep them actively unhappy in their work, unable to consider either trying to improve the situation or looking for something else. Sometimes the job doesn't even have the money going for it. In New York, I knew various people in their twenties and thirties continuing for years as grunt workers in the entertainment industry. Stuck in places where it remains difficult to advance, afforded little respect by superiors (who nonetheless depend on them), they barely make ends meet. Many of these jobs are dead end and boring, and yet bright young folk stay with them throughout their adult lives. I cannot imagine many of them looking to make even a lateral move.

It sounds strange, to be cowed by comfort or bullied by ease. But comfort has a way of sneaking into our pantheon of values and taking over. Most of us believe that we *deserve* a certain amount of comfort after what we've been through, and once we discover it at work, home, in love, recreation, shopping, whatever, we consider it worth making some sacrifices for. The odd thing is that often we will sacrifice the very things that are good for us and for others, simply because the coziness of the status quo seems like too much to offer up.

In college I was in one particular relationship for a year and a half. During much of that time, we were unhappy—bickering and fighting, me refusing to commit to her emotionally, she reacting with volatility to my coldness. On some level, I probably knew six months into the relationship that this wasn't going to work. But we continued—content to live in a kind of emotional détente where neither of us had what we wanted. We had the comfort of each other's company and the indefinite deferral of any day of reckoning. For a long time I was afraid to disturb that. Finally I saw that this was not what I wanted, and that I wasn't doing her any favors pretending it was.

## The Fog of Comfort

Sometimes the consequences of comfort-gone-bad turn powerful and horrific.

In 1994, after President Juvénal Habyarimana of Rwanda was killed in a plane crash, Hutu militias went on a killing spree in Rwanda against Tutsis and Hutus who sheltered them; some eight hundred thousand people died. United Nations peacekeepers asked for authorization to help stop the killing, but the United States and Great Britain blocked U.N. Security Council action. In the 2004 film *Hotel Rwanda*, based on a true story, the Hutu house manager of a five-star hotel in Kigali, Rwanda, finds himself sheltering large numbers of Tutsi and Hutu refugees from the unfolding genocide. In one scene, that house manager, Paul Rusesabagina (played by Don Cheadle) is talking to an American TV cameraman played by Joaquin Phoenix. Rusesabagina expresses certainty that there will be a military intervention by the West once people see what is really happening. The cameraman looks at him with a mixture of cynicism and sadness, telling him that reports on the slaughter will provoke little more than a sigh and no action at all.

There's something about being mired in our own comfortable world that dulls our sensitivity to other people's realities and especially to other people's suffering.

Once I was the priest on a weekend retreat for young professionals in a secluded locale on the Hudson River in upstate New York. It was early fall, about five o'clock in the evening. Crossing back to a supply cabin to pick up candles for a prayer service, I thought I heard a voice crying out for help. Was it my imagination? Where could it be coming from? Numerous steep hills intersected with one another at the northern edge of the retreat center near the supply cabin. There were outcroppings and switchbacks, bushes and small groves of trees. I couldn't see anything. I grabbed my candles and made to walk back to the main room, but the echo of the voice in my head bothered me. I went back to listen. Again I heard very distinctly what sounded like a man crying for help. It was coming from up the hill at some distance. I shouted back, tentatively. He heard me; the man shouted back, sounding both panicked and relieved. He told me he had fallen while hiking, and he was trapped. I called 911 on my cell phone. It took a rescue unit and a helicopter pilot hours to extract him from the ledge where he had fallen, but eventually they got him to a hospital. The man recovered.

Later, others admitted that they, too, had heard the man crying out but had done nothing. I had almost done the same. Why?

At times I wonder if a solid, comfortable middle-class existence can put a person in a kind of "comfort fog." Compared with our ancestors, we are far less troubled by infant mortality and the constant threat of death. In command of our destinies, we have access to all kinds of creature comforts and electronic conveniences. A half-conscious motivation grows to filter out the things that might disturb our peace. A plea in the distance should remain in the distance. A cry for help from a mountainside or atrocities in a foreign land might even register with us, but accepting them as a personal responsibility requiring action is quite another thing. Our programming resists, tunes out the needs of others. That cry for help sometimes has to get so blisteringly close that we will actually become ashamed not to respond.

Though maybe that is where its impact is most dramatic, comfort does not just dull our responsiveness to people in need. It can diminish our sensitivities in general, making us bored, indifferent, and unmotivated. It's a part of what happens when a brain wired to outwit predators and environmental challenges—for fight or flight—has too little to do. This is the mind losing its edge. It becomes accustomed to sticking to routine and the familiar—that formulaic romantic comedy or action film, the same place for lunch week after week, that radio station with the endless supply of easygoing ballads. Then there is the shying away from new people. That's work—asking them questions, understanding their answers, new opinions, making room in your life. Too much to consider.

Beware the fog of comfort. An elderly gentleman I know, ever perceptive, jokes about our human reluctance to adjust our opinions and perspectives, even if new information is available out there. "Don't disturb me with the facts," he says.

In fact, the fog of comfort is particularly renowned for deadening us intellectually. Take the example of Internet hoaxes or Web "urban legends." If you are like me, you probably believe that nearly every piece of information you want or need is more or less immediately accessible via the Internet. It's all out there for the taking. That sense of effortless "instant information" induces a certain dulling of the critical intellect when using the medium. I'm sure you have gotten the e-mails forwarded from friends over the years: that Bill Gates was paying $1,000 to everyone who beta-tests his tracking software by forwarding that e-mail, that Mr. Rogers was a Navy SEAL with confirmed kills and extensive tattoos, that bedbugs arrive on clothing imported from China, that President Barack Obama is a secret Muslim radical. And on and on. Most of these have floated around the Internet for some time—none has any basis in truth. I have been taken in by an urban legend or two in my time. After all, it came from the great mother lode of information—what else did I need to know? Of course, with contemporary search engines and Internet-hoax Web sites (like snopes.com), checking on the accuracy of such things should be simple. Not many of us bother. Too often these hoax and urban-legend e-mails are a comfortable fit with whatever beliefs or ideas are already lodged in our brains (that making money is a matter of luck, that people commit themselves to doing good only to redeem their past faults, or that certain politicians are out to get us), and so we surrender our skepticism and buy them wholesale.

Falling for Internet pranks is one thing, but the comfort-induced blunting of mental acuity can have more serious consequences. We can get lazy about vital information. The 2001 attacks on the Pentagon and the World Trade Center were almost immediately identified by the U.S. government as the work of the terrorist group Al-Qaeda, who subsequently claimed responsibility for it. While President George W. Bush asked the question if there could be some connection between the attacks and the Iraqi dictator Saddam Hussein, advisers and terrorism experts could not find such a link and publicly said so. It seemed unlikely from the beginning, since Osama bin Laden based his movement in a radical interpretation of Sunni Islam that was critical of Arab leaders like the pan-Arab secularist Saddam Hussein, who had cooperated with the West. Nevertheless, some members of the Bush administration continued to insist on a link, and Bush himself maintained that the Iraq War was part of a larger fight against terrorism. All along the media rightly cast doubt on such a link, though perhaps not as energetically as they should have.

Yet for years after 9/11 large numbers of Americans (62 to 76 percent, according to various polls circa 2002–2005) insisted in polls that Saddam Hussein was in some way connected with Al-Qaeda and the terrorist attacks of September 11. It could be that many people simply could not sort out an admittedly complex geopolitical quagmire—9/11, a war on terror with countless fronts, war in Afghanistan, war in Iraq, the Taliban protecting Al-Qaeda, Saddam slaughtering Shiites and Kurds in Iraq. It could also be that once the Saddam–Al-Qaeda rumors emerged, many people just stopped listening, showing no further interest in the facts.

Leaving the realm of politics, I can also report on the ill effects of comfort among my fellow clergy. In my former ministry I used to travel a lot across the United States and Canada. I got the opportunity to listen to sermons and homilies in all kinds of places and on all kinds of occasions. Some were beautiful— attuned to human beings struggling with spiritual questions in the midst of real lives. I heard a wedding homily where the preacher said she hoped and prayed that today would *not* be the best day of the couple's lives. While everyone initially appeared taken aback, she went on to explain that her prayer was for a lifetime of growth and love, where the best was yet to come.

A few of the sermons I heard, however, were terrible—wildly inappropriate, obstinately judgmental, shabbily thrown together. On Easter Sunday a retired priest cheerfully explained to a church filled with semilapsed Catholics about how skipping mass puts a person on the road to hell. Happy Easter, and welcome to our parish! Another priest brought out a small collection of ethnic stereotypes to illustrate a point, and one preacher disguised as a sermon a laundry list of complaints against the town in which we were sitting.

But more sermons I have both heard and heard reports of were mediocre rather than terrible. A bishop I heard preach on three separate occasions told the same jokes each time and used the same tired image of the church. Some of those present had heard the jokes and the image even more frequently than I had. A pastor strayed extensively from his point to talk about himself—at length. An assistant priest droned on about theological generalities, never stopping to tell a single story or make a single concrete reference. Polls and surveys say people are desperately looking for spirituality, but what they often get is pious platitudes, Scripture readings retold almost verbatim, childish exhortations to do good and avoid evil.

I fear that too many in the clergy are not using their brains much. Comfortable with our own ideas and perspectives, many of us stop listening and learning. No one holds us accountable for this. There are jokes about priests who haven't read a book or had a new idea since their ordination. Among the Catholic clergy, our preaching is rarely formally evaluated. For most helping professionals—doctors, social workers, psychologists, across the spectrum to group fitness instructors—there are legal or at least industry requirements for continuing education. People have their minds renewed and recharged so that they might better help those they serve. New ideas and techniques find their way into their work. Unfortunately, there are no such requirements for clergy in most jurisdictions. Theological continuing education may be available, but many do not take advantage. Clergy often feel too busy to do so (Catholic clergy confront a shortage of personnel almost everywhere in the world), but many have also gotten comfortable with what they learned in seminary. Minds freeze up. Our bishops and superiors feel cozy, too, and they do not wish to rock the boat by requiring continuing education. And so many remain immersed in a holy fog of comfort.

## Creeping Comfort

To understand how comfort goes bad, it might help to pay another brief visit to the history of comfort. As we found in the last chapter, we live a qualitatively different life today than people did fifty or a hundred years ago. We experience a more comfortable world than our ancestors, and that surely makes a difference in how comfort goes awry.

People then saw life in quite different terms. Living a century ago Albert Schweitzer quipped that happiness was "nothing more than health and a poor memory." Today we expect more. It's not that life no longer holds challenges—as long as life involves war, love, work, rush-hour traffic, gossip, and the need to figure out new electronic gadgets, we will find life challenging. But the shape of things alters as our base level of comfort grows. Instead of life commencing for a new human being with painful childhood diseases, now (at least for the middle class) it begins with the mildly unpleasant event of vaccination shots in the pediatrician's office. Instead of winters punctuated by freezing twilight trips to the outhouse and evenings huddled around the Franklin stove, now winter evenings are passed in warm living rooms, with the indoor bathroom reassuringly available down the hall (and a little deodorizing spray therein to take off the edge).

True, many substantial things remain the same—people still fall in love, have babies, pay taxes, and die—but life *feels* remarkably different. We don't expect it to fall as hard on us, and we are often right. Less everyday physical suffering comes our way, fewer painful indignities. This is how we live; we come to believe it the way things ought to be. We notice different only when the elements of comfort suddenly vanish. On the day and night of the Blackout of 2003 in the Northeast and Midwest, I wandered the sweaty streets of Manhattan with everyone else, amused to discover how little I could do without electric power.

My grandmother grew up in the 1920s. Her mother died of tuberculosis when she was fourteen. Her father lost his job during the Great Depression. Aside from siblings lost in infancy, she had a sister who died as a young woman, a brother and a sister (and a husband) who died in middle age. She was by no means atypical for her generation. My parents, on the other hand, are both still alive in their seventies. My brother and sister and their spouses are alive and healthy, my sister with a robust young child. We all live in an age of reduced child mortality and ever-increasing life span. In our generation, we regard suffering and death with surprise, as if they were abnormal. A young church receptionist quietly told me the story of a recent funeral, where the family of the deceased demanded endless attention from her and everyone else at the church. Apparently, death seems so extreme and extraordinary to us that we feel entitled to almost any indulgence in the face of it.

Even more telling, we grow stunned in disbelief when mass

suffering strikes in the heart of the United States, as if technology and affluence bought us a pass from such acts of nature. People shook their heads at the death and destruction visited upon New Orleans and the Mississippi Gulf Coast by Hurricane Katrina in 2005. Some even blamed the suffering poor of New Orleans themselves, an absurdity. Such vulnerability for Americans seemed unthinkable.

Thus does comfort creep out from our lives and into our expectations. It's not just physically everywhere. It's psychically all around us, too.

Comfort's omnipresence makes it the normal state of affairs for us, the condition for the possibility of contented daily life. We cannot do without our creature comforts. Stan Cox's 2010 book, *Losing Our Cool*, recounts how air-conditioning has turned from a luxury into a necessity, changing our society in the process. Even back in the 1970s, editors at a Detroit newspaper found that they literally could not pay people to give up television for a month. Comfort has become obligatory rather than a respite from the difficult world. In the 1980s my brother worked as a radio disc jockey in Southern California, and the format he worked then went by the name of "easy listening," a prescribed collection of soft-rock hits. Nowadays they call it "adult contemporary." It's "comfort music," and it is extremely popular, especially among those who are established in their lives. Most of us feel that we will take as much comfort as we can get. *Comfort* has become a kind of guiding value in our lives.

In fact, in almost any part of American life, you can find comfort hiding not so deeply in the shadows. It's the excuse, the motivator, the rationale. Comfort flipping on the television to unwind after work. Comfort choosing the same barbecue chicken burrito time and time again. Comfort keeping to inane small talk at the high school reunion so no one gets offended. The desire for a comfortable lifestyle pushing us to long hours at work. Avoiding acquaintances who give us an *uncomfortable* feeling. With comfort ever more available as a seemingly reasonable explanation for our choices, it's all too tempting to tend toward the easy way out. In other words, sometimes laziness is next to coziness.

Not always surely. And I cheer for comfort along with everyone else (I'm the one who orders that same barbecue chicken burrito). Still, I wonder if our creeping use of comfort has gotten out of hand. Back in my life as a parish priest, I would make up work in the office to avoid the things I found most challenging, like visiting someone at the hospital or making phone calls about fund-raising. Comfort gets in the way of the good we want and need to do. It keeps us away from the people we need to engage. It blocks the healing process. A parishioner I knew in New York City worked across the street from the World Trade Center on 9/11. His company had clients who died. He told me about how one day as he talked about the attack and the clients they had lost, his coworker angrily rebuked him. The man told him he was making him uncomfortable. It was time to let go, to forget about it, to move on. This happened six days after the attacks.

We cannot reverse the great march of comfort in society, and who would want to? But I wonder if this creeping comfort is making us all a little *high maintenance* at times, believing in the need to have our desires and preferences accommodated. I used to look at my toddler nephew crying because I took his cracker away, and uncannily he reminded me of all of us.

There are positive sides to this. Higher expectations for lifestyle

produce better results, more creative ideas, better goods and services to improve the quality of human life. But they can also
make us spoiled brats. A friend from London found herself in
the crowded Port Authority bus station in New York City on the
day before Thanksgiving, a busy travel day in possibly one of the
busiest travel centers in the United States. The thirtysomething
man in front of her in line, frustrated that things were not going
as planned for him, actually threw a tantrum, shouting at the
woman in the ticket window, screaming at those behind him in
line, declaring himself to anyone else who would pay any attention. He could not get what he wanted, and frustration slipped
into fury. My friend said to me, "Does he know what day this
is? This is on the day before Thanksgiving. What in hell does he
expect?" What do we all expect? It's a question worth asking.

## Adversity's Answer

At a conference I attended in Los Angeles in 2000, an older
African-American Catholic nun approached the microphone.
Seventy-one years old, she brought a few thousand Catholics to
immediate silence by beginning her story, "My grandfather was
owned by the Jesuits at Georgetown University in Washington,
D.C." More than a hundred and forty years before, Sister Mary
Paul Lee's grandfather had been a slave of the Jesuit priests who
taught young men philosophy, religion, and ethics at Georgetown
University. The story of the slave-owning habits of bishops and
religious orders in the Southern states is not well known among
American Catholics, and a great many people were hearing the
shocking news for the first time. If that were not enough, she

continued with tales of discrimination from her own life. Growing up in modest circumstances in Philadelphia, she attended a Catholic high school and played on the girls' basketball team, but she ended up banned from playing when the team traveled to Baltimore—the other school would not allow her to enter their segregated gym. After graduation, she sought to fulfill her dream of becoming a nun. Order after order turned her down on account of her race; she ultimately found her way to an all-African-American order, the Oblate Sisters of Providence.

This wizened sister frankly spun out these stories and more. Her tales were the beginning of a service of reconciliation for this conference, part of the Catholic Church's desire in that "Jubilee Year 2000" to come to reckoning regarding its own sins (Pope John Paul issued numerous apologies for historical divisions and crimes that year). But even more astonishing than her forthright tales of discrimination and racism in church and society was the hope and strength that remained with her. She acknowledged that things had improved over the years, though there were still many miles to go. She did not display doubt or anxiety. She told her story with dignity and did not regret it. She was a woman without illusions about life, and yet she embraced it fully. She was comfortable with herself, seemingly so much that nothing and no one could alter that fact.


Life's biggest challenges often seem like the powerful wind that will blow us away. But leaning into the wind, we find ourselves gaining wisdom and grace and the deep comfort that is strength.

In the original set of *Star Wars* films, the young Jedi knight Luke Skywalker starts out as an impetuous youngster, a dreamer who is bored and longing for adventure. What his adventures teach him, however, is how immature, selfish, and uncomprehending he has been. What he suffers—the early death of a mentor, exhausting boot camp in a swamp, narrow escapes from death in battle, a dark discovery about his paternity, the loss of his hand in battle, encounters with malicious and dark enemies—schools him in the most important lessons of life. In this crucible he sees both the universe and himself more clearly—ideals matter most, his own rage can corrupt him, key human connections endure even beyond death, adventure for its own sake is an illusion. He learns what we all learn, that struggle clarifies our values. Having endured and grown, Luke Skywalker is transformed into a focused warrior for his final battle, a moral confrontation that will require discipline, commitment, insight, and trust in his own goodness and that of others.

*Star Wars* is a science-fiction fantasy—not to be compared with real ordeals like that of Sister Mary Paul Lee. Yet the shape of the story tells us about the confrontation with adversity in our own lives. In a sense, our real lives begin when challenges erupt and drag us out of the comfort zone. Struggle ensues, and with it comes insight. We find out who we really are, who our friends are, what we really believe. Ultimately, change becomes possible. We emerge as different people, better prepared for the great work of our lives as lovers, parents, caregivers, members of the workforce, mentors, wisdom figures, shapers of society.

This archetypal story of struggling with adversity, being transformed by it, and thus being prepared for the ultimate challenges and work of life is basic to mythology, literature, and the arts. George Lucas, in putting together the *Star Wars* movies, claimed he was heavily influenced by the work of Joseph Campbell, the late expert on world mythology. Campbell claimed that all of the world's major stories amount to the same story—the hero's adventure (or that of the *heroine*, since in many of the world's myths, the adventurer is female). It begins with some sort of beckoning to the adventure, and the hero(ine) then heads out to face the dangers of the world, aided by a supernatural force or forces, pausing here and there to meet gods and goddesses, fathers and mothers, enemies and companions. An extra-special trophy of some sort is sought (the Sumerian hero Gilgamesh sought a plant that bestows immortality, Indiana Jones sought the lost Ark of the Covenant), and the hero must return home. But the trophies are not so important (a snake gobbles up poor Gilgamesh's plant before he can enjoy the fruits, the Ark of the Covenant ends up in a government warehouse) as the experiences endured and the wisdom found in seeking those trophies.

I don't know if there is only one story in the history of the world. The hero's adventure is certainly extremely common and old, but Campbell's theses are decades old, and particularly dependent on the now-controversial psychological theories of Carl Jung and Sigmund Freud. Yet the adventure of the hero is useful in our reimagining of the psychology of comfort and challenge. It reminds us that the *journey* of life is the thing, what we learn and in what ways we grow. In the adventure of daily life, unforeseen challenges loom and sometimes function as terrible threats. But in the end, they teach us what we could not learn in any other way. And on every journey there will be help from others. We will meet companions and enemies, demons and angels, fathers and mothers and brothers and sisters, literal and figurative. We will have great goals and dreams to focus our attention and to justify great risk. Along the way the goals will morph and change, perhaps even lose their importance as we grow in understanding.

One of the critiques of the hero's adventure in our own time is that it is essentially a tale for the elite, for the rich and famous. Regular people must work for a living; they do not wander across the world without a practical reason; they do not have ships and crews at their command. Yet in recent years historians, scholars, and writers have worked hard to increase the trove of "poor man's adventures" by recovering or re-creating the lost stories of people from outside the power structure who have been erased from history and literature. We now have versions of the tale of the slave ship *Amistad*, whose slaves revolted and won their freedom. Author Toni Morrison wrote of the adventure of escaped slaves after the Civil War in her 1987 Pulitzer Prize–winning novel *Beloved*. The 1984 film *The Killing Fields* brought the genocide of the Khmer Rouge to the screen from the point of view of one who survived and made the long journey to escape. In his 1991 novel, *Rain of Gold*, Victor Villaseñor recovers his own family's adventures of displacement, exile, and love throughout Mexico and California from the days of the Mexican Revolution.

The important challenge for each of us is to uncover the "hero's journey" in our own lives, the struggle with adversity and what it has taught us. A friend of mine came to this country from Latin America many years ago, hoping to escape the economic chaos back home and join her family here. A businesswoman in her country, she left everything behind with a vague plan of entering graduate school in the United States. Instead she found herself with insufficient English skills and few prospects. She told me that she had worked so hard back home, establishing herself in a successful career with all the trappings—apartment, money, new car. She came to the United States without any of it, and yet found that she didn't lack much after all. Her journey changed her values completely. By her own account she is a different person now, more rooted in the present moment. Before, she had time for success and acquiring. She still works hard, but now she also enjoys life's simple pleasures, and takes time to think about her life and care for the people around her.

Our "hero's journeys" need not be so dramatic; they might even be mined from our childhood. When I was in the sixth grade, I had a terrible crush on a girl in my class, a girl far more confident and popular than the awkward adolescent I was becoming. In desperation I inscribed her name "with love" in a red Velcro wallet I carried around with me. And then one day I dropped the wallet in the school yard during lunch period. It was found by another girl, a girl routinely mocked by other kids for being "ugly" (she suffered severe acne). She seized upon the opportunity to be the source rather than the butt of jokes, and she began spreading the news about my certainly unrequited crush. When I came back to class from lunch, nearly the whole class stood around her as she presented me with my wallet, my inscription held up for all to see. They jeered at me while my crush stood by and publicly disavowed me.

It was humiliating, though not the life-ending tragedy I presumed at the moment. Later I learned this was run-of-the-mill suffering compared with other folks, that terrible things were possible in the world, things I would eventually see and hear for myself. But I did not yet know this. Regardless, events like this one did make me recognize not only that people could be cruel but that the victimized often become the victimizers. Cutting down other people is often the high cost for belonging (at times

I paid), and life was unfair but could be endured and enjoyed. The struggles that taught me those lessons also planted the seeds for the better parts of the man I am today—compassionate to those who are weak, appreciative of the rights of marginalized people, unwilling to dismiss people because they are not behaving like everyone else. In the end, I am grateful for what happened to me then. What I learned was more than worth what I went through.

Nevertheless, I—like most people—would avoid adversity if I could. During my time in the seminary, I got fed up with a lot of the challenges of life in the church—the celibacy requirement, the church's lack of appreciation for the gifts of the women around me, the institutional inertia, the narcissism of many members of the clergy. I thought about giving up on the whole thing. One afternoon, a middle-aged nun of my acquaintance was helping me sort it all out. Knowing she had seen all the institutional sins of the church up close, I asked if she would do the same if she had to do it all over again. Her eyes began to look weary, and she did not answer. "It was a different time," she said. It was an unfair question. All she had endured working for the church had contributed to her character, had made her a shrewd and yet compassionate person. Yet this did not make her eager to go back and do it all again.

Many of the members of my religious order today are older men. Indeed, for seven years of my priesthood I lived in a house dominated by retired men in their seventies and eighties. More than a dozen of the men I have lived with in communities have died since then. Some of them I knew for a short time—they passed in and out of my life. Others I grew to know well, and I was fond of them. Most of them were good men who cared deeply about people. Having watched them all pass away, I think about life and death differently. I remember the liveliest and most loving among them, and I hope my life unfolds as theirs did. I think of their bodies waked in our order's living room while we told stories both comic and serious. How could I think of death as unusual or unapproachable after that? In fact, the whole collection of ritual and words with which we marked their passing bids me trust in a mystery greater than I can understand, greater than death itself. I cannot be but grateful for this. But I tell you, if I could find a way to erase the memory of their growing weak and dying, if I could shift off the weight of their absence, if I could forget all the funerals and walk on as if nothing had happened, I would do it.

We rest from our deeds. After a time of great struggle has passed, a certain kind of "comfort equilibrium" returns. It is true in all the great stories. In Homer's *Odyssey*, Odysseus returns home to Ithaca, his enemies defeated, and the story ends as he enjoys domestic bliss with Penelope and Telemachus. There is feasting and celebration. In J.R.R. Tolkien's *Lord of the Rings*, the hobbits retire to the shire once the ring of power has been disposed of and Middle Earth saved. Life seems to mean more to them. Not that this time of comfort and rest always lasts. The next challenge always calls to us, as it does to all the heroes and heroines. The English poet Alfred, Lord Tennyson picked up on this in his poem "Ulysses" (the Roman name of the adventurer Odysseus). In the poem the aging wayfarer gathers his old buddies and sets off again, leaving his son Telemachus to deal with broken water mains and divorce court. Adversity and challenge beckon again and again. So, too, with us: we go voluntarily or involuntarily. Going forward with openness makes things easier. What happens to us in its course is what teaches us to be fully alive. That wisdom is the most real comfort we have.

# Chapter Five

# Home Alone

*Ah! there is nothing like staying*
*at home for real comfort.*

—Jane Austen

## The Home as Comfy Castle

Can the comforts of *home* go bad?

As a child, I watched reruns of *The Flintstones* on television—that Hanna-Barbera cartoon takeoff on *The Honeymooners* in prehistoric period dress—and I distinctly remember one of Fred Flintstone's mottoes. "A man's home is his castle, Wilma," Fred would say, defending whatever mess he and Barney Rubble had created in the house. Like most programs of its era, *The Flintstones* left a certain ambiguity about whether Fred or Wilma actually ruled the roost. In both the Flintstone and Rubble homes, the men being in charge seemed at the same time officially sanctioned and tolerated by Wilma and Betty. But the part about the home being castle, at least, remained secure. Bedrock mirrored twentieth-century suburbia with its postwar dreams of home ownership and domestic peace. The show confirmed my assumptions growing up about the home as a realm protected from the rest of the world, especially the sometimes threatening public world of work and strangers. It was a fortress. There might not be any actual armed brigands ready to attack in the suburban California neighborhood where I grew up (on Flintstone Lane), but the single-family home with its garage, yard, fence, curtains, and shutters was built as a sanctuary. Within the walls you could breathe easy. This was a sheltering sort of comfort.

This arrangement didn't drop out of the sky into our neighborhoods. Instead, for English-speaking folk, it developed in both England and the United States. Historian John Gillis says that in the Victorian era people in those countries began to focus on the home as a separate and sacred place, physically and emotionally attended to by wives and mothers. Gillis believes that before that time, on both sides of the Atlantic people looked upon their homes as purely functional. Houses were way stations in the local village, with all kinds of people coming and going. The community often had more importance in people's lives than family—helping people get started, showing up at weddings and funerals. The historian of American families Stephanie Coontz concurs that family privacy only gradually became an ideal for U.S. families, starting in the nineteenth century. According to her account, after the Civil War, with overwhelming changes afoot in society and the economy, a lot of people in the new middle classes responded by more or less battening down the hatches. They gave up on being involved in society at large and focused their energies on cultivating moral virtues and bettering the economic situation of their own families. This was a new family-oriented application of that old idea of American self-reliance.

Other societal developments contributed to an increasing preference for private family living space. Reformers of society in the early twentieth century discouraged middle-class people from living in boardinghouses (up to then a respectable way to live) and poor people from sharing kitchens and apartments to save money. Having one's own space even became at times a condition for receiving welfare. Still, until the government-subsidized housing boom after World War II (thanks to the GI Bill, the Federal Housing Authority, Fannie Mae, Ginny Mae, and the Interstate Highway Act), the majority of American families couldn't afford to have their own single-family homes. Since then, families have invariably strived for it. Even as the housing bubble burst in the late '00s, more than 70 million homes in the United States were occupied by their owners, making two-thirds of all households owners rather than renters (Census Bureau, 2009 American Community Survey). Thus did the single-family house become the emblem of private comfort and domestic refuge.

But private comfort is a mixed blessing. The walls that keep the world out also seal us in. Having our own space has many advantages, but it also means less connection with others outside. The evidence of this is all around us. To walk many suburban neighborhoods in the early evening is not to see a soul. A New Yorker I know, accustomed to the bustle of pedestrian-filled streets, told me after visiting suburban Los Angeles that he thought it looked like a scene from one of the Evangelical Christian *Left Behind* novels, where most of the population had been taken to heaven in the Rapture. I know what he means. The town where I grew up is a safe place to raise children, but if you drive through its major streets, all you see are the trees and eaves of

houses peeking up over heavy brick walls that mark off one housing development from another.

Time for a stopover at home then amid this exploration of
comfort. Home, it seems to me, constitutes a "comfort zone"
more than worthy of our time and consideration. I recommend
pulling up a chair or a corner of the couch and putting up your
feet as we look into the world of the comforts of home.

As Jane Austen observed, there is nothing like home comfort.

It's that morning mug of coffee clutched over the breakfast
table. There I am with the morning paper in my hand, munching
on some breakfast cereal, wondering what has happened in the
world since the day before. With the fog of sleep wearing off and
the uncertainty of what lies ahead, coffee—its smell, complex
taste, opacity of color, density as a liquid—it's an oddly beautiful,
familiar, yet functional pleasure. I realize there are people who
don't drink coffee, who cannot stand the smell, but for me there
is nothing better than a mug of coffee at home in the morning.
For others, I know it's more the bed they just got up from, the
sheets and blankets pulled up around them in the cool air of
night or morning. Some people talk about the feel of cotton
sheets, others of fluffy down pillows. In more moneyed times, I
knew friends to blast the air-conditioning on summer nights so
that their bedroom takes on an unseasonable chill to help them
sleep. Coziness in bed. Home.

For a lot of people, comfort gathers around the things we have
in our homes, their associations with family, culture, and tradition, with history and places and people, from furniture and
photographs to fine art or commercial prints to keepsakes and
knickknacks. It is often precisely a sense of personal connection

that makes the difference. A fitness instructor who grew up in wealth much prefers her modest middle-class home to the mansion she knew as a child: "I'm connected to my home now; my home is a part of me. Everything that's in my home is a choice that's either for comfort—that chair that's so comfortable you can't get rid of it even though it's ugly—or it's there because it's beautiful and it's bringing me comfort because it's beautiful. I need to have that thing up there on my mantel. A painting my son drew could give me so much more comfort than a Monet original." I myself have a "downsized" habitation relative to what a lot of other people have, but I do have a collection of photographs and prints that have hung in my bedroom in different places I have lived around the United States. They are of sentimental not financial value. Old family photographs are dear to me—my parents' portrait taken in the early 1960s, in stylish black-and-white, my mom in a sleeveless dress with her hair elegantly up, my dad wearing a paper-thin tie with his hair buzzed. For the religious among us, there are the spiritual symbols and remembrances—my collection includes a framed reproduction of the image of the Virgin of Guadalupe, given to me by a seminary buddy; a small print by Sister M. Madaleva, a nun and artist my mom once knew, of the Corita Kent school. It contains a quote from the great Jewish philosopher and theologian Abraham Heschel. Having all these things around makes my room a place of both familiarity and meaning. The photos and keepsakes connect me with family, religious tradition, things I associate with who I am. I feel very much myself, at home.

Of course, home is not all about stuff. A lot of what makes a person feel at home doesn't have much to do with *things* but with people. What makes a home comfortable on a deeper emotional level are the memories of people who gather or have gathered within it. There are the remembrances of family seated around the dinner table for meals, of laughter, of people relaxing in the living or family room on a Saturday or Sunday afternoon. In several of my college friends' houses, there is a photograph of all of us together in the living room of my oldest friend and his wife. Smiles illuminate everyone's faces, a Christmas tree lit up in the background. Whenever I visit them at that house in San Francisco, I sink comfortably into their couch and think of that photograph.

In their old house, my parents had a celebrated family room, the center of comfort gravity in the home. There, various incarnations of cats lazily nosed up to four generations of my family. There, my now-deceased grandfather napped before afternoon football games. I am certain that these memories have as much to do with making that room comfortable as do the cushy furniture and omnipresent TV. Even the weirdly configured and ever-transient priest houses I have lived in soften up under the influence of pleasant memories. In the New York City home I shared for seven years with a horde of priests (many of them retired and *many* years my senior), a handful of us would gather in the late evenings to watch crime dramas in a fourth-floor living room. Jokes and sardonic comments provided as much entertainment as the programming. We bonded across the generations, and it endeared me to these men who had grown up and lived in worlds so different from mine. Later I moved to California, and the guys from the New York house called me one night, leaving a deadpan message that they were still waiting for me on the fourth floor. There was a new episode of *Law & Order* on that night.

# Home Alterations

It's an odd thing really. Though nothing functions better than home as a symbol of stability, consistency, and familiarity, life at home has actually changed a lot over the years. And it continues to change. We have already seen how houses went from being functional households for people who came and went, devoid of modern conveniences, to bastions for an ideal nuclear family built around indoor plumbing, heating and cooling, and the appliance-driven kitchen. The revolving-door households of old were not private space. But more recent changes begin to give home life a different feel even in our own times.

For one thing, the word *hometown* is becoming a misnomer. Most Americans now call many places home throughout their lives. We have become accustomed to people leaving home when they grow up, often moving long distances from their families and hometowns. Downsizing and the shifting of jobs overseas mean that the nimble worker must be geographically flexible. And people just plain move more than ever—one out of every seven Americans changed residences between 2008 and 2009. The truism that "you can't go home again" feels odd and convoluted these days. What is this "home" we cannot go to? One friend decided to return "home" after a stint living in Central America; in the interim her parents had moved from California to Kentucky. Another friend, when you ask her where she is from, simply does not know how to answer. What does *home* mean once you have lived in five or six different towns? For all of us it seems to have grown more complicated. A few years back I returned "home" to California, yet I lived four hundred miles from where I grew up. And I have spent more years of my adult life living on the East Coast than in California. What is "home" for me?

Divorce continues to be one of the most powerful social forces redefining people's sense of home. According to the Centers for Disease Control, a third of all first marriages are disrupted by divorce or separation within ten years. The divorce rate has always fluctuated through American history, but higher rates have stabilized in recent decades, suggesting we should not expect the widespread nuclear-family households peculiar to the 1950s to reappear. In fact, blended families have become more the norm in many places. Other social factors changing the makeup of life in homes today include the prevalence of two working spouses, the rise of cohabitation outside of marriage, and more households made up of gay partners, including those with children. There is also the phenomenon of single parenthood—8.3 million single mothers in the United States, according to the Census Bureau in 2009. On the other side of the spectrum, we have more homes made up of married people without children present—over half of married households, in fact. (No doubt this is partly due to an older population.) Nevertheless, we can say that a family household today could be single parents with children or couples with no children. This is not to mention the millions of grandparents who were the primary caregivers for their grandchildren.

The most dramatic development of recent years in terms of home living, however, has nothing to do with any of these well-known trends. It is the number of people living alone. In 1950, one out of ten households in the United States was a person living alone. In 2000, it was one in four households. This is more people than live in all of Texas and Arizona combined. If the traditional nuclear family remains the standard householder in our heads, then maybe we need to get over it. A quarter of the households out there are people living by themselves. If the idea was originally that the home functioned as a castle of comfort and privacy for a nuclear family, the castle in reality now shelters a variety of types of families, and increasingly, people who are lords of the manor all by themselves.


Some changes are harder to document by citing statistics, but they still have an impact. As a kid in the 1970s and early '80s, I used to go and spend a week or two each summer at my grandparents' house in the San Fernando Valley north of Los Angeles. Though I didn't know it, for a week or so, I had moved to the 1950s. Each afternoon, my grandmother and I would meet my grandfather at the Elks Club for lunch (I would have a "Roy Rogers"—that old faux cocktail for kids). He'd come home in the afternoon (in a tiny Datsun we called the "Yellow Submarine"); we'd have dinner and then play cards in the evenings—gin rummy, poker, rummy royal, and, as I got older, bridge. We played poker only for pennies, but my grandparents taught me everything I know about cards. It was great fun and very social. We would talk, laugh, and tease one another. I imagine if we had been back in Indiana, where our extended family and the friends of their younger days lived, we might have gotten together with others as well. But after moving to California—my grandfather moved in the 1950s on account of my uncle Tracey's asthma— they only had one or two couples with whom they socialized.

Later in my life I would make a connection between this kind of leisure and the old movies my mom and I watched on TV—the card playing, the fact that there was a club or bar where people would meet one another, even the fact that visits with my grandparents meant sitting around talking while people had cigarettes in their hands, or, later in the evening, my grandfather's scotch and my grandmother's sherry. I would also recognize this kind of leisure from the stories my grandparents told about their lives as young couples in their twenties back in Indiana, some thirty to forty years before.

Where I would not recognize this kind of leisure was from my own life and that of my parents. As for most people of my generation, leisure time growing up was dominated either by playing with toys with other children; by scheduled activities centered around school, athletics, or church; or by movies and television. With some exceptions, we did not play cards or games as a group, except simple ones among the kids. We did not sit around and talk, except at meals and on holidays. It wasn't that we became couch potatoes all the time and social life ended. Life was just different, more diffuse and spread out, connected by looser threads. There was always plenty to talk about. Most of the time we were just busy. At home we connected with each other around the business of everyday life.

And then sometimes the TV blared.

## Channeling Comfort (TV)

You cannot understand the comforts of home today without taking television into account. The number one leisure activity across the world, watching television is said to occupy about four hours of the average American's day. If you think about the biology of it, this isn't hard to understand. TV is almost perfectly designed as a machine to capture our attention. EEG studies show that the visual changes of scene and camera on television activate our "orienting reflex," an instinctive visual responsiveness that evolved to help us detect movement (probably in order to hunt). By itself, TV gets our attention. Most human beings who have been in a room with a television on experience this (according to my sister, especially men). To get how monumental TV's presence is in our homes, how nearly impossible it is to imagine a house without one, I recommend an old *Far Side* cartoon. The scene shows a middle-class family, including pet dog, gathered in the living room sitting on the couch and on the floor, all staring at a blank wall. The caption reads, "In the days before television."

People think of TV as an irreplaceable part of the comfort apparatus of their homes. Recall the Detroit newspaper that found back in the seventies that they couldn't pay people to give it up. After a long day at work, most people want to relax, to stop thinking, to vegetate. In my time as a doctoral student in theology, I spent all day long reading or teaching about arcane theological textbooks. When I finally gave it up late at night and turned on the tube, I was resolutely moving toward a horizontal position in my chair. I had that remote in my hand. I was *hoping* for an experience that would not demand anything of my brain.

Researchers say I would not be disappointed. Psychologist Mihaly Csikszentmihalyi has done a lot of work on television as an essentially passive encounter with a human nervous system designed to be at ready for saber-toothed tiger attacks and marauding enemies. That seems to be exactly what is so attractive about TV—it demands little of us but has a high comfort dividend. It's mesmerizing, fast-moving, involving. It gives us story, characters, images. It is a cheap investment of mental energy for a large payoff in diversion.

Critics like Csikszentmihalyi say this is dulling our brains. Their review of research shows that people watching television demonstrate low levels of the ability to concentrate and low electrical activity in the cortex of the brain. Heavy viewers report more sadness and irritability when they aren't busy, suggesting TV has the effect of people losing their "mental edge" during off times. There are differing opinions, though. Some argue that TV in recent years has been getting progressively smarter and that today's viewer actually has to think *harder* than the watchers of yesteryear. Authors like Steven Johnson looking at that trend point out that most dramas today have more plot threads and are faster moving, that fewer shows stop to patiently explain exactly what's going on. The witty verbal repartee of the golden age of film has come to TV. Even reality shows employ complex premises and subterfuges. More than ever before in the history of television, you really do have to use your brain. Thus, we still have the comfort we want, but it may not be the dumb comfort we assume when we speak of the "boob tube."

For a long time, however, there has been something missing in these debates about TV, either in the perennial controversies over increasing sex and violence in the programming or in the deliberations over whether or not TV "rots your brain." It is something obvious but paradoxically easy to miss—watching TV keeps us at home. It draws us away from other people. Then take into account the fact that, for those people who do have additional leisure time these days, TV seems to be swallowing it up entirely. You start to wonder: Could there be a connection between watching television and isolation? Some of the research points that way, especially for heavy viewers. And now we have the increasing phenomenon of lots of people watching their own sets in their own rooms. Thus it could be that our great electronic comforter creates a certain amount of *discomfort*, too—isolation and malaise. Instead of talking with family members, enjoying activities outside the home, socializing at a neighbor's, going out and having fun, people are at home watching TV.

People do watch television together. It can function as a common experience, both in the living room and even beyond. Popular TV programs provide a common topic of conversation, sometimes around the watercooler, for people who have little else in common. Globally, TV becomes a common experience, too. We watch world events unfold together, from the fall of the Berlin Wall to 9/11 to disasters like the Indian Ocean tsunami, Hurricane Katrina, and the Haiti earthquake. Without a doubt this makes the world seem more like a global village, like a globally shared experience. But TV can be a substitute for other shared experiences, including conversation, even substantial conversation. We discuss popular television programs instead of civic issues, spirituality, and our own relationships. Children rehearse information about TV programs instead of taking an interest in other people or in the world around them. Instead of facing our problems and resolving our conflicts, we talk about TV. We do this even with the intimate people in our lives. A friend tells me of a long, detailed discussion his extended family had about a Mafia television series at a family gathering. People were able to comment on the behavior and motives of the show's characters with remarkable clarity and insight. Someone, at a momentary lull, observed sardonically, "We know more about that family than we do about one another."

# Virtually Connected

After television, probably the technology with the most important social impact in our homes is the Internet. The Internet will ultimately rival television's record-breaking market penetration, if not surpass it. In 1997, 18.6 percent of households had Internet access. By 2003 it was 61.5 million households, 54.6 percent of the total. By 2007, 85 percent of American adults had access to the Internet. Commentators once predicted that computers and the Internet might stimulate a revolution in social comfort for our nation, reorganizing the way we communicate, form community, seek information, and shop. To an extent they were right. We connect with loved ones far and near via e-mail. People stay in touch with one another constantly via social networking Web sites like Facebook, which itself has 500 million users across the world. Many of us share on specific topics via message boards or hear the news from communities and groups we belong to via the Internet. A good subsection of people engage in computer gaming via the Internet, sometimes for hours or even days. The Web provides us with all kinds of opportunities to go trawling or trading for information. Blogs exist to communicate news, entertainment, and the opinions of pundits and regular folks. And most of us engage in at least some of that favorite American pastime, shopping, seated before our computer screens. All this happens, significantly, from the comfort of our own homes (or workplaces).

Our computers and Internet connections are now "comfort nonnegotiables," maybe even more than television. In a 2004 survey 64 percent of people said that a computer with Internet access was the one thing they would take with them to a desert island if they could (other choices were TV, radio, cell phone, newspaper, and a large supply of books). It shouldn't surprise anyone. Consider the comfort benefits of the Internet just for information seeking. While you may have to take care to ensure that material found on the Internet is *accurate*, you hardly have to lift a finger to get it. It all starts with a few words entered into the appropriate search engine (using the English verb, to *Google*). On my nephew's first birthday, conversation turned to what famous people had been born on his day and what historical events had taken place. Naturally, we wanted to know immediately. I zipped upstairs and in three or four minutes I knew, thanks to the Web. A newspaper *might* have done the job, but the Web was quick and comprehensive (incidentally, the prophet Muhammad shares his birthday, and a couple of U.S. Civil War battles were fought on that day as well).

Then there is shopping. Many things will never be bought en masse over the Internet, and many people I know would never give up the pleasures of dipping into stores, but no one will dispute that Internet shopping is a great convenience, especially on those days when you just cannot bear to enter a mall parking lot. This is not to mention what a boon the Internet is for used and difficult-to-find items. And it all happens quickly, on one's own terms, without having to budge from that chair in the bedroom or home office. We never do such things at work, right? ☺

The greatest "comfort advance" of the Internet, though, has got to be its power to provide "comfortable community," to connect us with other people while we remain snug in our rooms. Part of what makes that particularly revolutionary is that it arrives on the scene when a lot of older kinds of connecting and getting together have fallen out of favor—dining with the neighbors, belonging to traditional service organizations like my grandfather's

Elks, being a part of political clubs and regular community events. The Internet fits well with the chronic networking and looser ties a lot of people maintain today. It renders geography nearly irrelevant. At various points over the last few years I have kept connected with friends and colleagues living in Ghana in West Africa, Darien province in rural Panama, Beijing, Jerusalem, and Cochabamba in Bolivia. At one point I was having a day-by-day discussion with a priest friend in West Africa, delving into the reasons his local church continued to practice European-style ritual in the middle of rural Ghana. All this at home without long-distance charges. And now Skype and other services have even brought audio and video into this sort of long-distance communication.

A lot of us have the feeling, despite the criticism of some, that these virtual encounters are *not* purely superficial. Research backs us up. People do authentically care about those with whom they connect online. And in a world where housing segregation, political polarization, and cultural tensions conspire to keep people away from each other, the Internet gets people of different races, ages, and genders talking, not infrequently about matters of substance. People claim they can be more honest and direct about their feelings and opinions online, in part because they are protected by anonymity. The Internet really does comfortably bring people together.

Still, it has limits. As with the telephone, in practice we connect most frequently by e-mail with those we connect with face-to-face. I once belonged to a Listserv whose active members lived mostly in the same building. It's true that the Internet connects human beings across boundaries of race and gender, but it establishes other boundaries—online we meet with people based only on shared interests and opinions. And then there is the issue of discipline and decorum. A number of blogs look to me like nothing more than undisciplined writing. Those who have visited some chat rooms and message boards know that anarchy reigns there much as it does on talk radio, and there has long been a special term coined for electronic ranting—*flaming*.

And as for the much-vaunted frankness of virtual communication, the medium's seeming anonymity allows for a lot of unbridled honesty, but you can also choose to lie with impunity if you want to (I think of a group of high school students who falsely impugned a teacher's reputation). Overall, online connections allow for some of these less-than-optimum responses at least in part because they do not offer important elements of live human relationships—nonverbal cues, touch, the accountability that comes with frequent association. If I have to look you in the eye with some regularity, I am likely to think about the impact of my words and actions. On the Internet, people are at a safe distance.

Like television, the Internet is a mixed blessing. Ultimately it asks more of us than TV does, as it facilitates communication across vast distances, with new friends and acquaintances, even in ways that pleasantly surprise us. Yet human beings are social creatures with needs and concerns a computer cannot resolve. Communication, after all, is not mere words; the complexity of emotions cannot be represented with punctuation and emoticons. Typing words on a screen is not a conversation. And the kind of friendship (or love) we can have *only* online—that is a very small thing indeed.

## Sofa-Mail

My oldest friend and his wife both have laptops and Wi-Fi at home. One day over Sunday brunch, we were discussing geeky, technical things, and they sheepishly admitted that sometimes while they are both sitting on the living-room sofa at home, separately tapping away online, they e-mail each other. We all laughed.

"It's absurd," said my friend, "the message going all the way to Cleveland or wherever the server is and then circling back."

Later on I thought about this. I began to wonder if the time will come when it will not seem absurd, when it will feel normal to communicate screen to screen with people we could just as easily move our heads and talk to. Will it feel easier for couples to e-mail each other and not deal with the risk of face-to-face communication? What kind of solitary and communication-challenged creatures would we have become if that were so?

I used to have an office next door to my main coworker. "Using the intercom" for us meant calling out down the hallway. If we had business to discuss, we would do so in person, using e-mail and voice mail only to avoid losing track of key details. But I can envision a time when we would sit in our respective offices all day long, fifteen feet away from each other, never making personal contact. The momentum for this has surely begun. I had an acquaintance from Mexico who couldn't get over the fact that I habitually communicated with him via e-mail. Why didn't I just call him on his cell phone? I had the number. He marveled at the fact that a person would communicate to a machine when he or she could talk to a person.

On one level I can understand this. Like with my friends' "sofa-mail," it feels a little absurd not to just talk to him. Yet I confess that frequently I am more comfortable with short bursts of communication at a distance. At times I regret having to abandon texting when the situation becomes too complex to resolve in an exchange of words and phrases. I curse when I find myself at the gas station and the automatic payment system at the pump does not function. In a hurry at the supermarket, I avoid the pleasant and amusing cashier to go to the self-checkout, even though I am far from convinced it moves faster. More and more commercial transactions are automated. It's convenient, but at what price if we lose our interpersonal skills and our human warmth?

Private comfort is on the rise. The castle of the home has subdivided into proprietary rooms. In Western countries—and most especially in the United States—no one wants just *access* to creature comforts. We want to have our own. In a small village in Chiapas, Mexico, people might be perfectly happy to have a television available in the local restaurant for soccer matches and a favorite *telenovela*. Not so in the north. We each want our own, and technology and the economy have colluded to come to our aid. Individual units now exist for every situation—rooms, furniture, appliances, technology, all kinds of conveniences. Today lots of people have not only their own television, they have many, one for each member of the family or even for each room in the house. Everyone needs their own iPod or MP3 player. There are radios in our showers, telephones in our pockets and purses, portable DVD players for the kids in the car or on the airplane. In many hotels these days, guests do not pad down to the lobby for morning coffee—each room has its own coffeemaker. Each desk at work has its own telephone, intercom, stapler, computer, and modem with high-speed access to the Internet.

Children pick up the motif early. Each child in a middle-class home in the United States has her own toys, usually her own room, maybe her own computer. It makes sense—encouraging independence and learning—but the cycle also builds on itself. A teenager wants a personal collection of computer games and DVDs for his own computer or TV. Expectations increase. Should a teen have his own car? The list of things the young person believes that she needs grows longer, and the financial demands on the family multiply. Some families have trouble keeping up financially (see next chapter) as a result. Many of us assume this is necessary and good, even when it puts economic pressure on us.

This move toward individual comfort is not born in selfishness or out of a desire for princely living. It begins with a cultural assumption that privacy and individual space are the right way to live, the healthy way to live. It's the individualism that initially drove people to private homes carried to its logical conclusion. At one point it was considered perfectly natural for brothers to share a bedroom (just as it was once considered acceptable for families to share a kitchen). As late as the 1970s, television families like *The Brady Bunch* had all the boys and all the girls sharing bedrooms. In most cultures around the world, children still share beds with one another or with their parents. Now we want our space. It's the way we are. Independence is, of course, a key American virtue to be cultivated. When my family moved from one house to another in the mid-1970s, a major motivation was so that each child could have his or her own room.

Individual space affords tremendous advantages to children as they grow up. It teaches them how to manage their own environment. With individual ownership comes responsibility, learning how to take care of things without diffusion of responsibility. Individual comforts can also teach children how to develop the skills for being on their own, being quiet, having time and space to think their own thoughts. There is an individual kind of creativity (as well as a group creativity) that only practice can perfect. But simply having one's own space does not automatically deliver on these things. Children need advice and guidance, often some training in the mental discipline necessary to deal with spending time alone. A fast-moving world where we never stop fiddling with the iPhone and never take out our earbuds does not always help.

There are other risks to equipping everyone with private comforts and individual space. It can make us spoiled—accustomed to getting what we want, unwilling to share with others, unused to accepting the limits imposed by negotiating for the bathroom or the computer.

Private comforts, if we do not remain vigilant, could also push us further toward isolation. We may not be aware of how far they have pushed us already. Part of my doctoral studies was language study, and theology required German. It turned out, not surprisingly, that my German teacher was a fortysomething immigrant from Germany, a new mother recently moved into a suburban neighborhood not far from my university. One afternoon she hosted a party for our class. We talked and ate, reminiscing about some of our more classic mistakes and sharing details from our backgrounds. The teacher got to talking about her own experience living in the United States. She found people friendly but hard to reach. We go from office to car to house, she said, barely pausing to wave to our neighbors. Everyone is involved in his private world. Telling us all this, she suddenly looked tired, and she said, "This must be the loneliest place on earth."

There is something nice about privacy, something comfortable about having one's own space, one's own bathroom, computer, TV, and CD player. But too much ownership over these little fiefdoms may encourage us in a kind of adolescent fantasy of comfort and control: "This is my space. No one can interfere with my life here. I have gained exclusive control over my own chunk of the universe." This may be the ultimate problem with thinking of our homes as a place of refuge, or as Fred Flintstone put it, our "castles." We think it perfectly acceptable to squirrel ourselves away with our stuff, and we lose that sense of the greater world that we share in common with everyone else.

## Chapter Six

# A Comfortable Living

*A wise man should have money in his head
but not in his heart.*

—Jonathan Swift

## Of Penguins and Security

My brother and sister-in-law once took me to see a movie about penguins.

Penguin life in Antarctica presents significant logistical problems. Penguins feed in the ocean but mate and lay eggs on the ice. In the middle of winter. In the coldest place on earth. Emperor penguins resolve this discrepancy by fattening up through the summer, leaving the water in March (in the southern hemisphere the seasons are in reverse) and walking more than seventy miles to their breeding grounds. They mate, each female lays one egg, and the female transfers the egg to its mate. The male warms it under his feathers, as even a few minutes of exposure to the winter air will destroy it. The female then walks the more than seventy miles back to the ocean to eat and bring back food for the chick when it hatches. By the time she returns, the chick is hatching and dad is starving, not having eaten in more than four months. So now the male makes the multiple-mile trek to the sea to stuff himself and bring back food for the little one. By the time he returns, the chicks have been left on their own a bit, the mamas having once again set off for the sea and the food supply. Fortunately for the females, winter is now starting to wind down, the ice breaking, and this startling commute to the ocean is not so far.

This is not what I would call a story about a journey of comfort.

The penguins do all this by instinct. No doubt if they had to *think* about the Sisyphus-like nature of these hikes back and forth, many would reconsider their options. At least the demand for Penguin Prozac would rise.

As human beings, we *do* have to think about providing for the needs of ourselves and our families. We have to find work to bring home the bacon, calculate what we should do to keep the steady income flow, figure out where and how to get our food and shelter. We have to plan ahead. We make budgets, deal with credit—mortgages, car loans, student loans, credit cards. Looking far ahead, we store our metaphorical fish for the future in the form of 401(k)s, CDs, IRAs, and Social Security. We may not have to walk seventy miles over Antarctic ice, but thinking our way through financial matters remains a challenge. Penguin life does not leave much room to maneuver—one error or a little bad luck equals disaster. Sometimes, as humans, we have a bit more breathing room. Yet no one wants to cut it too close between income and expenses, especially in difficult times. Everyone wants a little bit of cushion. You might call that safety gap "financial comfort."

. . .

Consulting people rather than penguins, I have found that theoretically Americans agree about that definition of financial comfort. It's simple and it's personal. A forty-five-year-old Internet technology salesman told me, "It's comfortable for me if the bills are paid and I know that I made sure it's done." Others talked about the freedom not to *worry* about the bills getting paid. A teacher described financial comfort as a certain "minimum" of food on the table, bills paid, the car running. I would hazard a guess that for most people, financial comfort occurs when expenses and income meet plus a little extra—the cushion. How the cushion gets defined differs, however, based on varied experience and different expectations. One suburban mom I talked to was emphatic about distinguishing between comfort and luxury:

> Enough that you can pay your bills and have a little bit extra . . . a little bit of fun money, a little bit of surprise money, but not be greedy, not to say I have to have enough so I can have a $125 bottle of wine every night. That's greedy. [It's] that comfort level of having enough but not too much.

But a group of middle-class white men—all in their forties and fifties—thought that many of their peers defined financial comfort not as the opposite of luxury but as the opposite of being economically constrained. Comfort is fiscal independence, the freedom not to have to "punch the clock" or report constantly to your boss. While they all felt this sounded attractive, they also noted that in reality it amounted to a mighty big cushion.

.   .   .

Perhaps surprisingly for such a wealthy nation, Americans feel ambivalent about money. We both praise people's ingenuity for gathering a nest egg and then gossip about them for not having to work as hard. We simultaneously love and hate financial success. We complain bitterly about corporate corruption scandals, about outrageous CEO salaries and oil company profits, but the pull of wealth remains powerful for almost everyone. We think of most people we meet as "middle class" (whatever the true nature of their finances), making it safe to harbor stereotypes about self-indulgence and aloofness among the wealthy. Then millions of us spend our money buying lottery tickets hoping to strike it rich. We claim we do not need luxuries to be happy or financially comfortable, but studies show Americans ever attracted to the increasing number of material comforts offered to them. "They want to have boats and cars and bigger houses," claimed one man matter-of-factly about his peers. Our attitudes toward financial comfort couldn't be more complex. The teacher I mentioned earlier told me about one of his high school students, a very intelligent young woman. When he asked about her goals, she told him she had to do well academically in order to gain entry to a prestigious West Coast university's business school and then become president of the Bank of America. When he told her he thought the end goal might be unrealistic, she assured him this was only until she turned forty, at which time she would retire and become a special education teacher. Apparently only the wealthy can afford to be selfless.

This may sound like a weird kind of mental acrobatics regarding wealth, but it shows up everywhere in American culture. On the one hand, everyone knows and praises the "rags to riches" story, the tale of the Horatio Alger figure. We celebrate it in both history and popular culture—in iconic political figures like Benjamin Franklin and Bill Clinton, in movies like Clint Eastwood's *Million Dollar Baby* (2004), or even in childhood fables like *Charlie and the Chocolate Factory* (1964). But we also have what might be called the riches-to-ashes story. In its most tragic form, the deeply flawed rich guy engineers his own demise, hung out to dry by his own hubris. This is F. Scott Fitzgerald's novel *The Great Gatsby* (1925) as well as Orson Welles's film *Citizen Kane* (1941). In the less harsh version of the story the high and mighty learn from someone closer to the earth (usually via love or friendship) the superior wisdom of real-life struggles. In a way, this is the deepest American ambivalence and fantasy indulged—to have had your grubby hands on all the success but, faced with a transcendent experience of love or spirituality, to see its true irrelevance. You can see the point clearly in James Cameron's epic movie *Titanic*, where poor artist Jack Dawson (Leonardo DiCaprio) pulls wealthy heiress Rose (Kate Winslet) out of her joyless comfortable prison of a life just in time for her to let go, fall in love with him, have real fun, and then somehow escape icy drowning. On the lighter side, there is the 1981 comedy *Arthur.* Dudley Moore's Arthur is suspended in an alcoholic adolescence by the pampering neglect of his wealthy family until his deepening attachment to a struggling waitress (Liza Minnelli) rouses him to new life. But he still gets the money.

Maybe this all makes sense for a comfortable nation built on the suffering of slaves, indentured servants, poor tenant farmers, and immigrant workers, especially when many of the financially comfortable of today are descendants of those poor farmers, servants, immigrants, and slaves. The American dream churns along through history, bringing financial success to some, but also leaving others behind (whose stories often do not get told). Maybe that makes us all a little uncomfortable. Maybe it should. Maybe what this really means is that financial comfort turns out to be more complicated than we thought.

## Blessed Are the Poor, but I Wouldn't Want to Be One

In American culture, we have a history of idealizing poverty and the struggles of poor people. This is the nation that produced novels like Willa Cather's *O Pioneers!*, John Steinbeck's *The Grapes of Wrath*, and Alice Walker's *The Color Purple*. But no one really wants to be poor.

"I've been poor," says the son of a Midwestern farmer who grew up during the Depression, "and it stinks." My own father similarly harbors no romance about his background in poverty. He worked hard to get out of it; it left him with a lasting appreciation of other people's difficulties. Thus, he has little patience for the pull-yourself-up-by-your-own-bootstraps crowd. My grandmother used to talk a lot about her childhood in Louisiana, how the school principal would pronounce her name in a way that sounded funny to her Indiana ears. Behind the commentary on Southern dialect were the stories of carefree days. After that, like many other men in the 1930s, her father lost his job. Their nice upper-middle-class life—with servants and money—disappeared overnight. My grandmother talks no more about her childhood after that.

Poverty, of course, isn't just a phenomenon of the Depression or of the past; it's a fearful reality today. According to statistics from the U.S. Census, more than one out of every seven people lives in poverty in the United States, and almost 8 percent of households live on less than $10,000 a year. A quarter of blacks and almost a quarter of all Latinos live below the poverty line as opposed to about a tenth of Asians and a tenth of whites. More than 32 percent of all single women live in poverty; that goes up to 45 percent if there are children under five present. Being poor is something real and ominous that everyday people try to avoid and to escape.

Poverty means more than a lack of money for the basics. It also means no financial "cushion" to break your fall should disaster strike. To look at it from the opposite end, as the fifty-four-year-old director of a charitable foundation reminded me, financial comfort means an extra leg up when crisis occurs. If serious illness strikes your family, you can focus on getting the medical resources you need. You can seek a second opinion, look at specialists, and research treatments on the Internet. If you are poor, however, you take what medical care you can get (if you can get anything). Less hypothetically, if you were middle class in New Orleans when Hurricane Katrina came, you escaped the city in your car, traveling to a motel or to a friend's home. If you were poor, you went to the Convention Center and took your chances.

For poor people, a thin margin separates survival and disaster. Along that margin lie dilapidated neighborhoods, schools with insufficient resources, class and racial prejudice, fewer jobs, low self-esteem, and the lure of alcoholism and addiction as an escape. Sometimes the organized crime of the drug trade exists locally as an alternative (and lucrative) economy. Government and charitable services remain available but are bureaucratically complex, scattered, and sometimes unintelligible. It's clear to the poor that the world is designed for the middle class.

Many poor people, like my father, do not remain mired in poverty. He had the additional advantages of being white, having access to state-subsidized education, and coming of age during the great postwar economic expansion. But even others without those advantages sometimes find a degree of financial comfort. There were teenagers I knew at a Catholic parish in Harlem well on their way to a good education and success, though they watched their friends sell drugs on the street at fifteen. There were families I knew in the now-gentrified area of New York City called Hell's Kitchen who were veterans of the heroin and crack epidemics of the 1970s and '80s. Many of the children of these Puerto Rican, Irish, and African-American families had good jobs and were successful parents. Some of their brothers and sisters never made it. They never found their stride or confidence; some died from violence or AIDS; others were in prison or fell victim to mental illness. My point is that some poor people do exceptionally well, but for those who find themselves in a crisis, no protective financial cushion breaks their fall. There is no extra access to the resources and help that money provides. They become lost. I think of a lot of the men I met in prison ministry. They had no expensive lawyers or comfortable suburban background to shield them from jail time for a drug conviction. Once in the system, many of them appeared locked in it for life.

This reality of poverty makes financial security an understandable preoccupation. I once asked a young homeless drug addict in a downtown park about comfort. Though he was undoubtedly high, he said to me without hesitation and with clarity, "It's having everything I need and not having to think about it." But the spread of poverty in the United States makes financial comfort a worry for more people than just the desperately poor. No one wants to be poor, and the worry about it seems to hang over a lot of people's heads. Many working- and middle-class people feel particularly vulnerable when it comes to health care and job security. According to the U.S. Census Bureau, 15 percent of Americans did not have health insurance in 2009 (nearly a quarter of those with household income under $25,000). More and more employers find they cannot foot the bill as health-care costs rise, including major corporations driven out of profitability by the cost of providing health care to large numbers of employees and pensioners. Cities and states struggle with their budgets on account of health-care costs. Health-care disasters are the number one cause of personal bankruptcy. Even just watching the health-care crisis for other people can have an impact on the way we think about financial security and comfort. A case-worker for adult protective services told me about her work investigating the neglect and abuse of seniors. She said:

> What is financial security, I think, has been skewed by my work. I almost feel sometimes like I don't know if I'll ever have enough money when I get old to pay for the care I need at home and not to be in an institution . . . There are seniors that have an amazingly comfortable life, but their needs, their medical needs . . . force [them] to go into a hospital. Are they financially comfortable? Absolutely not.

Job loss functions in a similar way. How many homeless people's stories begin with losing a job? How many of us have exhausted our savings and gone deeply into debt during extended unemployment, dancing with poverty? As with health care, the prospect of unemployment frightens many people to the extent that they believe they can never have enough money.

Comfort implies security. We need to know that we will have at the very least housing, food on the table, and health care, with a sense that these things cannot be taken away arbitrarily. If they are taken away, a person or family wants to know they have the capacity and resources to regain them with some timeliness. Gaining a modicum of security like that will look slightly different for each person, depending on skills, education, savings, and family resources, as well as the children and other dependent persons under his or her care. It also depends on factors like age, immigration status, the type of field one works in, and whether or not recession dominates the economic landscape. There's no magic formula, but the precautions people take in terms of health and life insurance, savings, retraining and education, retirement, seem like rational responses to the need for financial security. They form part of that healthy cushion of financial comfort.

But how much of a cushion is necessary? How much is enough?

## Tyranny of Expectations

One summer I spent a few days in London. One night in a hotel room, I flipped on the television. Over the next half hour I watched, with increasing fascination, an evening drama about urban bus drivers. It had all the usual elements of office drama— tangled relationships, gossip, tyrannical supervisors, adultery, people getting fired, people fighting the system. Yet despite this predictability, I remained enthralled. I had never seen or even imagined a TV drama about bus drivers before (I later learned the BBC had one about postal workers). Here the drivers, men and women, were portrayed with all the usual human foibles but also as being content with the routine of a dependable job. And why not? Yet as I watched, it struck me that this would simply not work in the United States. Even back in the mid-1950s in *The Honeymooners*, Jackie Gleason's Ralph Kramden had to show a certain ambivalence regarding his work as a bus driver. American-TV bus drivers have to dream of something else, ambitious to improve their social situation in some way. In an American show there would be second jobs, night school, long commutes to the suburbs, or justifications for a lack of social mobility in the way of family obligations—sick mothers, children in college. At the very least the drivers would talk about their plans and hopes for their children, how much further the kids would go. All this would have to appear.

Restlessness for a better life is ingrained in the national mythology of the United States. That is why people come to this country. Nothing could be more American than a restless desire for a new and better lifestyle.

The greater mystery may be how Americans form our expectations about lifestyle in the first place. How do we come to expect a certain level of comfort for our families? How does a certain kind of car—a certain level of affluence—come to feel like a self-evidently comfortable life?

Sociologist Juliet Schor believes that it all comes down to comparisons with people we know that we make almost unconsciously. We see what other people have and we want it—that is, what our family, friends, acquaintances, coworkers, coreligion-ists have. Apparently many of us also have a habit of comparing lifestyles with the characters we see on television shows, at least with the ones we can relate to. To back up this seemingly absurd conclusion, Schor reports that as people watch more television they also tend to engage in more petty theft! In any case, in real life, this phenomenon of people coveting their neighbors' goods has a way of building on itself. As more people desire what others in their comparison group have and acquire it, there is more stuff around to see and to want. The coveting and the acquiring increase. Simply put, material comfort becomes contagious, and the contagion spreads like wildfire. Eventually various material comforts reach what journalist Malcolm Gladwell calls the "tipping point." They spread exponentially. It seems as if everyone has it, whatever "it" is—kids' sneakers that light up (or roll on wheels), fancy boots, a high-definition flat-screen television.

This habit of "comparison collecting" works out for some of us. For those with the upper income levels within their com-parison group—who are richer than most of their family and neighbors—it works in their favor. They could probably afford a lot more than they buy. For those who work or associate with people better off than they are, the situation can grow dire. They might end up mortgaging themselves out to dry just to "keep up" with their friends and colleagues. Or there may occur some kind of "fall from grace," where a person or family falls noticeably out of step with the lifestyle of their peers. According to Schor's studies, people feel ashamed for not keeping up.

This explanation of the relentless march of our American lifestyle makes a lot of sense. It shows why certain lifestyle expectations spread within a reference group—why there were once endless Volvos in the city of Berkeley (then Priuses), why so many gay men bought furniture at IKEA, why thousands of upper-middle-class urbanites thought sports utility vehicles necessary to drive on city streets. Yet it also demonstrates why it becomes difficult—or even shameful—to *not have* things. A college buddy of mine and his wife purchased a home, a modest bungalow in a Los Angeles suburb. It was a lovely house, a nice neighborhood, easy access to work for them, and an extra bedroom for the son who came along within a couple of years. But common acquaintances reacted with disdain to news about the square footage— 930 square feet. People both complained to them directly and gossiped about it behind their backs. One person even said to me, "Why did they bother buying it?" Though practically speaking my friend and his wife had all they needed, according to their "reference group" of friends and acquaintances, they were acting imprudently by not buying bigger. It wasn't even my house, and I felt the pressure.

In other parts of the world, Americans are routinely trashed for our acquisitiveness and materialism. Such a blanket accusation misses something, a dynamic of comparison and conformity that traps people without them even being aware of it. In the United States, *not to have is not to belong*, to be left out. It feels intolerable. Yet, for many of us, staying in the race takes an even greater toll.

What is the impact of these increasing lifestyle expectations on society as a whole?

Novelist Salman Rushdie is known among critics for writing about his native India and the clash of worldviews there between culture, religion, and modern Western influence. He is probably best known to the public for being sentenced to death by the Ayatollah Khomeini for allegedly attacking Muhammad and the Quran in his novel *The Satanic Verses* (1988). But in a later novel titled *Fury* (2001), the writer addressed the question of ever-increasing material expectations in New York City. In this first novel taking place in the United States, a depressed Indian émigré academic on the run from his family in England wrestles (for unknown reasons) with bitter, even murderous rage. Arriving in Manhattan, however, he finds he is not alone, that virtually everyone in the Big Apple seems to want to take a swing at someone else. His explanation: living at the end of the twentieth century, people have seen expectations ratcheted up by prosperity. It's unbearable. No one can possibly be satisfied. No one can be comfortable *enough*. Everyone feels thwarted, personally deprived, bored, depressed, and ticked off.

Is Rushdie right? Certainly he exaggerates our predicament— not everyone I know is ready to explode. But the malaise and pique he describes are not alien to the lives of people you or I know, nor indeed is that frustrating feeling that somehow life can never be enough. According to Schor, behind this frustration and disquiet lies a simple social pattern. Rising consumer expectations trap us in a work-and-spend cycle that makes people increasingly unhappy. She points out that surveys gauging personal happiness peaked in the 1950s, and she quotes stories about people earning six figures and still feeling anxious and pressured to make ends meet.

I am loath to draw conclusions about Americans' personal

happiness over the decades from a survey, but Dr. Schor's basic idea—unhappy people madly working and spending to keep up with ever-rising expectations—rings true. When I lived in New York, one evening I attended a party for people working in banking and finance, most married with children. I listened to them talk about the financial burdens imposed by the lifestyle they had to maintain—expensive suits, houses and apartments, private schools, summer camp for the children. I began to understand how a person with a six-figure income could lament not having enough money.

When can people stop thinking that they must have more? In the United States anyway, my sense is that this never happens. The restless American drive to improve one's situation—the same drive that has taken immigrants out of their tenements and into the suburbs, that has seen parents work double shifts so their children might be the first in the family to attend college—that drive to improve never goes away, generations after the tenements and the dead-end jobs. Americans never stop working toward a better lifestyle for themselves and their families, even when the driving ambition becomes unnecessary or even faintly ridiculous. The high school teacher I quoted earlier claims that many people he knows see becoming a millionaire as their goal—not as an exceptional thing, not a dream, just an ordinary goal for a bunch of middle-class guys. They have set themselves up to fail. Even in the richest country in the world, only a tiny percentage of people will ever achieve such wealth. But the ethos of America requires that people keep moving up.

Thus, the quest for a little cushion of financial comfort has gotten completely out of hand amid a tyranny of expectations. And the United States is not alone in this. Tracey Smith, a British writer who specializes in simpler and more ecological living, told me:

> Across the world, society tells us, we need to aspire to earn as much as we can, we need to have the latest gadgets, the quickest fix, fastest cars—and we can have the best loans if we cannot afford them, credit is thrust upon us from every form of the media. We are running ourselves into early graves in pursuit of these dreams, too, stress levels are higher than ever, use of antidepressants through the roof, and surveys on the quality of our sex lives is showing our rat race lifestyles are having a great impact.

When I traveled to Mexico City in 2001 and 2007, I noticed gigantic, well-stocked supermarkets springing up everywhere. And there was great interest in the latest computer wizardry and imported gadgets. Even the quieter places of the world are beginning to show signs of the impact of these rising consumer expectations. A Scottish nurse described her homeland as a very quiet, out-of-the-way, somewhat undeveloped place while she was growing up twenty-five years ago. She claimed, for example, she had never laid eyes on a piece of broccoli before coming to the United States. But now, she says, "Things are heating up. There are more cars on the road . . . People probably have more money on their hands than they used to, you know there's more consumer goods available, so it's definitely getting more like [the United States]." The rising tide of expectations is spreading throughout the world.

Yet there is also movement around the world to simply opt out.

# Downshifting from the Rat Race

When two jet planes brought down the World Trade Center towers on September 11, 2001, Tracey Smith and her husband, Ray, decided it was time to make their move.

Both Tracey and Ray had worked in the "square mile," London's version of Wall Street. In 2001, however, only Ray worked for a data connection company there, while Tracey stayed home with their three children in the London suburbs. With his long hours and commute, Ray would often find himself kissing the children good night after they had already gone to sleep. Both felt that something had to change—what they had was more a "mere existence" than a life. Like some other English couples they knew about, they had begun to investigate the possibility of moving to France and living a quieter, more ecological and family-oriented lifestyle—what is sometimes called a "downshifting" of lifestyle. But they hadn't quite made the break. On 9/11, Ray was at work talking on the phone to a client in New York City who was sitting in his office across from the World Trade Center. The first plane hit, and the man described the entire experience to Ray. A short while later Ray watched it on television. The whole thing proved transformative for him and for Tracey.

"We just couldn't believe how many wonderful mums and dads and sisters and brothers had gone to work that day and hadn't come home. It's a real prick of your mortality. Dear God, this life is so short," Tracey explained. "Our life was simple, but it was hard, we were struggling to just all be together. The kids were one, two, and three at the time, and we just thought, we're going to make our move. So that's why we made our big downshift." Within a few months they had left their life in London for a farmhouse in southwestern France. They grew their own fruits and vegetables, and they raised chickens. They sat and talked together in the evenings. Living on a fraction of the money they had earned in the past, they now had a luxury they had never experienced before: time for each other.

Tracey and Ray are not alone in their desire to escape the relentless upward surge of expectations in contemporary life. Tracey now writes on downshifting for national magazines and Web sites in the United Kingdom, and she has e-mail correspondents who have made this change across Great Britain, in the United States, Australia, and all over Europe. She tells me that in the United States, most of her downshifters live in California, Washington State, and Virginia. She does not normally encourage people to make the kind of radical shift she and her family did. To her, downshifting can and should come in baby steps. Tracey believes the main thing is "when they realize it doesn't matter how much money you have. You cannot buy time."

Juliet Schor also ran across the phenomenon of downshifting in her investigation of Americans' quest for material comforts. She speaks of people waving good-bye to the rat race, the pressure, the endless upgrading, the brand names, and the culture of disposability. Schor reported in 1998 that about 19 percent of American adults had downshifted *by choice*. They did it for a host of reasons, a lot of them having to do with stressful lives and overwork. Some do it so one parent can stay home with children. A few attempt to change priorities and seek more meaningful lives. A lot of these people described to Schor the palpable relief they felt at not having to do work they hated or didn't believe in anymore. Others celebrated the joy of a lifestyle that did not tread so hard on the environment or one that enabled them to spend more time with their children. Professor Schor also took a look at those people who had "been downshifted," who had had it done to them, so to speak, by job loss or family economic problems. Even among them, nearly a quarter found that they actually preferred their new downscaled lifestyle.

A lot of those who downshifted by choice in Schor's study did not stick with it. Tracey Smith told me this was true in England as well. She said that one of the major moving companies that helps people make the move to rural France told her that nearly two-thirds of those who went were back within a year.

I asked Tracey why she thought people had so much trouble making the downshift work. I assumed she would say something about people's attachment to their old lifestyle or the social position that goes with it. Rather, she said, people attempt too much too quickly. They are not prepared. Chiefly, they have not thought about how to make a living in their new lifestyle. "We all need to earn some money at the end of the day, it doesn't matter how simply you're living." Interestingly enough, she also felt that many people downshift to resolve relationship problems. That farmhouse in the country sounds like a romantic solution to ailing marriages, but it feels a lot less romantic once you get there and have to clean your own septic tank. Finally, she suggested that many people simply do not bring the practical skills and orientation necessary to live outside the "disposable society" of the city and the suburbs. They cannot fathom actually getting out the tools once something has broken or attempting to barter repair skills with friends and neighbors.

So goes the downshifting story from England and France. But downshifting in the United States looks a little different. It often goes by the name *voluntary simplicity*, and it does not always involve abandoning the city and moving to the country. As a result, downshifters may find themselves still connected to the world they knew before the shift. Moving to smaller quarters across town or to a less busy city some distance away makes for a different experience than taking off to France. And it creates its own difficulties in tensions with family, friends, and acquaintances. Usually the social tensions level off at bewildered incomprehension and the occasional sarcasm, but sometimes it goes further. I know a young woman from New York City who tried but could not hold on to her old friends after she downshifted; not having the money for frequent dinners and brunches out, she simply could not find financially compatible activities to share with them.

Despite the complications, it can be done. Tracey called her downshift to France "the biggest adventure of our lives . . . the most amazing four years of my life." She returned to the UK only because her work promoting downshifting kept calling her back there. Now she and her husband live in a small cottage in rural southwest England. She volunteers for the Magdalen Project, a local organic farm that hosts meetings for stressed-out corporate workers. Rather than feeling envious toward a more opulent lifestyle, her children brag to their classmates about the kind of life they have together as a family. Tracey looks around at all the stress people experience with their busy lives, and she knows it does not have to be like that. Her own experience motivates her to "try to help people achieve a simpler, happier disposition for their own health and well-being and for the love of their families." She engages in no guilt mongering or scare mongering in her writing. She advises people, "Ditch the guilt for what you're not doing and feel good about what you are doing." Downshifting and living a more environmentally sustainable lifestyle can begin with small things—fewer hours of TV and more family time, recycling instead of throwing things away, spending more time with friends, changing jobs to have less of a commute. Not everyone is equipped to move to the country and grow vegetables as she did.

## The Bread of Comfort

Another way to get off the train of rising expectations is to make a greater commitment to share.

"Money is the ability to help other people, and that in itself is really wonderful." That's what the fifty-four-year-old mother of a grown daughter said during one discussion I initiated about financial comfort. She directs her family's foundation, providing services to adults with disabilities, Boys' and Girls' Clubs, and the frail elderly since 1980. She derives great satisfaction from this work, which she considers herself fortunate to have the means to do. Not only does this work help the less fortunate, something she remembers being taught to do from girlhood—her family had a *tzedakah* box for charity at Sabbath dinners—but it also continues a legacy begun by her parents and continued by her and her brother together. All three are now deceased.

As this philanthropist's comments about *tzedakah* boxes on the Sabbath suggests, Judaism has a lot to say about sharing with the less fortunate. In fact, most of the religions of humanity (and some major philosophies) see providing for the needs of hungry, homeless, and poor people as a duty and a privilege. They recognize that such acts turn a person away from superficial preoccupations and cultivate virtue and depth. The emphasis is strong in the three so-called Abrahamic religions—Judaism, Christianity, and Islam—though not always there in practice. In the Christian Bible, Jesus contends that paradise belongs to the one who offers food, drink, shelter, health care, or a prison visit to a person in need (Matthew 25:31–46). Traditionally, Christians gave 10 percent of their income "to God" (the church word for this, *tithe*, is simply Middle English for "a tenth"). Catholic churches now recommend 5 percent to the church and 5 percent to charity. Throughout the Jewish Scriptures, people are instructed over and over that their own spiritual well-being depends upon their care for widows and orphans, those who in ancient times had no one to provide for them. Jewish law states that 10 percent of one's income goes to charity. Similar sentiments about widows and orphans are expressed in the Quran, and every Muslim is required to offer a percentage of his total assets each year for the poor (known as *zakat*). They do not see this as charity (*sadaqah*) but as fulfilling one of the five pillars of Islam.

According to UNICEF, there are tens of millions of street children in cities across the world. I met one a few years ago in Mexico City, on a side street not far from the Basilica of Our Lady of Guadalupe. I was visiting a friend there, and that afternoon a friend of his drove us around town. She had carefully guided her sedan into the left-turn lane when the boy—who looked about seven with a beaming smile and dirty face—approached it. He put his grimy hand out for money. She reached into a bag on the car seat and pulled out the loaf of Italian bread we had purchased to eat at the dinner party she planned. The child took the bread, thanked her, and moved on to the next car.

She explained that rumors said that local organized crime syndicates "employed" the street children, taking the lion's share of their earnings from begging on the street. Our host reasoned that they could not take the bread.

The story of the street kid reminds me of how complicated sharing the "bread of our comfort" can be. When I worked as a parish priest in New York City, con artists attempted to scam me out of money with sob stories more times than I can remember. Yet thousands of people with real needs lived in that same city. How do we share under those circumstances? Some people's solution is to color all the needy in the tones of the shysters, even though, for example, families with children are one of the fastest-growing groups among the homeless. Many people opt not to share because they do not know where the money goes or because they haven't a clue how best to give, not wishing to encourage dependency or vagrancy. We have ambivalent feelings about certain kinds of requests for money. Not many New Yorkers shed tears in the 1990s when Mayor Rudy Giuliani managed to eliminate the ubiquitous "squeegee guys," who would come and wash your car windows for a donation, with or without your permission. I occasionally give money to beggars (feeling that there but for the grace of God go I), but I know a lot of very good people will not. Probably a sizable donation to the food pantry, the homeless shelter network, the local poverty relief organization functions as a more effective way to bring comfort to the needy. Not to mention volunteer work for these groups.

Activism also matters, and in many cases is an even more effective form of sharing. Throughout the 1980s wages declined precipitously for janitors in Los Angeles, so much so that jobs formerly at a living wage with health benefits ceased to exist.

Especially with the lion's share of jobs occupied by female immigrants—people without political clout and arriving in L.A. in large numbers—improving the situation looked impossible. Activism, however, made the difference. The Service Employees International Union launched the successful "Justice for Janitors" campaign in the late 1980s. Central American and Mexican immigrant janitors and their student, civic-leader, and clergy allies demonstrated in the business districts of Los Angeles, intending to put pressure on the larger and more well-known companies that hire janitorial services rather than the janitorial services companies themselves. Particularly after a widely publicized beating of activists by police in June of 1990, sympathy spread for the janitors' cause. The companies were forced to negotiate. Wages improved and benefits returned.

Often such activism accomplishes more than simple giving. How much do governments spend helping hungry children in comparison to building weapons or servicing their national debt? Often very little. A donation to Doctors Without Borders, Oxfam, or one of the religious relief groups like Catholic Relief Services or American Jewish World Service will certainly help suffering people hit by the plague of AIDS in Africa. But this ends up being a drop in the bucket compared with the impact the rich nations have when they invest in AIDS prevention, poverty reduction, and allow for patented medicines to be used at cheaper prices. Polls show that Americans routinely overestimate the amount the United States gives in aid to poor countries. It is actually less than a tenth of a percent of gross national income, and most developed countries give far more. Working together to change the conditions that foster AIDS or large-scale poverty may not look like a form of sharing what we have, but the powerful pressure of citizens on their own governments in solidarity with the poor makes a big difference.

Both sharing and activism depend on people finding common ground—even and especially if that common ground begins with our common humanity.

Legend has it that in 1943, after the German occupation of Denmark began, the Nazis decreed that all Jews had to wear the yellow Star of David to identify them for deportation to concentration camps. King Christian of Denmark had been one of the few European monarchs to remain in his country after occupation, and each day he appeared on horseback riding around Copenhagen alone. After the Nazi decree regarding the star, he appeared on these daily rounds with the unmistakable mark of a yellow Star of David on his sleeve. Everyone understood this as a gesture of solidarity: other Danes followed his example, donning the mark themselves, making it virtually impossible for the Danish Jews to be identified and deported.

It is a wonderful story of leadership and compassion; but the story isn't true.

The Jews of Denmark were never required to wear the yellow star (except those who ended up at the Theresienstadt camp in Czechoslovakia), and the king never rode about on horseback wearing the star himself. What is true, however, is that nearly all of the Jews of Denmark survived the Holocaust, spirited out of Denmark to Sweden by friendly Danes who were incensed by this German offensive against Danish traditions of equality and tolerance. Ordinary people assisted in the rescue, hiding families, feeding and transporting people, caring for Jewish homes in people's absence. Many risked their lives. Probably we cannot say that no anti-Semitism of the kind found elsewhere in Europe existed in Denmark during the era of fascism, but we can say that as a general rule Danish Christians saw Nazi targeting of the Danish Jews as *their problem* rather than something to distance themselves from. And they acted.

Solidarity is that gesture or action that communicates to a besieged group "I am with you." President John F. Kennedy's speech during the Soviet blockade of Berlin in 1961 was a gesture of solidarity. He famously said, *"Ich bin ein Berliner,"* by which he meant to say, "I, too, am a part of Berlin," though purveyors of urban legends erroneously claim that the syntax of the phrase made it sound like he said, "I am a jelly doughnut." His words brought great comfort to the surrounded people of West Berlin. The young and energetic president of the United States was with them and would not abandon them to the Soviets.

When people are under attack or even just hurting, to put some distance between us and them may seem like the most natural reaction in the world. Why should their problem be mine? It may require a great deal of empathy and focused energy to put myself in their place—it may be quite *uncomfortable.* On the other hand, it may come surprisingly naturally once we put aside certain fears and anxieties. When I was a parish priest in New York City, I was called one day to visit a homebound woman dying from cancer. Our backgrounds couldn't have been more different—she was a native New Yorker, of Puerto Rican heritage, female, middle-aged, divorced, and the mother of grown children, sick with a terminal illness, spiritual but not terribly religious, by personality direct and fairly heedless of other people's opinions. I was an imported Californian, a young white man, never married, childless, healthy, religious by profession, by temperament cautious and sensitive to the opinions of others. Yet in the months that I visited her before she died, we connected. Something about the force of her personality—a tenacious liveliness—captured me.

This sense of solidarity may be the most important quality we can share with someone. Acts of help work only when accompanied by true compassionate understanding. Otherwise help has a condescending edge to it—implying a superior, at times almost godlike position from which assistance is handed down. That sense of common humanity gets lost. The giver forgets that the tables could easily be reversed. A wealthy suburban church community in California became accustomed to sending money and food to their sister parish in a more troubled urban neighborhood on the other side of town. Perhaps many members of the affluent congregation felt virtuous for giving, and it was a help for the poorer church. But it could hardly be termed "sharing." Most members of the rich parish had nothing to do with these people. They really knew nothing about them. Then one day the people of the poorer church asked the wealthier parishioners to come visit. This was an invitation to be in solidarity rather than just to dish out assistance. A lot of parishioners were actually afraid to go, but those who did had a wonderful time sharing food and conversation. Each group saw more of the humanity of the other, their everyday joys and worries. In the end, it was a great comfort to both.

## Freedom and Financial Comfort

"John" is a retired garbageman in his fifties, a fact he reports with pride. He always appreciated that his job afforded him a stable living for his family, and that it brought him into contact with all kinds of people, not infrequently the homeless and destitute. At times he tried to help them. I met John at a medium-size state prison in New York State. He was a volunteer, directing spiritual retreats for inmates. I had been asked to come to help John and his team—to listen to the inmates' confessions, to talk to them, to comment on religious topics wherever necessary.

This retired garbageman (he rejects all the euphemisms, no "sanitation worker" for him) passes most of his days involved in some act of service. He likes working the retreats for the inmates in particular, and he is good at it. Not mincing words, punctuating his talks with rapid-fire humor, he tells the inmates that he knows they think they can put their lives together on their own, but they can't. He entertains them with a colorful account of his own conversion. He did not need God, but God came to him anyway, on a retreat such as this one, and afterward everything was different. It's a classic conversion story, the details of which confidentiality forbids me from reproducing here. It was deep and dark enough. And yet now he stands before them without any nervousness or anxiety. He takes time with each inmate outside the sessions. He calls them brothers, tells them he cares for them, and declares that it does not matter to him what any of them did to get there. Each of these declarations is tested by the inmates during the retreat, and he seems to pass.

John comes back to one point again and again. Like most people, he used to have a life tethered to many cares. But his faith made him free. Using that word—*free*—in a prison is risky. This is a crowd skeptical of freedom. But John does not worry about that. He offers direct feedback, both positive and negative. My impression is that he *is* truly a free man. After I found faith, he tells them, I found I wasn't so scared anymore. God is with me. And you know what? I'm free. He opens his arms as he says it. No one can take that away from him. He's not afraid to die or anything else. God is going to take care of him. He tells them that even if he were in there, he would be free.

Most of the men on the prison retreat are between the ages of seventeen and thirty. I can see that the faces of some of them are masks; they are reserving judgment, or perhaps they only came to take a break from the daily grind of life under the state's regime. But others don't try to hide it. They are rapt at John's words. They look at him, and they do see freedom. And they want it. They want a more stable life for themselves. Most of them have children, some have long-term girlfriends or wives. They want to offer more to them than they have in the past. They want that faith that will move mountains, that will make all things possible, that will get them through every day they have to spend inside. They want to be free, free so that no one or nothing can touch them.

This may seem like an odd story to drop in the middle of a chapter about financial comfort.

In a world with swirling expectations for financial and material comforts, we may never be satisfied. We might in fact find ourselves exhausted by the work it requires to maintain a certain lifestyle. Every day in this world people get up, commute long distances to work, toil at a job they dislike, commute back home, arriving barely in time to eat a bite, relax for an hour, and then turn in to get up and do it all over again. We begin to feel like machines. Sometimes good reasons exist to live like that. Sacrifices must be made for the education and welfare of children, for the opportunity to move into a safer neighborhood. As Tracey Smith and the downshifters in Juliet Schor's research found, however, at times we wake up and realize that we work ourselves to the bone only for the sake of having more stuff, or at least for the privilege of keeping up with the lifestyle of others who make a lot more money than we do. Why do it?

When I was working for hourly wages as a teenager, I remember asking one of my coworkers why he worked two full-time jobs. I wondered if he was helping to support his family or saving up for some kind of dream. He looked at me as if I were stupid, and said, "So I can buy more things." As he described the myriad stereo equipment he had recently bought, I wondered when he had time to enjoy it. But I kept quiet.

My own experience suggests that most people look for something more in life than simply buying *more things*. We want to feel the freedom that John exhibited, a letting go of fear and worry, a firm sense that we will survive and be happy no matter what comes our way. No financial cushion, no matter how large, will provide that. In a way, that is what those old riches-to-ashes books and movies tried to tell us. Orson Welles's Kane could not buy back what he lost in childhood; Fitzgerald's Gatsby could not secure the love and loyalty of Daisy. Those guarantees always lie just beyond our reach, like the light across the water in F. Scott Fitzgerald's novel.

This is not to say that financial security isn't important, that saving isn't a good habit, that people shouldn't buy life insurance, that health insurance shouldn't be affordable and accessible to all, that some kind of social safety net shouldn't be preserved for future generations. These are all excellent habits and necessary social structures, but they will not fulfill our deepest expectations or afford us happiness.

Nor do I think a person has to have exactly the type of Christian faith John had in order to feel free. But probably everyone would agree that freedom requires a certain amount of letting go. Fear and worry will always try to tear us down, to take away our happiness. Solid spirituality keeps them at bay. So does love. As the Bible says, "There is no fear in love, but perfect love casts out fear" (1 John 4:18, NRSV). There *is* a comfort for us in love, in spirituality that brings real freedom.

So we turn to relationships and to spirituality as the journey into comfort continues.

# Part Three

# Way Beyond Easy Street: Real-Life Comforts

*Too much of a good thing is . . . wonderful.*

—ATTRIBUTED TO MAE WEST

# Chapter Seven

# The Comfort of Company

*It is not good that the man should be alone.*

GENESIS 2:18, NRSV

## It's Not Good for the Man to Be Alone

At Jewish and Christian weddings, you almost always hear the above words from the book of Genesis. At both, this is generally how you hear it translated, though literally the Hebrew text says that it is not good for the *adam* to be alone (where we get the name Adam), a word that means "human being," regardless of gender, like the Latin *homo* or the Greek *anthropos*. It is not good for the human being to be alone.

Translations aside, maybe not everyone would agree with the sentiment. A friend who moved to New York from the Philippines was initially mystified by Americans' frequent need for what we call "space" (really, time alone). Americans consider it a perfectly reasonable thing to ask our friends or family to leave us alone for a while. Many of us actually look forward to sequestering ourselves in our rooms. This strikes people from other parts of the world as odd if not downright antisocial. In many places, it's considered impolite to leave someone alone, a failure of companionship or hospitality. On the other hand, that peculiar American need for "space" can be contagious. People immigrate here, go back to their home countries, and feel crowded and overwhelmed. Even my Filipina friend found herself infected by the alone-time virus in some small way. When she moved to Latin America and attended a big meeting of the organization for which she worked, she attempted to take a few minutes away from the din. People kept approaching her and politely asked her how she was. The situation had been reversed.

Even within more individualist cultures like the United States there are variations on how alone people want to be. Some kinds of work require more solitude—astronauts, farmers, monks—and they tend to appreciate it more than most of us. Western men famously want more alone time than women, and beyond that there are individual personality differences. Some of us want to think things out thoroughly before we ever open our mouths; others think out loud, finding it difficult to draw conclusions without the give-and-take of conversation. Age sometimes (but not always) makes a difference. Many teenagers and college students I know dislike being alone and look for distractions when faced with the possibility—they switch on their MP3 players, whip out their cell phones, or flip on the television. An elderly man I know spends most of his days in silence thinking and working alone at home. After a lifetime working with people, he finds it a peaceful and creative space.

Regardless of these variations, being permanently cut off from the company of others isn't good for us, and we intuitively know the impact isolation has on us psychologically, leaving us prickly and depressed. There are the medical effects. The incidence of strokes, high blood pressure, and various diseases increases as people spend more time by themselves. One review of research in the journal *Science* found that extreme isolation doubles the risk of sickness or death. It is not good for the human being to be alone, at least not too much. On the other hand, positive clinical effects go with *not being alone.* There is a basic connection between both psychological and physical health and the company of others. Having other people around makes us feel healthier and more contented. As a sixty-year-old long-married attorney told me, "If we want to talk about comfort, we should really talk about love." She elaborated that she did not mean just romantic love but "something bigger."

Our experience and scientific research back her up. Friendships engender happiness. The people we care about often complement us and make us better people. I have a friend, a colleague of mine in graduate school, who is a very kind and positive person. When she comes around, it brings out a kinder and more positive side of me. Don't we all know shy people who delight in their more gregarious spouses and excitable people calmed by life partners of a more quiet nature? I know a restless architect with a thousand interests who is grateful that his wife's homebody ways rein him in. Other people often bring to us complementary perspectives as well as security, understanding, energy, companionship. Medical research has shown that people with loved ones in their lives are more likely to survive serious illnesses like cancer and heart disease—and are more likely to survive period—than those without the same social connections. At least one study found that the better the *quality* of a person's relationships, the less likely she was to get sick. The quality of relationships clearly makes a difference—nasty friendships and bad marriages take their toll on people's health and life—yet, on average, having people around is a comfort.

## Families by Any Other Name

Most of us intuitively know all this—that we are better off with people in our lives. In fact, a lot of people's deepest fears are organized around being abandoned, alone, friendless. Yet we live in an age and culture where close relationships are more and more challenging to maintain. It's an individualistic age. Our connections seem weaker and more diffuse. Yet many people do maintain strong connections in the face of today's questions and pressures, developing for themselves a kind of "family of choice."

In the contemporary age of mobility and globalization, transnational institutions and markets have created a whole tribe of international wanderers. You know them if you aren't one yourself—in the United States the parade of economic migrants and itinerants I have met includes medical doctors and Catholic priests from India, farmworkers and businessmen from Mexico, Italian college professors, Spanish museum curators, Singaporean lawyers, bankers and housecleaners from Colombia. A friend of mine who works for the United Nations belongs to this tribe.

Having lived in the Czech Republic and Finland, she originally hails from a London suburb. She has traveled extensively through Europe, East Asia, the United States, Africa, and South America; her work has often functioned more as a reason to take her where she wanted to go than as an honest-to-goodness career choice. Yet despite all this wandering, my friend has an incredible gift for making and holding on to friends. She maintains connections with a large number of people all over the world. When she recognizes something in you she likes, she makes a commitment to you as a friend. You will be invited along on lunches and Saturday outings, to gatherings on New Year's Eve in foreign cities, and to dinner when her parents come into town (who also have a gift for hospitality). You will be introduced to other friends, many of whom will become your friends as well. Even when you are separated by the miles, there will be the occasional e-mail, card, or phone call to ensure that you are doing well and still in the circle.

My friend makes it sound easy, but it's not. Even for her. As with most people, she has had the perennial anxieties over work and love. But I like to think that she lives more contentedly than many of her contemporaries because of this advantage she learned from her family: that relationships are central in life, that some kind of sense of family is key, that if family does not lie close, you must, in a sense, create it for yourself.

Another friend puts it more frankly. She reports that when she left home to become a missionary sister, a wise older nun said to her, "Make home wherever you are."

In the political arena we hear people urging us to "return to family values." This is indeed noble, but in an age of spectacular divorce rates, high mobility, and both parents working, it is unrealistic (and a bit sexist) to expect people to return to the social roles and expectations of times past. You cannot put the genie back in the bottle. Even the sense of family that predominated then, the nuclear family, was for many people a betrayal of the *real* family—the extended family—that they had known in their home countries, in small towns, or in their childhoods. But we should not forget that there is truth in the family values rhetoric—a hunger for connection and belonging. Human beings must have *family*—a network of relationships where we are accepted and belong. Children need caregivers, adults companions on the life journey. Yet in our time the social and economic factors that held families together—geographic stability, prohibitions against divorce, women depending on men for income and men on women for homemaking—do not hold us together so well anymore. Many people believe family and community ties are breaking down. Others say they are simply being reconfigured.

If traditional families of blood relationships do not always hold together, families of *choice* fill in the gap. Those in the adult world have the right and ability to choose with whom they will associate, and they often bring good people into their lives (and into the lives of their children), especially if families are not around, or only around in a limited way. An Internet technology salesman from Northern California described this as the "tribe" phenomenon. He noted that most of his friends in California moved there from somewhere else. Their families live far away and they see them at most a handful of times a year. So for regular companionship they depend on the "tribe," a group of close friends that regularly gather at the holiday parties, who keep tabs on one another, who are the ones to show up for funerals, weddings, baptisms, and bar mitzvahs. The bond among them is genuine, but the salesman admitted to some differences between the tribe and blood family. He felt more willing to make naked demands on his family back in North Carolina than on his friends here. While he had no doubt they would pitch in if needed, he felt in the tribe that natural "give-and-take" of friendship rather than sheer duty.

When my British friend lived in New York City, she found herself at the center of a group of friends who met in a ceramics class. They serve as a kind of family of choice for one another— they support one another, show up at each other's wedding or art openings, celebrate birthdays together, send flowers and gifts at the right moment, and keep information about the group moving. Similarly, a priest I knew with a challenging biological family situation had a small group of friends with whom he vacationed every year. In a way they were like his family. They called him frequently just to find out how he was doing. I think he owes half his sanity and health to them, and they do not even live nearby.

Even a person's biological family can become a family of choice. Since the traditional notions that family is about inheritance, community alliances, and political and economic gain have pretty much collapsed in the West, new possibilities open up for relationships within our families. Family members can become friends, especially once children are older. I was reminded of this hearing the family situation of a former stock trader who left it all to work in patient care with the sick and dying in New York City hospitals. Born in South America, he immigrated to the United States as a teenager. He and his siblings still have memories of their extended family all gathered around in the town where they grew up. Perhaps as a result, even as they have scattered, his brothers and sisters remain in close contact. They celebrate holidays together and talk together on the telephone to their mother, who has now moved back to South America. They seem to have created the combination of independence and togetherness they all want.

None of these people is spectacularly wealthy, but in each of them I have observed a certain joy and comfort that I believe comes at least partially from that network of relationships, far and near, that give a human being a platform on which to stand. If my family of choice accepts me and I know who I am, I can relax in that and move on to accomplish good things in the world. I am *rich* in a different kind of way.

## Comfortable in Common

Yet not everyone can be family. Not everyone makes me feel more comfortable or less alone. Everyone has had the experience of that awkward conversation at a party so that after three or four minutes you were looking for an escape route. As a priest, I sometimes feel like *I* am that person for other people. At wedding receptions I find myself shouting over the music talking to elderly family members of the couple while the younger guests serially avoid me, sometimes looking at me as if they're afraid celibacy could be contagious. In any case, not everyone makes a person feel at home.

A computer analyst says he thinks of people when he thinks of comfort, but only *certain* people. It has to do with trust. A friend of his describes it as the ability to "let your hair down" with someone, to let down your guard and not worry about what you say. A woman married many years with grown children talked about the comfort that comes with a shared history over time. All of them agreed that having people with whom you are comfortable makes a qualitative difference in your life. A computer analyst, a single man in his fifties, told the story of a camping trip to Yosemite National Park. A self-described "Southern boy," he hates the cold, and yet during this trip cold rain fell while slushy snow covered the ground. Yet he felt so at ease with his friends on the trip that he hardly noticed. As he described the experience, "I completely forgot about the cold. We were so comfortable with each other that I marveled about it later. That I went through that and we all did, and we were just having the best time of our lives."

Much of what lies behind this mysterious interpersonal comfort seems to be an awareness of commonalities. We feel comfortable with people when we see what we have in common with them. In the 1980s, a group of well-known sociologists—Robert Bellah, Richard Madsen, William Sullivan, Ann Swidler, and Steven Tipton—argued that people in the United States tend to congregate in "lifestyle enclaves," middle-class communities where people associate based on their similar approaches to recreation, dress, and consumer tastes. Americans apparently feel more comfortable together when they know they all like to ski on vacation (or go to Las Vegas) or all enjoy football or have minivans. Not that it all comes down to lifestyle. Beliefs and values seem to matter a lot to people. At a political rally in San Francisco, I met a volunteer worker in her twenties who described herself as comfortable right there in the midst of the noise and crowds. She drew my attention to the sense of common purpose and values around us. A fortysomething patent agent described the comfort he derived from gathering for Easter dinner with others who shared his Christian faith. "So you can be overtly Christian and it's okay," he added.

Similarly people have said to me how *uncomfortable* situations of interpersonal disagreement and conflict over values and beliefs can be. One highly educated woman in a group I was consulting over lunch stopped short in describing her view of spiritual comfort, concerned that getting into the details of religious belief might be "embarrassing" or even divisive there at the table. A group of men I talked to expressed their concern about inadvertently offending a woman with feminist sensibilities. The aforementioned patent agent said that he and one friend of his, in order to avoid vociferous arguments, have agreed simply never to talk about politics or religion. Interestingly enough, sociologist Nina Eliasoph claims that Americans tend to avoid talking about politics in groups for fear that potential disagreement will disturb the unity of the group—that it will make things so uncomfortable that people will choose not to come together at all. True as that might seem, it clearly does not tell the whole story. As one Northern California man pointed out to me, many people actually relish pushing their cause on others. Though he admitted that this made *him* feel very uncomfortable.

## How I Found Acceptance as a Pain in the Ass

Initially we almost always find greater comfort with those people we share something in common with, whether it be a lifestyle, personality traits, or beliefs and values. A limited number of times in our lives, however, something else happens. We develop a stronger bond that transcends just having things in common. Time passes. A common history develops. Knowledge and acceptance of both strengths and weaknesses, gifts and vulnerabilities—it all figures in. As one woman in her fifties said of her relationship with her husband, "There is initial love, the thrill of every day, of meeting someone in a romance, and then thirty-four years later it's so comfortable, so nice. And you've gone through [a lot], you've grown together." Whether this happens with a lover or life partner, with close friends, or even among the members of our family, these experiences of love and connection mark and change us. They comfort us—but in a deeper way than just removing anxiety or forestalling conflict. They strengthen us, make us the people that we are.

Many years ago, before I entered the priesthood, I got into a fight with my then girlfriend at a church event we were both attending. I cannot remember who left the meeting first in a huff and who followed down the street. In any case, we caught up with each other about two blocks away. It was a warm summer evening. I remember the streetlamp was out, and it had grown unnaturally dark. She turned to me in the shadows, and I braced myself for a blast of her fury. It came, but what she said took me entirely by surprise. "You're a pain in the ass," she blurted out, "but I love you anyway, Brett Hoover." And she chuckled. I had no idea what to say. I was still angry but also oddly comforted by her words. After all, frankly, I *am* a pain in the ass. Yet here was someone who knew that, who knew me as I am and accepted me, who knew my strengths and weaknesses and dealt with me in the complexity of it all. How could I not feel gratitude for her love and acceptance?

At Christian weddings, people almost always choose to read from Saint Paul's great hymn to love in his First Letter to the Corinthians from the New Testament. Even if you are not a Christian, the words may be familiar to you: "Love is patient, love is kind" (1 Corinthians 13:4, NRSV). Within the "hymn to love" also lies an extraordinary passage about life's essential incompleteness. "For now we see in a mirror, dimly, but then we will see face to face. Now I know only in part; then I will know fully, even as I have been fully known" (1 Corinthians 13:12, NRSV). The metaphor may seem off to us. This passage makes more sense when we remember that in biblical times the only mirrors people had were polished metal; the reflection they saw remained blurred and indistinct. Paul knows only too well how in this world our knowledge of others and even of ourselves has definite limits. Everything, to some extent, remains dim and incomplete. Yet love, when honest and true, serves as the closest thing we have to seeing clearly and completely. As a wise woman said to me one afternoon over lunch, love "illuminates your being." Most of us who have experienced it know what she means. We feel a supreme comfort when we both know and are known in that deep, intimate way. Relief comes over us—we are not alone in the universe. Someone understands. As Plato described true friendship, we feel—if only for brief moments—as if there were "one soul in two bodies."

Such loving comfort may indeed be one of the greatest of human comforts, but it does not come easily. An actress and fitness instructor I know said baldly, "Loving is hard." When pressed to explain, she said, "When I say that loving is hard it's probably because of all the things around it, the external things, the pressure." One of her students saw it slightly differently: "It's that those difficulties and hardships exist, and love is what allows you to overcome them." Another student was more specific: "I mean I was not loving my child instantly—fifteen hours of labor, C-section, seven days in the hospital. I was far from feeling the love [at first]. My husband was doing a great job." However one looks at it, love and intimacy are a challenge. In the United States, most people expect to find them in the context of marriage, yet half of all marriages fail. A survey of gay and lesbian friends and acquaintances suggests similar struggles for long-term fidelity. Romantic comedies and love songs may give people the idea that intimacy is easy and natural, but in reality most of us have to learn intimate sharing the hard way, as a skill that requires practice and struggle to become good at it.

Why should it be any different, especially when it comes to the connections and collisions of men and women in love? When I lived in New York City, I knew a lot of men in their twenties who spent the lion's share of their time hanging out with their buddies. They felt comfortable talking out problems—theirs or the world's—amid jokes over a beer or between barrages of sports statistics in front of a game on TV. I watched these guys get married, one by one. Initially this always proved a shock. Suddenly an empathetic and emotionally articulate human being shared the guy's life and wanted to know all about him. The arena of intimacy now looked very different from shouting opinions in arguments with six guys at a Mets game. Nor was this easy on the wives, who had their own customs of friendship and sharing. As one friend of mine put it, "Sometimes it seems like men and women are really from two different cultures."

## A Touch of Comfort

As a teenager, I attended a spiritual retreat for high school students. It was about an hour from home; I went with a large group of my classmates in the opening weeks of our freshman year. At the time I detested or was afraid of about a quarter to a half of them. I had never been one of the popular kids, and in junior high school so-called friends ridiculed me continuously. At the same time, like most early adolescents, I was desperate to belong.

Retreats, like summer camp, have a way of doing away with old social hierarchies and bonding teenagers together. Indeed, on that weekend, anything began to seem possible. Saturday afternoon, after an emotional set of testimonies from different teens, the retreat leaders set up an open mike. Some of my classmates got up to speak, open up their lives as I had never heard them. One of my junior high school friends took his turn. He made a public apology to a person he had hurt and asked for forgiveness. I thought he must be speaking about me, but I could not feel certain.

As the session came to an end, my classmates collected near the front of the room, hugging and celebrating with a strange new emotional freedom. I suddenly wanted to be there with them, yet I remained uncertain of myself. Did I belong or not? (Do we ever stop asking this question, even as adults?) I took some steps toward the group but stood at a distance. Fortunately, someone broke through my insecurity. A girl I had known all my life, someone who, perhaps not coincidentally, had suffered as a young child with leukemia, spied me as she moved through the teenage hugging festival. She smiled and motioned with her hand for me to come forward. She threw her arms around me. I belonged.

You do not forget moments like that, no matter how many years go by, no matter how much the wounds of childhood get left behind. The moment when touch brings healing, comfort.


"For me the most comfortable thing in the world is having my daughter in my arms. The most comfortable sensation that I have ever experienced in my life." So said one of the nurses I interviewed in San Francisco. Listening to her, I felt she captured something essential about touch and human comfort. Too often we look on touch (especially in Anglo-Saxon cultures) as a kind of "nice extra" or some kind of passing experience of security or pleasure. But to this nurse, touch was clearly something that calmed and sustained her. It gave her strength.

People are funny about touch. Attending a weekend conference for Catholics and Protestants in Albuquerque, New Mexico, I caught some of my colleagues sneaking back from an event in the room next door at the convention center. Amma, the renowned "hugging saint" of India, had people queued up waiting for an embrace. My colleagues wanted a hug. Yet somehow they felt embarrassed about it, as if the desire itself were childish.

How people feel about touch varies a lot, and it certainly varies by culture. New Yorkers do the one-cheek kiss (as opposed to the French, Belgians, Iranians, and Eastern Europeans, who do both cheeks). Californians seem always to be hugging (much to the bafflement of people from elsewhere). Midwesterners prefer a firm handshake. Southerners will put their arm around you, slap you on the back, and call you "darlin'," but this is a sign of camaraderie and friendliness, not of intimacy. New Englanders, at least stereotypically, hardly seem to want to touch anyone at all. Many Americans of color will complain that these analyses of regional culture are really about white people, and they are not wrong. At the African-American Catholic parish in Harlem where I used to help out on Sundays, the enthusiasm for handshakes, hugs, and kisses meant the kiss of peace lasted a good ten minutes. The situation wasn't so different for the Caribbean Latino community at the same parish. Take the subway to the gentrified precincts of midtown and majority white crowds were quite comfortable with the polite handshakes within your pew that Catholic rubrics recommend.

And beyond culture, what about individual differences? I know of one couple, an old friend of mine known for magnificent bear hugs, while her other half would never dream of giving you more than a formal handshake at a respectful distance. The truth is, the way in which touch means comfort for a person depends a lot on a dozen personal and cultural preferences. Moreover, some people's traumatic experiences with touch, through sexual assault or abuse, make them understandably shy or wary.

Yet who could conceive of love without touch—any kind of love? Touch encompasses in an extraordinary way the physical, emotional, and social elements of comfort and packages them in a way that has *meaning* to most of us. Certainly we physically need touch. We suffer without it. Maybe more than we know. I had a college professor in the mideighties who complained that the biggest failure of the sexual revolution was allowing young people (he pointed dramatically at us) to charge right into intercourse without sufficiently benefiting from the prolonged touch of foreplay.

But it also matters that we associate touch with affection and how we *feel* about others. It is a sign of the emotional bonds between people, a gesture of love. I sat at a Fourth of July concert and watched the mother in the row in front of me place one arm around one young son and stroke the hair of her other son, asleep on her lap. Touch is also a social gesture, a sign of trust in different kinds of relationships. In business, people shake hands on a deal. Couples must *consummate* their marriages or they can be legally annulled. Because touch signifies trust, however, it can be abused. At times what ought to be an expression of love becomes an expression of power. The most abusive forms of this are well known, but anyone can find their use of touch compromising. A loving pat on a child's head becomes condescending;

the firm handshake turns into a demonstration of strength and superiority.

Nevertheless, despite the risks involved and the cultural complexities to consider, we simply cannot do without human touch. And who would want to? In a crucial way, we are our bodies—we communicate and learn and love through them. This seems self-evident, but it has not always been so. Ancient Stoic and Platonic philosophers—whose thinking then became a part of Christian tradition—tended to separate the physical aspects of life and love from its spiritual nature, even at times going as far as to condemn sexual desire or make of it an inferior, animal thing. Recognizing that very human tendency for strong emotions to get out of control, they made an ideology of "taming the passions" and refused to see the good in what we feel. Yet show me a person who can love without her body. Even the mystics used sexual metaphors to describe their spiritual ecstasies. Jesus and most other great religious figures touched people to bless and heal them. If comfort is physical, emotional, and social, then inevitably, wonderfully, the comfort of love involves touch.

## Mentor Me Mucho

What does the Declaration of Independence have to do with comfort?

Many Americans forget or do not know that Thomas Jefferson was a nobody when he wrote the Declaration in 1776—a thirty-three-year-old junior delegate to the Continental Congress. The act propelled him to fame. Elected to the Virginia House of Burgesses at twenty-six, he was then elected to the Continental Congress on the eve of revolution. So was Jefferson as remarkable as history says? Or was he lucky, in the right place at the right time? A later president, John F. Kennedy, thought the former. When he was entertaining a roomful of Nobel laureates at the White House, he famously quipped that it was the greatest gathering of minds at the White House "since Jefferson dined alone."

Benjamin Franklin is the founding father best known for being the "self-made man," the one who out of modest circumstances achieved education, wealth, and fame through his own efforts. The patrician planter Jefferson could not claim that by a long shot. Instead we might look at Jefferson as a model of the "interdependent man," the productive recipient of the generosity of others. On the other hand, we'd best not consider him a model of ethical behavior (on account of slavery, adultery/concubinage, and intellectual dishonesty).

Part of the credit for Jefferson's meteoric rise goes to a cadre of talented and politically savvy mentors he had. While studying at William and Mary in his late teens, Thomas Jefferson became acquainted with three of the most important intellectuals of his age: Francis Fauquier (the governor of Virginia), William Small (professor), and George Wythe (lawyer). Jefferson had private meals and conversations with these older men. From them he learned about the Enlightenment as well as some of the key lessons of his life. When he studied law under Wythe, he became so proficient that he almost single-handedly reformed the law code of Virginia while George Washington and others were off fighting the American Revolution. Many of the changes he proposed were initially rejected but were eventually incorporated. Jefferson's law protecting freedom of religion in Virginia is said to be the model for the First Amendment of the U.S. Constitution.

Thus, Jefferson's great success as a lawmaker, statesman, architect, educator, and philosopher started with his tutelage by learned mentors. When he grew old himself, Jefferson understood the importance of offering guidance and care to the next generation; he saw to the construction and program of study of the new University of Virginia. In fact, he insisted that this accomplishment should appear as his epitaph instead of another prominent fact of his life—that he had been president of the United States.

It is impossible to say if Thomas Jefferson would have written the thoughtful and inspirational document he did if not for the capable care of those who mentored him as a young man. At the time that he wrote it he possessed self-assurance, a grasp of the newest political ideas from Europe, a sense of order in thought and word, and an awareness of the current political situation. His teachers had taught him well and had helped him develop his gifts at the right moment. What he later did depended upon the confidence, strength, and comfort they had afforded him when it mattered. Mentoring is an odd kind of comfort—a support and a kindness that functions like a seed planted for the future. It helps a young man or woman cement identity, learn the boundaries of their abilities, and absorb lessons about what is possible while building up the confidence to do it.

There are other stories. In the economic boom times of the thirteenth century in Italy, the unhappy heiress Clare di Favarone met secretly for a year with the radical friar Francis Bernardone, the man we know today as Saint Francis of Assisi. He became her spiritual teacher, and eventually she abandoned home and family (an almost unthinkable act for an eighteen-year-old woman of that era) to help with Francis's project of promoting a new spiritual movement. In the chaotic China of the sixth century BC, a man we know as Confucius joined the movement of youths engaged in ritual dancing. Watching their moves, he developed a complete philosophy about rhythm, ritual, harmony, and duty. He became the leader and mentor of a large band of young men. Eventually these men became the backbone of Chinese society as it was restrained and reformed in the coming years. In this way the philosophy and tradition of Confucius became a guiding force in the development of the culture of China and several other Asian cultures.

Because we so strongly believe in the power of the individual in Western cultures, we downplay the importance of mentoring. It comes up now and then in discussions about children who have lost one or both parents. Yet mentoring is a time-honored form of love and comfort for young people. It has played a strong part in the most important movements in the history of the world. Even as we ignore it in daily life, it appears in shadow in our religion, our mythology, our movies and popular culture. The phrase *passing the mantle* as a description of the transfer of authority comes from a mentoring story in the Jewish Bible. The legendary prophet Elijah, capable of all kinds of miraculous utterances and deeds, receives a message from God that he has to find the young man who will replace him as prophet. The wisest characters in religion and mythology do not resist their own retirement but seek to equip the next generation to replace them. Elijah seeks out a young man named Elisha. Unceremoniously he dumps his cloak over him as the younger man plows his fields. Elisha immediately gets the point, feeds the neighborhood with the meat from his oxen, and runs after Elijah to learn the prophet business.

After years of mentoring, as Elijah prepares to move on to celestial pastures (in a fiery chariot, by the way, if you haven't heard the story), his apprentice asks for a double amount of his spirit ("spiritual supersizing," you might say). The wish is granted, and as a symbol of having taken Elijah's place, Elisha picks up the mantle—that is, Elijah's miraculous outer cloak. The passing of the mantle enables Elisha to accomplish powerful things, including socially useful miracles like purifying the local water system and the more personal sign of cursing a gang of nasty youths who mock his bald head. The youths are then eaten by bears. Don't mess with God's messenger.

These tales make the point that those who wish to accomplish things must put their hours in with their models and teachers. In the symbolic bestowing of a double portion of Elijah's spirit, we also learn the ancient principle that it is the destiny of the student, after submitting to the teacher/master, to eventually outstrip the mentor. Again, this comes as a comfort rather than a threat to the mentor, who knows this is how one's legacy for the good survives and grows.

In the mythology of the movies, the diminutive Yoda stands out among the mentors of the reels. His inverted sentences and surprising behavior teach the Jedi apprentice Luke Skywalker his spiritual lessons in the first set of *Star Wars* movies. His pint-size stature and reptilian complexion first teach Luke Skywalker that appearances deceive and that real power comes not from one's own strength but from dependence on the (divine) power of life around us—in this case, the Force. Yoda invites Luke to let go of his preconceived notions and teaches him detachment, discernment, strength. In the end, Luke learns that fear is normal but that it can also kill your faith. Finally, in a vision sequence, Yoda shows Luke Darth Vader, whom he battles only to find his own face in the severed head of the evil master. Before he ever learns that Darth Vader is his father, he has already understood that evil draws its power from our own fear and hatred. The later set of *Star Wars* movies reminds of another important fact about mentors: they don't always know the answer. Yoda finds himself unable to anticipate or prevent Anakin Skywalker's turn to the dark side of the Force, and he fails to defeat Palpatine, who then becomes the evil emperor while Yoda cowers off to exile.

Self-esteem begins as a gift. We emerge into life confident and secure because along the way someone showed us that we came into this world not as a mistake or a burden but as a gift. Our presence in the family and in the world was good. "I want to teach my daughter to be comfortable with who she is," said a former teacher and mother. Those who do not receive that gift have the added burden of searching for it during the balance of their lives. Many find it—through the things they accomplish, in other relationships that turn out more positively, through the discovery of some vocation or purpose that gives their life meaning. Even those of us who *did* have that gift of self-esteem as youngsters need to have it confirmed. Thus, the anatomy of mentoring begins with that gift. As giver/mentor, one offers support. We tell young people of their worth, challenge their self-deprecation, affirm their achievements and insights. We want them to develop confidence, the ability to act and react on their own. Through our presence in their lives, we let them know that they are not abandoned, not forgotten, not left behind. We invite them to understand the wonderful gift that each human being is. The more that sense of being a gift has been disparaged or discouraged by abuse, poverty, racism, immature parenting, abusive peers, or other factors, the more a child or young adult will be in need of that message.

But life has its limits. Not every thought and feeling a child has is good. Fulfilling every desire is dangerous. A child has to learn respect, self-discipline, and the flexible boundaries of a good life. This is the second important element of mentoring—setting limits. A couple of years ago I sat behind a young father and his toddler son on a train from New York to Philadelphia. The father allowed the son to wander a bit in the aisle of the train, but at each moment he had an eye on the boy. If the boy began to bother others or get too close to the exit door, the father would call him back or step up to hold him back if necessary. While affirming the importance of exploration and curiosity, he also wanted to teach his son, literally in this case, that life has limits.

In the post-1960s world, setting limits has suffered as an authentic and loving task of parents and other adults. Children behave disrespectfully without any negative consequences from their parents, teachers, coaches, or relatives. I do not know why. Maybe adults today want to be buddies rather than guides for their children, or perhaps they are seeking the love *they* missed out on as children. No doubt many adults feel too tired from their long working hours to focus on discipline. Whatever it is, lots of adults seem reluctant to act as the enforcer of limits. It is an *uncomfortable* role.

When parents are not willing or able to set limits on their children, the young need help from mentors. Even when parents *are* willing, the young still need some help. After all, being a parent is no easy job, more so in the complicated world of today. Maybe we all have some responsibility to the children in our lives—our students, family, neighbors, community members. In my work as a parish priest, I found that local teenagers coping with a confusing urban environment appreciated adults who set limits. Amid what feels like chaos, narrowing the path to where it becomes manageable looks to them a lot like an act of love. And it is.

. . .

"I don't just tell you the rules," our gray-haired campus priest said to us one afternoon, "I also teach you the rules for breaking the rules." He obviously saw his job working with college students not only as teaching us about faith but also preparing us for life. He, too, was a mentor. I was nineteen, old enough to understand how complicated life could be, and I began to appreciate his way of passing on the complex lessons he had accumulated through long experience. It amounted to showing us how to navigate the nuances and ambiguities of adult life. In some cultures, extended family members other than parents do this kind of training in people's lives. Aunts and uncles, grandparents, older siblings pass down the wisdom of real-life experience in little parables, demonstrations, and commentaries on observed behavior. In our meetings and discussions with our priest back in those college days, there were all those things, plus his maxims. One of his favorites taught us how to negotiate authority in the real world: "Sometimes it is better to ask for forgiveness than permission." In more recent years I find myself passing that one on to college students. The point, I suppose, is that mentors save us from having to learn all our lessons via costly mistakes.

Some of it works that way. But a lot of wisdom in life comes only from the *interpretation* of our mistakes and failures. As a twenty-three-year-old fund-raiser for a national charity, I did not exude confidence in my work, a crucial attribute for a fund-raiser (as in sales). However, by receiving constructive criticism from my boss and from an older friend, I gradually improved. Unfortunately, at the end of ten months I remained so far from my quota that my dismissal was assured. To save everyone embarrassment, I resigned. In the debriefings with mentors and friends that followed, I began to understand that businesspeople in particular needed to see in my self-assurance and command of the facts that their money would go to good use. Reviewing feedback from my boss, I later saw some of the signs that I had initially missed—especially how my clothes and attitude had communicated youthfulness rather than initiative and business sense. People wanted a fund-raiser who appreciated their generosity but also would stroke their egos a little. When I took the job, I anticipated a future promoting a worthy cause. I underestimated the complicated balances of working with real human beings, and failure coupled with the wisdom of mentors taught me how to deal with that for my next endeavor. The learning was hard at first, but it was actually a great comfort in the long run.

A balance of challenge and support remains the key ingredient in bringing real comfort—that is, strength and confidence—to young people. All of us know inside that a healthy adulthood amounts to an acceptance of responsibilities for one's own good and the common good. That's why parents keep at stuffy jobs to support their families; that's why teachers repeat lessons for the umpteenth time if their students need them to; that's why people keep in touch with old friends in trouble, appear at the hospital at a moment's notice, and travel great distances to be at a family funeral. Sigmund Freud said that life was all about love and work, and therein lie the big commitments. Yet as adolescents we struggle with duties and responsibilities, and sometimes in early adulthood we do as well. Having absorbed that powerful impulse to maintain easy comfort, the young have trouble letting it go. Thus, left to their own devices, younger people sometimes eat ramen noodles for lunch and put off general education classes indefinitely. They need challenge as well as support.

The priest at our college parish was often pretty tough, telling people not to be naive, to use their brains, ridiculing positions he thought were immature, and raising his voice if he thought it would do any good. One day, after a flurry of complaints from my fellow students, I jacked up my nerve and put the question to him. "You know people say you are an SOB," I started. Without flinching he replied, "I *am* an SOB. So what? I know who I am, who I'm not, and what I am here to do." I didn't know how to respond. I waited for some canned response about helping students reaching their potential, but instead he raised his voice and gave me a passionate answer I saw he believed. "You think I'm tough? You haven't met the real bastards of the world. Surviving me will be nothing compared to the strength you need to deal with them."

Strength is found in surviving and learning from the challenges presented to us. Some of those come from life, but others are produced, like the emergencies in a flight simulator or the crisis scenarios presented in training at work. Traditionally, if you wanted to learn any art or craft, you apprenticed yourself to an expert. The master would start you slowly, apportioning you the most basic tasks of the art, allowing you to learn through simple practice. But after you picked up the foundational skills, a good teacher would purposefully put before you challenges just beyond your skill level. Then, in the correcting of mistakes and errors, you learn.

Life is an art. To live it well we need to struggle with challenges tailor-made for our set of strengths and weaknesses.

Real mentoring means issuing the right challenges, those the young person really needs. Selfish mentors issue challenges to cement their own power, to guarantee that their students fail, or, worst of all, to entertain their own sadism. The good mentor pays attention; she explains. Challenges cannot be arbitrary; the young person's trust in the mentor will be broken. As a mentor, you need to observe someone and grasp their particular needs. What will someone need to stay strong and live well? I know a twentysomething man with a tyrannical father. He has found through experience that a calm, measured response to his father's histrionics serves him well. That is an important skill for him to learn. But he has not yet found his own voice, to speak confidently, to have opinions and express them. He needs a mentor who will value his opinion but who will also desire it of him. He needs support, but it will do no good for the mentor to avoid criticizing him—he has to learn confidence in the face of his father's criticism—but the criticism must be constructive, to the point, judiciously issued, waiting for his response. He must always find a listening ear and be treated with respect. Only a sensitive and observant mentor will be able to do these things.

The biggest challenge to the mentor herself is keeping the focus on the young person. Always temptation will arrive to focus on ourselves as mentors. We will want to challenge in a way that pleases us, demonstrates our expertise, resolves dilemmas we had in our youth but are not of the present. I once was helping a young immigrant improve her English; I urged her to practice by reading and offered to lend her a novel or two. I wanted her to read *The Great Gatsby*. It's *the* American novel, after all. She asked me if it was sad. Well, yes, it was. There was quite enough sadness for her right now, thank you very much. Did I have anything else? I passed up Hemingway and Steinbeck as well and handed her a Harry Potter novel. She needed to improve her English, not follow my agenda for learning the classics of American literature.

## Lasting Comfort

During the years I lived in New York City, my parents visited several times. On one particular visit, I gathered a few friends—most of whom they knew from previous visits—and we had dinner together at a favorite Mexican restaurant on the Upper West Side. It was a Sunday night, fairly quiet for Manhattan. After a round of the restaurant's excellent margaritas, we settled in and began to tell stories and talk. I loved joining these two worlds of mine together. My parents were curious about this eclectic group of friends of mine—a witty doctoral student in theology, a freelance children's-book writer with boundless energy, a quiet massage therapist prone to bursts of laughter. We got on to New York City itself, too, beautiful and odd. My parents had become more accustomed and more attached to the place with each visit. We enjoyed a tasty dinner, paid the bill, and began walking to catch the subway about eight o'clock or eight-thirty, still early by New York standards. As the sun was beginning to set, I stepped into Ninety-third Street to cross. Down the block to the west the sky was brilliant red like fire over New Jersey. We all paused there in the middle of the empty street and looked. My mom raised her index finger in the air as if to point at the sun, and facetiously I touched my own finger to hers, like I was completing some sort of human circuit. We laughed. Pretty soon everyone else had touched their index fingers to ours, and we had constructed a human carousel in the middle of Ninety-third Street. My theologian friend jumped underneath the formation (where, being short, she fit well), and my dad snapped a photo. The photograph sits on my shelf still—smiles all around, fingers joined, scattered city lights and buildings like dark hulks behind us, the sunset sky on fire.

That evening of celebration and care was one moment in my life and in the life of my family and my friends. For that moment, we felt connected by beauty, laughter, and our bonds of family and friendship. And then the moment ended. The sun went down; my friends dispersed to their various trains; our dinner was over. The next day my parents returned home to California. Isn't that the nature of all experiences of loving comfort? We are loved in particular moments of our lives. We touch, we connect, and we are mentored in particular moments. Then the moments pass. Yet I would not call these moments irrevocably lost or fleeting. We are changed by them, if only a small amount at a time. We carry these memories of loving comfort in our minds and in our bodies; they become a part of us. This is why I hold on to the photograph from that evening. I know that single, silly moment had a tiny part to play in persuading the weary man in me to hope, to trust in life's goodness, to continue believing in God, even as life presented obstacles both oppressive and complicated.

Very often on the journey into various "comfort zones" within these chapters we have seen more of the escapist side of comfort. This is the comfort of the beer and the aspirin, the comfort of our stressed-out selves in search of comfort food. This is the comfort of action movies, of "chilling," and of the nap on that perfect spot on the couch. That kind of comfort is wonderful, but it has no long-term power to satisfy us. No one remembers these moments with carefully preserved photos of couches or meatloaf or air-conditioning. Loving comfort, on the other hand, feels like an entirely different thing. On the surface, it operates like those other kinds of comfort—we get distracted and feel good. Where love works differently is on the inside. As these moments of care pile up, we believe in them. We feel more loved. They shore us up from the inside out. Some work so powerfully that we remember them for years.

This was confirmed for me when I talked late one spring to a table of suburban women in the restaurant of a Northern California fitness club. These were my homegrown experts on love and comfort. All of them were married, several for many years. Most were mothers with children, from toddlers to college students. They trusted that various gestures of comfort they had offered would make a difference in their children's lives. Near the end of our discussion, one woman, a sixty-year-old lawyer, summed up much of our discussion with the sudden declaration that love was comfort and comfort was love. I was skeptical: it seemed too easy and too sentimental. After all, many people find love difficult rather than a comfort. But she elaborated. She insisted she was not talking about some kind of infatuation or familial obligation but about "that love that sort of illuminates your being, that makes you want to give, that gives you that warm feeling, and that you get back, too."

The other women heartily agreed. Intrigued, I began to put aside my skepticism. Moments of loving comfort do change us from within; they illuminate us. I thought back to what one of them had said early on in our conversation. A woman in her late fifties, married with a grown daughter, she had defined comfort in a unique way. She said, "Comfort is almost to me a state of being . . . Comfort is almost not things around me but within me. To be comfortable with myself, I have to like myself—in order to be comfortable in any situation." She was describing comfort in terms of its old, medieval definition—strength. The love that truly is comfort, that changes us, that "illuminates our being," is the love that makes us strong.

# Chapter Eight

# Comfort in Crisis

*A silent look of affection and regard when all other
eyes are turned coldly away—the consciousness
that we possess the sympathy and affection of one
being when all others have deserted us—is a hold,
a stay, a comfort, in the deepest affliction, which
no wealth could purchase, or power bestow.*

—CHARLES DICKENS

The first person to hear my notions about comfort for this book disliked them, though in his kindness he remained supportive. We knew each other through a church where I had served, and liking the sort of things I had said in sermons, he encouraged me to do more writing. So I told him the broad outlines of this book. A gentle man in his fifties, he had long worked for a major cancer hospital. Despite the fact that much of his work occurred at a desk, it still dealt with the stories of families devastated by cancer. And he worked closely with the head of psychiatry at the hospital, the woman charged with the emotional and psychological well-being of countless people undergoing terrible suffering—some hovering at the edge of life, others in the process of losing even their children to cancer.

My notion of a complicated and ambiguous comfort left him cold. Who could blame him? To him comfort served essentially one purpose: peace and healing for people in pain and crisis. Anything else felt like a distraction in the world in which he dwelled.

He explained this to me, and I understood. And he is right. Comfort would feel like a pretty empty word without this important sense of consolation for the afflicted. The "journey of comfort" we have undertaken in these chapters would seem like a shallow venture indeed—lacking depth and humanity—without some understanding of real comfort in crisis.

And so we begin at a well-known moment of crisis, familiar to many people around the world—the terrorist attacks of September 11, 2001.

## Weigh Me Down

Her husband, her mother, and the rest of her family were there, as well as a whole cadre of fellow flight attendants from United Airlines. The church was packed. Somewhere in the crowd sat our local congressman. I took a breath and began the funeral sermon for Deborah Welsh. "This wasn't supposed to happen," I began, my voice shaking. "She should be here with us now. Lots of other people should be here with us as well. I imagine a lot of you, like me, are feeling like the poet from the biblical book of Lamentations. He had watched his own country be laid waste in war, and he said: 'My soul is bereft of peace. I have forgotten what happiness is.' (Lamentations 3:17–18, NRSV). We are shocked, as if the ground beneath our feet can no longer be trusted."

Among the biggest temptations in offering comfort in a time of crisis is the desire to "fix" things, to solve the problem. It does not work. Comfort in crisis is not a "fix." It's a salve, a soothing empathy. Healing and hope come not from knowing the answer but from knowing we are not alone.

I studiously tried to avoid easy solutions that evening in September 2001, about ten days after the attacks. It wasn't difficult. The crisis remained fresh, even raw, in those days. Every park railing, every hospital emergency-room window, nearly every public space, was plastered with a multitude of photocopied paper flyers, each one announcing in bold letters: "Missing." There was someone's name, a photo. The photos were hastily gathered from family archives; they showed people on casual vacations, in official military portraits, at weddings and formal dances. It was as if an entire county of people in tuxedos, gowns, uniforms, and Bermuda shorts had suddenly disappeared. Of course, by that time the truth had dawned on most of us. We were walking the streets of New York City surrounded by the smiling faces of the dead.

I was living on Fifty-ninth Street in midtown that Tuesday in September, a few miles from the World Trade Center site. Late in the afternoon I got the news about Debbie. Deborah Welsh was a regular in the parish where I worked, a friend, and a long-time flight attendant for United Airlines. As the government grounded airplanes all day long, her husband grew worried when he heard nothing. Surely it could only be an oversight, a lack of cell-phone coverage somewhere? Yet in fact she had been the lead attendant on Flight 93, the plane that crashed that morning in a field outside Shanksville, Pennsylvania. The passengers had rebelled against the hijackers. A mutual friend called me from California with the news that Debbie's plane had been one of the four ill-fated, hijacked planes. As the words came out on the receiver, my friend's voice dissolved into tears. I felt myself go blank inside. It seemed impossible that someone as lively and vibrant as Debbie could be gone. On the other end of the telephone line, my friend wiped her tears and urged me to go see Debbie's husband immediately.

I found him with their dog outside the apartment he and Debbie shared. I offered to stay with him for a while, and we sat in a local restaurant while he talked and tried to make sense of it all. There was little to say. I had no explanations, no solutions. He talked; I sat and listened. After a few hours I left him in the care of friends, a couple who lived nearby. They agreed to stay by him until the next day.

Other things happened in the days after the attacks. Debbie's friends held a party to remember her, and they passed out photos of her. I remember standing on a roof garden talking with some of her friends while the military's F-16s whooshed overhead amid the otherwise silent skies—all other air traffic had ceased. I officiated at another service for a young bond trader who had only been married a couple of years. He left behind a wife, parents, many friends. Another priest I know officiated at a funeral service for the wife of a psychologist, a man who had just lost his first wife a few years before. And the firefighter memorials soon began—so many that they did not cease for months.

.   .   .

Even as the immediate crisis around the attacks subsided and life in New York City returned to a semblance of normal, there were many signs that things remained amiss. I read in the newspaper in January that the debris from the towers had just stopped burning. People moved away from New York permanently, feeling that the city would always remain a target. A few frightened souls came to my office to talk, distraught. They complained of generalized anxiety, despite their lack of connection to anyone who had died. Months after 9/11, the New York City Board of Education found children in the city still traumatized by the event.

All through this time my family kept calling to see how *I* was faring. Their supportive presence did not evaporate, one of the great human temptations in crisis. We all give in to it, forgetting about people's pain once the initial drama fades. This happens frequently with illness and grief. Yet mourning, healing, recovery, survival—these remain the long-term business of our lives. But who has the patience to wait along with someone as he or she goes through them? For every tale I hear of the professor husband who left his job to care for his sick wife or the girlfriend who married her dying boyfriend, there are the countless other cases: the cancer patient whose friends fail to visit; the divorced man whose friends cannot understand his dark moods; the diabetes patient whose family simply does not want to hear any more about her illness. Let's face it: whatever the crisis, we would all prefer to move on as soon as the funeral ends, the case is closed, or the patient moves home from the hospital. Yet the bereaved, the sick, the disturbed seldom have that luxury.

Real comfort in crisis then depends on a presence that remains with us, hanging in there. A phone call a few weeks after a funeral may offer more comfort than one right before it. A family friend on the other side of the country e-mailed me one day saying, "Call me. I am terribly bored stuck at home for eight weeks after foot surgery." Naturally this type of long-term comfort in crisis is a lot harder to keep on top of. Comfort in the first blush of crisis seems easier. Most of us feel inoculated from fear and anxiety in those intense first moments. But then later, the fear of pain and suffering catches up with us. We begin to question and doubt ourselves. Can I really handle the emotional pressure? Visiting a sick friend there may be odors, tubes, machines. In New York City, the buses used to line up near where I lived to transport family members to visit their loved ones in prison. I admired people for making the trek over and over again, and I wondered how many—after a while—just stopped.

"I don't know what to say." Many people tell me this when their loved ones are in crisis, and they do not know how to help them.

But comfort in crisis almost never depends on the right words. Rather it depends on being present. In Spanish the word for condolence is *el pésame*, which etymologically means "weigh me down" or "burden me" with your sadness. It is a promise to share a friend's sorrow. A customary expression of consolation to the grieving is *Te acompaño en tus sentimientos.* It means literally "I accompany you in your feelings." It does not say that I understand or I know what you should do. It does not posit any kind of solution. It says that I will be beside you while you feel what you must feel. I will feel it with you.

## Shit and Angels Happen

At one time in my life I used to take weekly yoga classes from a Catholic priest and his cousin. It was billed as "Prayer of Heart and Body," and they did a marvelous job of making yoga accessible, enjoyable, and spiritually meaningful to our crowd of body-inhibited Christian folk. About halfway through the year, however, the cousin was injured in what you might call a "yoga accident." In a different class, a wayward headstander kicked her right in the nose. It broke her nose in such a complicated way she was left with debilitating headaches and the prospect of surgery. Reflecting on her predicament, she searched for a deeper meaning in what had befallen her, but she could not discern it. Her coteacher and cousin, the priest, decided to offer a spiritual explanation of his own. "You know," he said, "sometimes shit just happens."

Indeed it does. A lot. There is a Haitian proverb, straight from the troubled history of that Caribbean nation: *Dèye mòn gen mòn*, or "Beyond the mountains, more mountains." In other words, there are no long plateaus in life—coming upon one crisis might only point you to another (in all fairness, Haitians apparently also use the proverb to speak of opportunities). Or as an American might put it, "It's just one damn thing after another!"

Crisis is a normal part of life. We will always find ourselves climbing mountains again. Some people do believe that if you only prepare adequately, work hard enough, have sufficient money, avoid upsetting God, have good karma—then bad things will not happen to you. But experience belies that. Experience suggests that what the priest said was true: shit happens to good people, to bad people, to the vast mass of us who lie somewhere in between. Were it not like that, human beings would not always be trying to account for it. There would be no Book of Job, no popular paintings of the Crucifixion, no *When Bad Things Happen to Good People* (or fame for Rabbi Harold Kushner), and probably no such thing as Buddhism at all. All these things came from people struggling to make sense of the presence of mishaps and emergencies, interpersonal disasters, disease and suffering, grim and malicious tragedy through the course of a lifetime.

When crisis strikes, we get that "end of the world" feeling—like time has stopped and we cannot imagine why the world ought to go on turning. It does, of course, and only when another person comes along to offer reassurance does that disorientation subside, as if that person provides a still point in a very unstable universe. In the most difficult of times, disaster can leave us feeling disconnected and hopeless, and yet human connection can provide a surprising amount of reassurance that defies easy definition or explanation. I suppose there is a part of each of us much like my young nephew. As a toddler, he would confidently stride off to explore the world, to see what ball-shaped objects he could uncover in the courtyard or the living room. Trotting off, he would suddenly stop, trapped by his own insecurity, and he looked back to make sure someone was watching, mommy or daddy or his grandparents.

Insecurity strikes bitterly in crisis, and the reassurance of people we love is one of the few things that salves it. A thirty-something friend of mine was walking along the streets of lower Manhattan in the months after a breakup with her boyfriend. Two friends walked with her, telling her over and over again how everything would be all right, how she did not need to worry. She was troubled, but the words seemed to be slowly trickling

into her head. Just weeks before my cousin's wedding, her grandfather, the town barber and family patriarch, died after a difficult
illness. At the wedding I scanned the reception hall. This great
rallying of family and friends seemed to be providing reassurance
for her and her immediate family after the loss of the beloved man.

In my own life I hit a rough spot a few years ago, struggling
with a combination of severe work stress and difficulties with
friends. One day I sat in my office in front of the computer, feeling desperately unhappy and sorry for myself. My friend Theresa
suddenly appeared. Aware of my being down, she offered me a
wrapped present. Inside was a tube of Elmer's Glue. She smiled
as I raised an eyebrow. "You've seemed a little broken lately, like
you were falling apart. I thought . . ." She smiled. I began to
laugh, not only at her odd sense of humor but also in appreciation
of her ability to empathize without needing to know the full
details of my current problems. She had appeared like a comforting angel that day, and I told her so: "You were an angel today,"
I said. "Everybody should get to be one sometime. Today was
your day."

## On Sending the Angels Away

Shit happens, and so do angels. A lot of us, though, lose out on
the comfort of our angels because we just don't know how to
accept their help.

It's an old story. When I edited a spirituality Web site, people
would e-mail in from all over the world seeking help in the midst
of crisis. They had suffered unexpected deaths in their lives, were
suicidal, had eating disorders, felt spiritually anguished and abandoned by God. Anonymity sent them to us—and many stub-

bornly resisted seeking help face-to-face, no matter how much we encouraged them.

While I lived in New York City, I knew a man who suffered from a long complicated illness through his sixties. The illness, which he was reluctant to talk about in detail, involved kidney failure (he went for regular dialysis) and weight loss, and it eventually killed him. The saddest piece to that drama was that he had stubbornly refused to see a doctor for a long while. Some of his friends claimed this resistance to seeing a physician was "an Irish thing"; whether it was or not, it had tragic consequences. At times those of us who knew him grew angry with him for neglecting his health as he did, but more recently I think of his story as more similar to the rest of us than we might care to admit. Few of us wish to acknowledge our vulnerability. Especially we men hold to self-reliance and independence as if our lives depended on it. Instead our lives may depend on letting go of it.

Why is it so hard to admit that we need help? A lot of us who grew up in the United States believe in self-reliance. We have the idea that it is truly shameful to ask other people for assistance; if we can't make it on our own we have somehow failed egregiously. Idioms and sayings reflect this: "If you want a job done right, do it yourself." "Pull yourself up by your own bootstraps." "The Lord helps those who help themselves." Apparently, even God is said to respect American attitudes of self-reliance. Such rugged individualist leanings appear across the dominant culture of the United States, from cowboy movies to libertarian politics to simple everyday habits. A friend from the Philippines found it amazing (and potentially dangerous) that while driving I would reach for a drink, change the radio, even search the seat pocket behind me for a map rather than asking her for help. Thinking about it, I realized she was right.

Of course, realistically no American—no one really—can fully practice what we preach. We all live in a complex web of human relationships—at home and at work, in school, through businesses and government. Pure self-reliance is not optimal, necessary, or even possible. If infection strikes, most of us consult a doctor and take antibiotics, and we do not think this is a breach of self-reliance. Nor do we think that way about getting a loan to buy a house or asking the teacher to explain points of grammar in French class or getting friends to help us move. People seek out these services just as an ordinary part of living in society, and others offer these services. Why should we think any differently, for example, about psychotherapy? Why should we view marriage counseling other-wise? Yet many people look on it as a sign of weakness rather than as a sign of marital commitment. Why would we look on a support group or Alcoholics Anonymous as a crutch rather than a valuable relationship for addicts? Yet people do. The moral distinctions we make between different kinds of assistance—a mortgage loan vs. psychotherapy—are in a sense arbitrary. In real life, human beings need various kinds of help at different times in our lives. The most logical thing in the world is just to get it.

Perhaps it is time to take another look at those old idioms and sayings about self-reliance. Maybe the Lord does help those who help themselves. On the other hand, maybe our preoccupation with helping ourselves has gotten in the way, so that neither the Lord nor anyone else could help us even if they wanted to.

## The Naked Woman in the Psych Ward and the Dark Side of Comfort

Sometimes what finally breaks down resistance to accepting help from others is the generosity with which it is offered. As a small child, the blind and deaf Helen Keller was unruly, resisting all efforts to calm and help her. Yet Anne Sullivan's kind and persistent efforts to connect her with the outside world broke through. Sometimes even the tiniest signal of a person's desire to offer assistance pushes us to accept the listening ear, the gesture of support, or even, shock of shocks, advice. Throughout much of my life I have kept my fears, worries, and problems to myself; yet more than once I have been persuaded to reach out by friends who simply walked with me and cautiously made inquiries about how I was, signaling in their way, "Talk to me."

Often it doesn't take much to get people to reach back. We're programmed as human beings to do it. For the most part, when a crisis hits, people want both to help and to receive help. We complain for the lack of either. If those who need help do not get it, they feel abandoned and forgotten. If those who can help are not needed, they feel useless and sidelined. People need to be needed. When, on the day after Christmas 2004, a tsunami swept across the Indian Ocean killing hundreds of thousands of people, first-world folks eagerly contributed to aid organizations, a few even traveling to Indonesia, Thailand, or Sri Lanka to help. In January of 2005 the international aid organization Doctors Without Borders had collected so much emergency aid for the effort they actually asked people to shift their contributions to other worthy causes or even to stop contributing. People want to help, especially when they cannot escape knowing about the crisis, when it appears on every television screen and in newspaper headlines around the world.

But offering comfort gets more complicated than most of us would like to admit. Fast-forward six months from the tsunami strike to June of 2005. Oxfam International, another relief organization, released a report showing (not surprisingly) that poor people had suffered disproportionately from the disaster but also that much of the reconstruction aid was helping those better off—landowners, businesspeople, those who had been in the public spotlight. A lot of reconstruction had apparently proceeded without a strong eye to the reality on the ground—these were places with millions of people mired in devastating poverty. Oxfam noted what everyone should have known from the beginning, that the relief and reconstruction ought to have focused on the poorest. By the summer of 2005, groups like Oxfam attempted to change that by refocusing the aid community's attention.

All of this serves as a reminder that every provision of comfort in crisis can have a dark side. Ready to lend a hand and desirous to be needed, people swoop in with the goods and the aid they think others should have, but it may not be what they need. It's like the absentee parent who arrives to equip his distraught children with toys or sneakers when what they really need is health insurance. In the complicated arena of the real world, proffered comfort has to negotiate the vagaries of how people actually live. At the parish where I lived at one time, we had both a food bank and clothing distribution once a week, both supplied by affluent folk from the neighborhood. Many of our neighbors could be impractical and uncooperative in their giving. I do not doubt for one moment their good intentions, but the donations of worn-out shirts and shoes could not help poor folks trying to get jobs or homeless people trying to protect themselves against the cold. Moreover, if people could not drop off their donations on national holidays and late at night, they would get downright hostile to the church, as if we had begun the food and clothing service for *their* sake instead of asking them to help us serve poor people. All this convinced me that too often comfort in crisis seems more for the needs of the giver than those of the receiver.

It probably would not hurt if we took a second look at our motives when we offer help. Comforting those in need can spring from hidden motives, gather us attention and accolades, and fulfill complex needs that have nothing to do with true altruism. Of course, no one's motives are pure. Many politicians, for example, notoriously confuse their desire to serve with their need for attention or their desire for power. At the same time, even politicians with mixed motives may accomplish a great deal for the common good—the outlawing of child labor, Social Security, the passage of civil rights legislation. These government reforms affect millions of people. You might think of it as providing "megacomforts" to the people.

Still, there is such a thing as "comfort collateral damage"— harm inflicted when people do a poor job of negotiating their way through their desire and duty to comfort. I have been there myself. Shortly after my ordination as a priest my pastor charged me with officiating at the funeral mass of an elderly woman I had never met. As was becoming my custom, I chatted with family members at the wake service, searching for information about her, hoping to make the funeral sermon more personal. I found that she had endured a difficult marriage with a man with a drinking problem. Without having looked into this thoroughly, I mentioned it at the funeral service. Her in-laws angrily interrupted my lunch the following day. It turned out that not only had her husband been a bit of a drinker, so had she. Naturally, *her* family members had failed to mention that. On the one hand, it was an innocent mistake; I had no way of knowing, and my intentions were good. On the other hand, I had succumbed to the temptation to oversimplify, hoping to be received as a sympathetic priest and preacher. But instead of comforting the bereaved, I distorted the truth. Collateral comfort damage.

On another more bizarre occasion I managed to dodge the bullet of collateral damage, but I could see how the situation could have ended differently with a more unscrupulous priest. I was making regular visits to the psychiatric ward of a local hospital while the regular priest-chaplain was away. I stopped by to see a young woman, someone in her early twenties, pretty, talkative, but with that spacey-happy demeanor one can attribute either to psychosis or to psychopharmacology. I had seen her uneventfully before, but this day she immediately greeted me enthusiastically, sat me down, and, all smiles, placed her hand on my knee. "I know why you've come," she said. That sort of clairvoyance is unwelcome in a psych ward, and I removed her hand from my knee. "I'm here to pray with you," I insisted, a little weakly. She sat down on the floor, placed both hands on my knees, and made like she was coming in for an airplane landing on my lap.

At that moment I decided that ethically it was my responsibility not to be seduced by a highly medicated mental patient. I stood up and told her that I was sorry but this was a prayer-only visit. I turned for the door. She called out to me. As I turned around to wave good-bye, she lifted her hospital gown all the way up. She had nothing on underneath. It occurred to me that there was a certain kind of classic male fantasy in this blend of seductive assertiveness and impromptu striptease. It also occurred to me that the fact that it was happening in the psych ward took a lot of the allure out of it. Nevertheless, a visiting clergyperson unaware of his own power in the situation or the importance of sexual boundaries might easily have let something happen to gratify himself. Imagine the psychic harm to the young woman once she recovered her senses and realized what was going on.

In fact, many people *do not* become aware of their power in helping situations. They do not see how their ability to comfort and listen may bestow on them a kind of aura of strength and attractiveness in other people's eyes. In such cases, flirting or propositioning may say less about real sexual attraction and more about being impressed by power or about gratitude. In either case, the relationship is hardly a normal connection between equals. Thus do we have the tragic history of therapists bedding patients, social workers their clients, teachers their students, clergy their church members, and so on. Not that you need be a helping professional or engage in sex to cause "collateral damage" in the world of crisis comfort. Some people make a career out of preying on vulnerable people, and they do it for a thousand reasons—to convert them to a religion, to press them for funds, to persuade them into a business deal, or simply to demonstrate their superior power so they can feel better about themselves.

In any case, the key to comfort in crisis remains integrity and personal honesty, both within oneself and with others. If I know who I am, what I need, and what I want, I am much less apt to confuse all that with the needs of the person whom I am comforting. This does not erase the challenging work of sorting out the needs of two different people, an activity that can still tax the brain, especially when a relationship is complicated or ambiguous. At one time I received daily e-mails from a church colleague and friend who was also a volunteer in the organization I worked for. Via her e-mails, I had become a kind of sounding board, a living journal where she reported on the long and difficult year she was enduring.

A couple of months into this, the ethical dangers of this suddenly occurred to me. A dependency was developing—it no doubt appeared to her as if I would always be there to listen. Yet I was not her psychologist or her best friend, and I worried that she passed up other opportunities to develop friendships and connect with people because she had this outlet in me. I also realized that I would not have let it continue if I had not reaped some benefit from it, if it had not enabled me to feel important and trusted, like a great dispenser of consolation and advice. I needed to understand my role in her life with greater honesty. I was a colleague and a friend, sometimes a consolation. I was not a therapist, not a life coach, not a spiritual director. The habit needed to be broken, and a long conversation between us ensued, tense and difficult. Ultimately she agreed with my diagnosis of the situation, but the pattern was set and not easy to break. It took some work on both our parts.

## Good Mourning

Etched into the wall of the parish church where I grew up are the words of the priest who founded it: "If I should pass from this mortal orb, give my regards to the faithful." Yes, he really did talk like that—he had what you might call a gift for Victorian vocabulary. You may have also noted what a friend of mine loves—his use of the word *if*. "*If* I should pass?" mocked my friend, a New Yorker with a wonderful flare for the dramatic. "Was there some doubt? Was he in negotiations with God about this?" If he was, he did not succeed. The priest died several years ago, at an advanced age, in a car accident outside the hospital where he had been visiting a sick parishioner. According to my mother's report, he was given a hero's farewell. And now, every time the people he once served enter the church he built, we receive his "regards" right there on the wall.

As my grandmother used to occasionally note (before her own mind and body succumbed to Alzheimer's disease), the only thing you gotta do is die.

Yet as the twentieth century wound down and the twenty-first century came to life, no fact has seemed harder to accept than this one. In a world in which we put our trust in the official ideology of technological and economic optimism, in a world where enchantment and spirituality seem relegated to fantasy and science-fiction movies, how can we possibly account for death? It becomes something abstract, cartoonish, something we refuse to think about lest it ruin our day. So has it been for some time. In 1973's *The Denial of Death*, the anthropologist Ernest Becker claimed that much of the psychological turmoil in Western culture finds its origin in a deep and total denial of death. Even before that, in 1969, the psychiatrist Elisabeth Kübler-Ross had exposed the great discomfort most Americans feel about death and dying, suggesting there was much more to *mourning*— and to comforting those in grief—than most people thought.

Consolation in a time of grief and mourning is perhaps the prototypical meaning of *comfort*. But does everyone really know how to do it? Kübler-Ross surprised everyone when she published her book *On Death and Dying* not for the dying themselves, but for the medical professionals and clergy who worked with them. She wanted to give practical advice on how to comfort and care for the dying and those who mourn. *On Death and Dying* became a runaway bestseller; hospitals, seminaries, medical schools, and universities all around the world began to teach people to recognize her famous stages of grief (denial, anger, bargaining, depression, acceptance). I remember studying the stages in high school. Kübler-Ross's book revolutionized the way Americans comforted the dying, and many contemporary notions such as hospice and palliative care have roots in her groundbreaking work.

Naturally, Kübler-Ross did not tell us everything we need to know to comfort those who mourn. Her research does remind us that one can approach death with a sense of hope and peace, and that most of us have the natural resources to get there. But since her seminal work was published, we have learned that things do not occur in as tidy a sequence as her descriptions suggest. She herself admitted as much in later years. Death, like the rest of life, is messy. One recent study, for example, did not find most people starting off in denial or disbelief, and it identified *yearning* as the dominant negative emotional experience of mourners. In a lecture I attended, a Protestant minister gently skewered Kübler-Ross by declaring there were actually three stages of death: "Before you die, dying, and after you die." The other big realization since Kübler-Ross started us on all this is that these stages of grief really apply in some way to almost any experience of loss. You don't have to die or watch someone do it to know the anger and depression of loss. You see it in divorce, immigration, job loss, hysterectomy, and any number of other kinds of loss or separation. In any case, the observations about the phases and seasons of grief can help us all in our efforts to comfort those we know and love.

The kind of comfort we can bring, of course, depends on where someone is in the grieving process. Grief is said to begin with denial or disbelief or shock. People mutter, appear half present, forget things. They may isolate themselves. I remember a semi-narian who lost his brother in an accident wandering around in a fog for weeks. Such a state of affairs may tempt a helpful (or intrusive) neighbor or family member to try to clear the fog with the heat of reality. Denial is not fashionable these days—we have our T-shirts telling us to "snap out of it"; we disparage our acquaintances who act like "Cleopatra, the Queen of Denial." We forget that denial and shock serve to insulate the mind and heart from the blow that not only deeply hurts but irrevocably changes everything. Usually such news is hauntingly final in its impact. Thus, as trauma specialists remind us, to force someone to deal with the starkness of reality before they are prepared can actually harm them. Better to be patient, to listen, to be present as our loved ones slowly digest the difficult information of life. Also, different cultures have different standards for the communication of information, of directness and indirectness. But people need not lie or pretend either. Ultimately, reality is the teacher, not us.

Of course, sometimes it is not the mourner who needs to hear from reality, the teacher, but rather the friends and neighbors who do. The roles get reversed—the mourner cannot escape the harsh reality of loss but everyone around her tries to make light of it or ignore it. This constitutes a particular danger in cultures like that of the United States that tend to hide from death. Most cultures prepare their dead for burial at home. We have mortuary professionals who take care of every detail. More and more, coffins stay closed at wakes and funerals. Terminally ill or grieving people get isolated not from medical necessity or a desire to be left alone but because friends and family cannot deal with their own pain. Spouses leave. We all deserve better than this.

Once, when I had the privilege of offering spiritual counsel to a woman mourning her mother's death, I understood something. For her, it was as if the world had suddenly come to an end. When people suffer great loss, that is how it feels—like everything in the world should stop and recognize this drastic change in the universe, this end-of-my-world. Part of the cruelty is that the world does not stop. For everyone else, each day goes on just like before. A part of bringing comfort is to recognize this: the weight of the pain of loss even as we must go on as before.

For many people the most difficult part of mourning is anger, the flash point. And many of us already have trouble with it. It feels irrational. Stricken with grief over her dead husband, a woman wonders why she should be ticked off at his physician or at her daughter or at God or even at her dead husband himself. But all this is actually quite rational. She has suffered a terribly unfair loss and chaotic disruption of her life, and she displaces her anger over this on anyone and everyone. Many men react similarly upon losing their jobs, since work provides the key to men's basic identity. Anger may *feel* threatening in these situations, but it provides a powerful release valve for the frustration and disappointment that envelop us in experiencing loss. After all, doesn't a grieving person have a right to be angry? Death, as a priest colleague of mine once observed, both literally and figuratively stinks. Comfort to an angry grieving or dying person might simply be letting him or her fume. It might also mean assuring them that the anger will indeed pass. Kübler-Ross felt that a hidden fear of death in those of us who come to comfort can prevent us from accepting the fury of loved ones. Sometimes comfort also means not taking it too personally if that anger ends up accidentally aimed at you as a proximate and convenient target. And sometimes people hang on to their rage tightly and for multiple years, so that comfort might mean inviting them to let go.

Interestingly enough, a lot of grieving anger, especially when it comes to death, gets put on God, something which presents a spiritual or theological problem for some people. Yet that is as it should be. God can certainly handle it. Most people are not expressing their opposition to God so much as getting their feelings out (I'm sure God's feelings are not so easily hurt). Maybe anger can even serve as a prayer. In Judaism, there is a long tradition of "holy argument" with God over the unfairness of life. It's considered understandable, considering the difficult way things often turn out. There is even a Yiddish proverb: "If God lived on earth, people would break his windows."

Not only do individuals mourn but also families and communities, even cities and countries, and anger is inevitably a part of that. I spent several months working and doing research in a Midwestern community drastically altered by Latin American immigration over the course of a decade and a half. Many (white) people had grown angry about this. Suddenly their little city was filled with signs in Spanish, unfamiliar food and music, and customs they did not understand. No one had anticipated these changes. Surprise and frustration boiled over into anger. There was yelling about people not speaking English. There were complaints about the young immigrant factory workers who roomed together, partying at all hours. Perhaps not surprisingly, the anger allied itself with the anti-immigrant chatter appearing on conservative talk radio. "Illegal is illegal," various people would tell me. The pundits, in effect, gave them permission to vent, even to be cruel at times. In truth, undocumented immigrants were already integrated into the life and economy of the city. They had homes and jobs, children in the schools. While original townsfolk needed a place to take their frustrations over the changes, they would also have to learn to live together with the newcomers for years to come.

.   .   .

*Bargaining*, according to Kübler-Ross, is a form of postponing the inevitable—that is, acceptance of the situation that causes the grief. After my grandfather died, my Alzheimer's-stricken grandmother needed care and a new place to live. As my parents tried to figure this out, my grandmother kept coming up with unrealistic possibilities. "Maybe I will move back to Indiana," she said, speaking of the state she had left thirty-two years before, where there was no one left to care for her. She attempted to negotiate an arrangement that would delay her grief and forestall the complete loss of her independence. Yet both were inevitable. In grief, people often attempt to negotiate a "stay of execution" in exchange for good behavior, religious commitment, atonement for past sins. Past guilt accumulated over time frequently figures in. Comfort may amount to walking through the fantasy with the person. When bargaining during grief, people often follow it through until they accept the absurdity of it. Most of the time they really know. My grandmother knew she could not move to Indiana. To call bargaining silly, though, or to demean it, does not help. It's a normal thing, and we can reassure people of this when they have passed through it. It's all a part of coming to accept what seems like an unbearable truth.

Most people find *depression* the most difficult part of mourning, either their own or that of those whom they love. When there are no more escapes or alternatives and no more distractions, one stands face-to-face with death or drastic changes. That opens up a tunnel of hopelessness that each person has to pass through on her way to facing the inevitable. This struggle with hopelessness is hard for people; it runs counter to the natural optimism of many of our cultures. People often find themselves isolated when depressed, other folks not wanting to be around them. They begin to feel responsible for their own sense of despair, like it's their fault. Yet it all makes sense as a response to grief. Grief itself is, in a way, accepting the unacceptable.

When my grandfather died, my grandmother suddenly found herself no longer a wife, without him constantly at her side. She had not only lost her husband; she had lost a part of her identity. My mother reassured my grandmother with her love and activity as much as she could, but it was difficult when so much had radically changed. My grandmother just kept saying, dispiritedly, over and over, "I sure do miss him." Sometimes in depression even appreciation and alternative activity prove insufficient. Cheer of any form has little impact. The only comfort that helps in this place is touch and company. Many years ago I watched while someone I knew went nearly silent for a long period of many weeks after a breakup. There was nothing to say. Those of us who cared about her just kept calling to check on her; those who could came to see her. With this difficult stage of the grieving, it is simply being with someone that makes the biggest difference.

In *Death and Dying*, the final stage of Kübler-Ross's schema is *acceptance*. What could that possibly mean? Anyone who has ever lost loved ones knows that you never really accept their loss, never stop missing them; time just eases the strain of not having them around. After a while, I suppose, we do stop railing against the separation we cannot alter. It's almost as if the battery inside us that powers the pathos of grief gets slowly disconnected. People begin thinking about the next stage: finding strength within— often through a "Higher Power" or in specific religious convictions. The dying may begin to look passive; some want to be left alone. Preparations have turned to the inside. Whatever the manifestation of this new phase of acceptance, a new kind of searching and hope has begun. Friends of mine who have lost spouses or parents often divide their lives into before and after. They are different people. In this new life, the sadness does not disappear, but they seem to have learned to carry sorrow as strength. This becomes, for a lot of mourners, the last and greatest comfort of all.

The greatest challenge, on the other hand, lies in the fact that not everyone involved in a death or experience of loss arrives at acceptance at the same time. Thus, a man whose wife has left him may appear to his friends to be "wallowing" in depression and anger. His friends simply are ready to move on, but he is not. A terminally ill patient accepts the reality of her imminent death before her family can manage it. They demand she continue fighting when she may want to let go. Parents and grown children notoriously come to accept the reality of a divorce at different speeds. In these kinds of situations, extended family and friends can offer comfort by showing a great deal of sensitivity and patience. There is no master plan for grief. It calls forth from human beings strange and powerful emotions. Often the best consolation we can offer is to show the people we love by our presence that we respect the difficult space that they must pass through.

## In Search of a Bemuddled Peace

I was on the phone in California, talking to a writer I knew in New York. He had cancer, lymphoma; he was frightened. I listened to his tale of a narrow escape from death in the emergency room, when the doctors did not know what ailed him; next came the true diagnosis, then the chemotherapy that his body appeared to tolerate well. Unfortunately it had not conquered the disease. At the time we spoke, he had encountered a kind of precipice, various uncertain treatment options to sort through. We both knew how serious the illness was, and that people die from it.

But something curious happened to my friend. Passionately he searched out the best facilities and experts in New York City for his particular type of cancer. He found himself more efficiently and tenaciously fighting the medical and insurance bureaucracies. He passionately wanted to live, even as he knew he could die. He appreciated support, even as he knew not everyone would have the capacity to remain by him through the whole ordeal. To me, he sounded stronger, spiritually grounded, even as he complained about his own lack of trust in God. Having found comfort through friendship and faith in the whirl of his threatening reality, he seemed to be experiencing not serenity, but an odd composure, a bemuddled peace. Anxieties returned to somersault him, but they shared the space in his head with a tentative and rising confidence.

Part of this bemuddled peace the writer found I attribute to his own inner resources, the strength he already had, which he generally disliked to acknowledge. The other part came from the fact that he had support; friends, family, as well as colleagues and members of his faith community who accompanied him as he journeyed through the dreadful territory of his disease. He did not have to be completely alone with what he felt, experienced, or endured. Even those who could not understand or found it difficult to hear about his illness still stood by him in their own limited ways.

Can any of us ask for much more than this in a complicated world?

. . .

Starting in the 1980s, there was in the New Age movement a bit of momentum around peace issues; people seemed taken with the idea that greater focus on inner peace could inch humankind toward world peace. In college, visiting disciples of the international guru Sri Chinmoy rented campus rooms to instruct young people in meditation, assuring them that more peaceful individuals made for a more peaceful world. Perhaps the most popular manifestation of this effort was a bumper sticker, "Visualize World Peace," apparently first distributed in the mid-1980s by the Carmel Temple in Texas. (Of course, nothing this popular in the United States goes without a parody, and so we also got "Visualize Whirled Peas.")

To me, visualizing inner peace, let alone world peace, at least in the glowing terms of deep serenity, seems elusive. One might gain a modicum of calm, a bit of tranquillity, but I think deep inner peace is a lot to ask. But I would not want to give up on peace entirely. So instead I vote for the writer's bemuddled serenity, his tentative confidence, his bit of comfort worked out in a complicated world.

Some months after that phone call from New York, my writer friend died suddenly of complications from cancer-related infections. His prognosis had not been terminal, as far as I knew. No one expected this, especially so soon. He was forty-seven. I lived in California at the time, but we had talked briefly on the telephone not long before he died. He sounded dazed as he lay in his hospital bed. Having trouble focusing, he asked me if we could continue the conversation a few days later when he was home. He never made it home. His death was messy. Young and brash, he was in the middle of several incomplete writing projects.

In the days and weeks after his death, many came forward remembering this talented, irascible New Yorker. His life had touched more people than I realized. Though he could be difficult, all agreed that inside him dwelled an irrepressible goodness and kindness. We were glad that he had walked the earth in our time. Ultimately I realized that remembering him in that way strengthened in me the things I had seen in him: a bemuddled serenity, a tentative confidence, and—dare I say it—a fragmentary sense of peace. May we all know that incomplete version here on earth as he rests in its full realization in a much better place.

# Chapter Nine

# Spiritual Comfort and a God for Grown-Ups

*I hear and behold God in every object,*
*yet understand God not in the least.*

—WALT WHITMAN, *SONG OF MYSELF*

## A Pastiche of Spiritual Comfort

Vastly different kinds of people believe in the benefits of spiritual comfort. It is not merely in the realm of concern of pious old ladies or Bible buffs. Nurses in San Francisco mentioned it to me, as did a group of suburban moms I talked to. I heard about the need for it from inmates in an upstate New York prison. A recovering alcoholic swears by it, telling me he would not get up in the morning if not for the comfort of a Higher Power in his life. A mother of young children I talked to in a railway station seemed uncertain about the existence of God, but she felt the presence and need for spiritual comfort. And then there was the college student who drove me along a Northern California freeway many years ago. We crested an overpass and a spectacular vista of San Francisco Bay suddenly came into view. She sighed with contentment, then turned to me and asked, "How can anyone see that and not believe in God?"

Mark Twain once noted (reported in chapter two) that a fortifying dose of ham and eggs increases the spiritual comfort inherent in these divine vistas. My traveling companion that morning on the freeway was not having breakfast as she drove (this was fortunate; traffic was heavy). But neither am I inclined to dismiss Twain's connection, however humorous his intentions. Up to now we have heard about the various forms of comfort and their roots in physical comfort. Why should spiritual comfort be any different? A temptation with spiritual matters is to place them in some rarefied realm flying high above everything else. It's the same impulse that leaves people surprised when they meet their priest or minister at the supermarket (or pass him or her en route to a public restroom). In reality, there is no grand division between spiritual matters and all other matters. Spirituality connects to everything we do. Human beings' true-to-life experiences of spiritual comfort tell that story.

One suburban mother in her thirties related to me how she saw spiritual comfort in terms of a heightened awareness of the world around her. It begins, she said, with pure physical sensation, a bodily awareness of the immediate physical environment. But it eventually moves beyond to include the emotional and social world, too—joy and pain, a presence or lack of chemistry with other people, being attuned to her children. Another woman

from the same town found spiritual comfort in going to synagogue *and* going to exercise classes. She described the former as
a familiar and physically coordinated experience of ritual—
beautiful music, a comfortable temperature, a lack of ambient
distractions. Then body, spirit, and mind could come together.
She reserved a more purely physical explanation for the gym-class
experience of spiritual comfort—the chemical flow of endor-
phins.

Once, in a frank exchange, a friend from college admitted to
me that though she found real comfort in going to our church,
it had little to do with religion. "Religion really isn't that important to me, I know," she said sheepishly. But she really appreciated
the friendships and connections; they were a source of emotional
support and solace for her. On the other hand, a small band of
extremely devout Catholics I met in New York City saw spiritual
comfort exclusively in religious terms. Comfort came through
the supernatural graces bestowed by the Catholic sacraments and
prayer practices—going to mass, receiving Communion, praying
the rosary, going to confession. It was God's action on the soul.
Yet even for them, these spiritual acts included other components;
their sacramental Catholicism had a strongly physical and emotional cast to it through its images and statues, its embodied
prayers and rites.

Diverse opinions make it difficult to say too much. People
seem all over the map when it comes to spiritual comfort. Then
again, people are all over the map when it comes to spirituality,
especially in the United States. Over 90 percent of Americans
pledge their belief in God in surveys. Almost three out of four
believe in an afterlife. Yet around a third feel the need to worship
that God at weekly services, even fewer among younger people.
Television programs and films regularly address existential ques-

tions, biblical history, esoteric myths, exorcism, life after death, even angelic visitations; yet very infrequently do programs show you much about people's *ordinary* spiritual lives. Half of all volunteering and half of all individual charity in the United States take place through religious institutions, but many people object if such institutions get government funding. A rabbi friend informs me that many secular-minded American Jews donate regularly to Chabad houses, the ubiquitous Jewish house centers associated with the ultra-Orthodox Lubavitcher movement; yet these same givers are not observant themselves nor do they attend any sort of synagogue. Many Americans claim they see the United States as a "Christian country," and yet an overwhelming number of the nation's most important historical figures rejected orthodox Christianity—Benjamin Franklin, Thomas Jefferson, James Madison, Ralph Waldo Emerson, Henry David Thoreau, Abraham Lincoln, Susan B. Anthony, Mark Twain. Unraveling spiritual comfort in such a beguiling religious environment feels like an impossible challenge.

Still, when we train our sights on spiritual comfort, some things do come into focus. To return to Mark Twain's humorous example, it cannot be just ham and eggs. It has to be ham and eggs while admiring a sublime landscape. For almost everyone, spiritual comfort involves some push beyond the ordinary way we look at experience—the everyday, the mundane. Like all forms of comfort it begins with the physical and the emotional, but it also has another dimension to it, something not always easy to name or describe.

After 9/11, a friend—another priest—and I went downtown to volunteer for the Red Cross. After a long afternoon listening to the family members of the "missing," to overworked police officers and frustrated volunteers who could not offer anyone good news, we left the National Guard Armory. We turned downtown, walking absentmindedly toward Ground Zero. We walked for a long time, often in silence, sometimes stopping to talk with people who saw our priest garb and hailed us. Around eight o'clock there was a brief dinner near Union Square, and then we kept walking. The night grew dark and the streets quiet for Manhattan. Suddenly the street was blocked off with the bright lights and smoke of the "pile" in the distance. We turned and looked for the subway home, both of us feeling strangely comforted. The physical walk, the company, the emotional release of so much exercise had done us good. But there was something more in the alternating rhythm of silence and talk, in the way the light and crowds thinned as the night wore on, in the odd way our gait had purpose even as we had no definite destination. This was "spiritual time," time away from time. That night even our Roman collars—usually a scarlet letter of weirdness in New York City—served a different function, a hopeful sign to those who greeted us, whatever their religious affiliations. Everything seemed to mean more and conspire to bring us and others hope.

Spiritual comfort does not always steal us so completely away from "regular life" like that, but it does pull at us from realms of depth and faith, peace and security, love and forgiveness, meaning and hope. Like other forms of comfort, it also has to do with relief, solace, and order amid the negative experiences of life— hope in times of grief, a rhythm of life to dispel the chaos, a reason to believe in forgiveness in a cold and vengeful world. But it all happens with an added transcendent dimension, a depth dimension. Spiritual comfort always involves our awakening to a realization that life means so much more than our narrow everyday preoccupations. This is why as Jesus heals the physically blind in the New Testament, he also points out how much more

"blind" other sighted people are—that is, narrow-minded, prej-
udiced, focused on their own privilege and power (see, for
example, Matthew 15:14 and Matthew 23:16–19; John 9:1–41).

Of course, mucking about with this depth dimension of life—
with meaning, order, transcendence—this remains a tricky business. A thousand charlatans and petty tyrants masquerade as
spiritual comforters. We get those spiritual extortion e-mails urging us to rely on the power of prayer, only effective if we forward
the e-mail to fifteen people within ten minutes. And for each
obstacle to real spiritual comfort on the outside, we are bound
to encounter a good half dozen within. After all, at the edge of
mystery, a multitude of fears and illusions lie in wait for us. We
make God over in our own image, or at least often according to
the icon of our own fears and anxieties. Spiritual comfort is not
so easy as it appears. In the Hindu scripture the Katha Upanishad, Death speaks to the youth Nachiketas and tells him, "The
sharp edge of a razor is difficult to pass over; thus the wise say
the path (to the Self) is hard."

Yet just beyond that edge lies a connectedness to all people
and all things, and a wordless comfort deep and unfathomable.
Ultimately that is the source of human strength and transformation.


## Psycho-God


"The fear of the LORD is the beginning of wisdom" (Psalm
111:10, NRSV).

In traditional English translations of the Bible, Jews and
Christians are told to "fear" God. For Catholics, "the fear of the
Lord" ranks as one of the seven gifts of the Holy Spirit (from the

old Greek and Latin translations of Isaiah 11:13). This usually produces a certain amount of confusion and anxiety in children until someone tells them that "fear" here really means something closer to "awe." The key prayer from the Catholic rite of confirmation attempts to clear up the confusion: "Fill them with the spirit of wonder and awe in your presence." The spiritual point, I think, is essentially the same one that my driving companion on the freeway made. Somehow struck by the divine touch—through beauty, love, understanding, gratitude—we become amazed, wowed, thunderstruck. *How is this possible?* The experience of wonder and awe deepens our awareness and brings us comfort. The world suddenly seems to have a purpose and order beyond our immediate consciousness. There is more to it than we thought. Probably most of us have had some kind of experience like this, even if we do not explicitly connect it with religion or a personal sort of God. The Bible says that the "fear of the Lord is the beginning of wisdom" because these sorts of experiences jolt us from our small-mindedness, from a desire to live in a narrow and carefully controlled universe. Everything is bigger than we thought, and we remain only a part of it. Not the center of things.

But in the world of religion, someone has to take a perfectly *comforting* spiritual lesson and turn it into a prison-camp motto. I met that someone working in a Texas hospital one summer. This tall, renegade Southern Baptist attempted to convince me that I should literally fear God, as in when God showed up I should run screaming in the other direction. This articulate middle-aged white man had come to town from the surrounding countryside to visit a sick relative. He had no use for poetic license or for the dazzling symbolism in Scripture. God was a hard, demanding father, ready to punish or even destroy at any moment.

If not suitably frightened, we would surely end up arrogant and adventurous, in moral and spiritual peril. I asked him if he thought it was perhaps possible to obey God without wetting your pants in terror. "No," he said decisively.

Seldom do believers in what I call the "Psycho-God" lay out their point so clearly, but there it was. God was the iron-willed judge, the fascist dictator of heaven and earth. This was a spirituality organized around waiting for the other shoe to drop.

It's not limited to renegade Baptists in Texas either. One afternoon, while reminiscing with Catholic friends in their late seventies, I got them onto the topic of their Catholic upbringing in the 1930s and 1940s. They remembered the old days of mass in Latin, the priest with his back to the congregation, memorizing the Baltimore Catechism, and a whole lot of focus on sin and hell. The husband of the couple had attended a Jesuit high school in Los Angeles in the 1940s, and he remembered a Jesuit seminarian telling him and his classmates, "No Catholic enters heaven headfirst; it's always back end first, backing away from hell."

In truth, this is pretty standard stuff in religion. Very specific images of hell form the basis of an entire chapter of James Joyce's *Portrait of the Artist as a Young Man*, as he portrayed sermons of his Dublin youth. Great Awakening preacher Jonathan Edwards famously preached sensually and vividly about hellfire, about "sinners in the hands of an angry God," convinced it was necessary to convert people from the particularly egregious pastimes of his era, such as hitting the taverns. After 9/11, some Christian fundamentalist preachers put the blame squarely on feminists and homosexuals—God's punishment had come upon the United States for its moral corruption. A great many of us have had some personal experience of this type of religion in our lives, whether it be Evangelical promises of hellfire for those who do not accept Jesus as personal savior, Catholics threatened with eternal punishment over "mortal sin," Jews and Muslims rigorously schooled in guilt by demanding parents. A religion of fear *attempts* to teach us something about God. God becomes a bit like an unpredictable and mercurial alcoholic parent. You creep around your life with this feeling that you never quite know what will set him off. That is why I call the image of God this "fear religion" gives us the "Psycho-God."

Even more important may be what "fear religion" teaches us about *us*, about human beings. As the man in Texas said, God cannot trust us. We are forever disobedient, angry, and rebellious, children who are happy to get away with whatever we can. Only fear keeps us in line. In real life, most of us only pass through acting like that, as a stage in adolescent development or in our alienated youth. But you have to grow up. And with that, we need a more grown-up relationship with God.

What often makes the religion of fear most attractive—and to some extent comforting—is an increase in the level of chaos. The more people feel helpless at the mercy of wild external forces, the more a hard-nosed religion and a frightful God look like an improvement. When trouble strikes, who doesn't want a fearsome divine force who can kick butt? It's the amplification of an impulse deep in the heart of religion. At the start of the Bible, we hear that the earth was a "formless wasteland," in Hebrew the *tohu vavohu*, primordial chaos, and the "mighty wind" or "spirit" of God (*ruach elohim*) pushed the chaos back. Believers have always felt a certain comfort in faith that brings security and order when chaos floods the world. Yet the purveyors of the religion of fear take it all a step further, envisioning the God that pushed back the chaos as militant and on permanent patrol. Insecurity around us suddenly makes their vision more palatable to the general public. Let the specter of terrorism loose with the threat of war without end and suddenly extremist statements appear perfectly normal. In the years after 9/11, an Evangelical preacher in Ohio called not for Christians to challenge terrorists but to "eliminate" Islam entirely. In fact, when I (in horror) shared the story of the preacher with a group of Catholics in California, one of them piped up and agreed with him, saying "That's what I think!" The Psycho-God is on the prowl.

But this brings us to the problem. Putting our trust in an angry Supreme Being will likely *generate* as much fear as it dissipates. There will be as much anxiety as comfort in the end. Jim Jones, the 1970s leader of the suicidal People's Temple cult, promised his followers again and again that he would protect them from the chaos. They surrendered to him their critical thinking skills, their personal authority, even their ability to make moral decisions. And there is a certain relief in this letting go of adult responsibilities. Yet in return came the horrifying turmoil of total dependence on an unstable authority figure, and eventually mass suicide when he persuaded them all to drink cyanide-laced Kool-Aid. In the 1990s there was the drama of Afghanistan and the Taliban. After Soviet forces had destroyed the country's infrastructure, mujahideen fighters made incessant war among themselves, closing the schools, emptying the markets, leaving the nation in ruin and chaos. When the Taliban took control, interviews with people on the street showed that many folks genuinely welcomed their leadership, repressive as it might be. It appeared that God had pushed back the chaos. But they had traded fear of chaos for fear of the Taliban. There would be little comfort after all.

That realization initially proves very uncomfortable—that in search of security we have opted for a hellish world of fear. But it also opens the door to a new way of seeing things—a better way. We find not only that the Psycho-God doesn't offer us much, but this really wasn't God at all.

## The God of Comfort and the Comfortable God

Before the 1960s Vatican II reforms, Catholic rules about receiving Communion were pretty strict—a person had to fast from midnight the night before. Though it wasn't church law, Catholics were also often told they could not receive Communion unless they had just gone to confession. The fear was that people might desecrate the holy sacrament by receiving it with some grave (also known as "mortal") sin on their conscience. And the mortal sins multiplied in those days—missing mass on Sunday and masturbating were chief among the commonly committed offending acts. You can guess the trajectory of all this. People went to mass, but they tended to get leery about going up to Communion. After all, a person could end up in hell on what today seems like a technicality. Receiving Communion was like a special occasion for many people.

And so it was for a nun of my acquaintance when she was a little girl. She had prepared the previous day, going to confession, getting very excited like a good little Catholic schoolgirl. Then disaster struck—she accidentally swallowed her morning toothpaste, thus technically breaking her midnight fast and making her ineligible to receive. She broke down in tears, and this was the state in which her father found her in the bathroom. "Why are you crying?" he asked. She sobbed out, "I can't go to Communion because I swallowed the toothpaste." He looked at her, stroked her hair. He just said, "God's not like that."

God isn't like that—not the metaphysical hunter of souls, spiritual executioner, custodian of the other shoe, ever ready to drop. Once a person lets that go, everything looks different. The Catholic nun still tells the story about the toothpaste and her father's commonsensical but liberating remark, decades after it happened. When I was five years old, one of my playmates lived a few doors down from the public school where we both attended kindergarten. I hated playtime at his house, since he always kept me doing his bidding by threatening to chop me in half using his knowledge of karate. I took it for granted that in fact he could do this. Yet one day I grew so fed up with him that I spontaneously rebelled, and he got up to carry out his threat. I thought my life as an intact body was coming to an end. When his blow failed to bisect me, I blurted out the obvious: "You can't really chop me in half." He smiled and shrugged his shoulders. After that, not only did the playtime balance of power shift, but my whole pint-size view of the universe seemed different. Without this constant threat to my bodily integrity, I felt both relieved and empowered. A malevolent universe had suddenly and unexpectedly turned benevolent.

Several people who have been able to "shelve the Psycho-God" along the way in their lives indicate that this sense of release is exactly the point. The Great Author of Creation suddenly looks like someone who might love and nurture me instead of threaten me. A writer and former priest shared with me how as a young man and as a young priest he was haunted by the old Catholic teaching that masturbation—indeed even the smallest self-stimulation—was a terrible sin. He remembers reading a book about all the physical problems that masturbation engendered and rushing to a neighboring priest's house at dawn for confession lest he end up in hell for officiating at morning mass in a state of mortal sin. The whole thing kept him in a state of fear and anxiety before God. Yet as the 1960s and the Second Vatican Council progressed, he and his companions in the priesthood knew something was wrong. He remembers taking a walk with a seminary classmate, talking about their sex-driven morality. They began to say to themselves, "This is crazy. Is this what God wants?" Hearing other people wrestle with silly rules and minutiae in the confessional helped as well: "I wanted them to believe that God really loved them, that God wasn't a 'bean counter,' that God wasn't ready to throw you into hell." Somehow it was easier to believe in a merciful and loving God when he realized he wanted other people to experience God that way.

This transition can appear anywhere people are taught to literally fear God and then find release, but not surprisingly it shows up disproportionately in the stories of people who start out life in situations of fear, neglect, and abuse. This unfortunately makes sense. When the people from whom we expect love are cruel to us, why would we expect anything different from God? Yet what surprises me is how often—contrary to all our psychological and spiritual theories—deep in their hearts afflicted people really know otherwise. Even as they feel unworthy and ashamed and await their judgment, they know something is spiritually amiss. As if the truth were waiting there all along. They are only waiting for the great reversal, the counterexample that will change their minds about themselves, the universe, and about God.

In Alice Walker's novel (and the subsequent film) *The Color Purple*, no one seems more beaten down than the main character, Celie. Men have pummeled and molested her all her life. Yet even as she writes her journal to an indifferent (and white) version of God, this journal itself is part of a reaching beyond the battered life she endures. And then she meets the dynamic singer Avery Shug, her husband's lover, who shows her many things, including a very different way of looking at God. Midway through the book, Shug tells Celie about the moment she realized that God was not a church-obsessed old white man unconcerned with black people. God was present in nature, inside Shug herself, connected to all things. Shug found a God who loved her and all creation. Celie is in awe of Shug's spirituality, and it jumpstarts a spiritual transformation that delivers her to a God of Comfort. She immediately finds the courage and strength to stand up for herself for the first time.

Jewish mystical tradition explains such a transition with the *sefirot*, a kind of tree or network of vessels of divine energy connecting God and the human world. At midlevel on the *sefirot*, in perfect symmetry lie three vessels—*din* or strict judgment, *tiferet* or wise and merciful love, and *hesed* or loving-kindness. According to kabbalists, people may respond more strongly to each of these types of love depending on their life experience and place on the road of spiritual development. In Christian lore (based in Jewish traditions), this transition is called *metanoia*, conversion, a move closer to the Living God, "a God merciful and gracious, slow to anger, and abounding in steadfast love and faithfulness" (Exodus 34:6, NRSV). In the New Testament, this God is the ludicrously generous shepherd who leaves ninety-nine sheep to go looking for the poor lost one (Matthew 18:12–13).

Such announcements of divine love and mercy are not found in Judaism and Christianity alone. Though the Buddha does not speak of a personal God, his gentle preaching of the dharma to

Yasa, a rich merchant disturbed at heart by the ugliness and pain of the world, has a similar feel of awakening to compassion and mercy. The classic stories of the Sufis in the Islamic tradition focus on the surprise and joy of these mystics as they uncover the crazy and undying love of God. Fear or anxiety may always haunt certain sides of religion, but the spiritual depths of a tradition almost always lead us to the comfort that comes with love and mercy. Human beings are not brought into the world as a mistake, and religion comes as a path to liberation from what ails and disturbs us. In the Abrahamic traditions of Judaism, Christianity, and Islam, God calls to and inspires the goodness within us. God sends friends, angels, and kind strangers. Human beings are endowed with intellect, imagination, and compassion to resolve the disasters that befall us. The Living God is a God of Comfort.

The God of Comfort, however, can also become the Comfortable God. Once a person discovers a spirituality oriented to love and mercy, it's easy enough to envision a Supreme Being docile enough to domesticate. Does that sound strange? People of faith have always struggled with the desire to reduce God, to make the Living God into the Mellow God, a meek and pliant pal to bend to your own will. Film director Kevin Smith mocked this in his 1999 film *Dogma*, when a cardinal played by George Carlin rolls out a winking statue of Jesus making the "thumbs-up" gesture, part of a supposed church public relations campaign to make Catholicism more fun. The Comfortable God becomes like a parent unwilling to discipline, who only wants to be pals with his child; or maybe the psychotherapist with unconditional positive regard but little actual advice for her client; or perhaps, even worse, a lovable pet—cute and loyal but not particularly concerned about what the owner does or why.

The contemporary turn of these images may give the impression that domesticating God is a modern problem, but nothing could be further from the truth. People have wanted to keep God under their thumb as long as human beings have believed in God. And while religions have their own divinity-domesticating tendencies, they also have their theological guardrails to prevent it. Eastern Orthodox Christians have their "apophatic" tradition, maintaining that human beings should say as little as possible about who God is. Protestant and Catholic theologians have their hairsplitting debates about the mystery of God for the same reason, and the Buddha rejected the idea of a personal God altogether.

Yet the Comfortable God sneaks up on you, particularly in our own era. Sociologist Christian Smith claims that North American teenagers today lean toward a spirituality called "Moralistic Therapeutic Deism." According to Smith, these teens believe in God, but they see God as a largely irrelevant character who only zooms in to solve problems when things get particularly sticky. Most of the time the Creator hangs back, wanting people to feel happy and act nice. In Smith's accounting, God serves as a combination "divine butler" and "cosmic therapist." But don't blame the kids. This kind of spirituality works perfectly well in our society. Our daily lives appear to function quite well, thank you very much, without divine intervention. We do not live in the spirit-and-saint-haunted worlds of nineteenth-century Latin American campesinos or medieval Europeans. We like our spirituality divorced from our daily lives, away from the daily grind of work, relationships, socializing, politics, and the marketplace.

We pride ourselves on making ethical choices uninfluenced by spiritual concerns. God rules in a realm all his (or her) own that mostly concerns Sunday worship and proper doctrine. You can pray, even attend services, and then go out and cheat your employees (or your wife). God will feel bad for you and forgive you. God will certainly never get angry.

I suppose this would have to be strictly theologically true—anger is a human quality we project onto God. Yet I have my doubts: to rob God of outrage in a world as broken and merciless as ours feels like saddling ourselves with some kind of divine pantywaist. Saint Augustine once said, "Love God and do what you will," but he surely never assumed that we would take him so literally. Augustine, of course, assumed that loving God made all the difference, and to him God was neither pantywaist nor psycho. God had personally pursued him through all his years of searching and now God wanted everything from him. Augustine believed God desired the same from all who were destined for salvation (he believed in predestination).

When I lived in New York, I knew a woman, a musician, who always talked about God as if God were her best friend or her upstairs neighbor. Yet many of us do not live in a world as enchanted as that of Augustine or this woman. We have a harder time finding God in the everyday. Indeed, many people leave behind the religion of fear never to take up religion or faith at all; they put it in a nice box on a shelf somewhere. It's easy to see why. We need to know that both religion and faith really are relevant to our daily questions and dilemmas. We want to know whether they will help us maintain hope in crisis, behave positively to others, treat strangers with graciousness, spend money wisely, let go of resentments and prejudices, and say the right things to our children when they come with questions. What we need is a spiritual wake-up call, something to show us that faith really could be a matter of life and death.


I offer a friendly warning that I am about to relate a horrible story.

The people of the village of El Mozote had been studiously neutral in the ongoing civil war in El Salvador, mostly on account of the inhabitants' commitment to Evangelical Christianity, which tends to be apolitical in Latin America. Both sides in the war knew about El Mozote's neutrality, and the villagers had received assurances from government forces just days before that they would be left alone. Yet on December 10, 1981, members of the Atlacatl Battalion, an American-trained unit of the Salvadoran armed forces, entered the village just after fighting with a band of guerrillas nearby. Having run out of lists of suspected collaborators in the area and unsure what to do next, the soldiers simply killed everyone—hundreds of people, including every man, woman, and child in the village except for two survivors. The survivors' brutal tales of what occurred were later corroborated by forensic evidence. People had been shot, burned, bayoneted, decapitated, and hacked to death. One of the two survivors, Rufina Amaya Márquez, saw her own husband killed and heard the screams of her children as they, too, perished. Later, as she hid from the soldiers in the bushes, she heard them tell of a young girl, repeatedly raped and then shot, who all the while sang Christian hymns, defying them and holding to faith in the face of unspeakable suffering. Her faith and courage frightened the soldiers.

The type of evil perpetrated at El Mozote—like atrocities committed in other places and times—staggers the imagination and requires a human accounting. In this particular case, the survivors and their advocates pushed for investigations while the Salvadoran government resisted them. But such brutal human suffering demands a kind of spiritual accounting as well. After the Holocaust in Europe, most Jewish intellectuals found their religious outlook radically altered by the experience; it happened to some Christian theologians as well. Very often when people witness unspeakable suffering, they no longer feel at home with God as they once knew God. In our contemporary world, terrible injustice may make a nice and nonjudgmental God look more weak and incompetent than kind and merciful. People may either lose faith in God altogether or look for a God who is not so indifferent to human suffering, who expressly takes the side of the oppressed.

Beginning in the late 1960s, a group of theology professors in Latin America started a movement now known as "liberation theology." It developed through the seventies and eighties in response to the terrible suffering of poor peasants across Latin America and to the violence and oppression perpetrated in places like El Mozote. Liberation theologians, who for a time had bishops on their side, felt that as long as such terrible evil existed in the world, spirituality could not simply be a matter of saying one's prayers, going to church, and believing in the proper doctrines. If God truly was love, as Jesus had said, then God could not be indifferent to the misery of millions of people. God simply had to take their part. The God of compassion and tenderness surely was also indignant at all this evil and demanding of a better world. True religion would "comfort the afflicted and afflict the comfortable."

It was not, as some critics in the United States and Europe accused, that these theologians believed that God loved the poor and hated the rich. Rather they thought that no one, least of all God, could witness the carnage of innocents and remain neutral. Again and again they returned to their critique of international capitalism, its legacy of devastating inequality, and the wars and oppression that had arisen as a result. Naturally, as the U.S. government poured financial and military resources into fighting leftist movements and regimes in Latin America, the theologians' free use of Marxist social analysis, their criticism of U.S. foreign policy, and their disavowal of the free market system made a lot of Americans nervous. Yet the liberation theologians did not simply dismiss the United States, but worried that first-world materialism was making life in the north unhappy and empty. Whether we agree with their politics or not, the spirituality they presented offers an honest challenge to an overly comfortable religion and a domesticated God. To them, the God of Love has no interest in condemning people on little rules and trivialities, but God does wish to hold human beings accountable for their lack of consideration for one another, and for their unwillingness to see the sufferings of others and share the good things they have. These theologians speak of a God who hears the cry of those who died at El Mozote and who will not let the rest of us forget. In a world of such suffering, what kind of people would we be if we did not remember and if that memory did not leave us more than a little uncomfortable?

## Of Death and Pasta

I moved to the San Francisco Bay Area about a year after I graduated from college. Immediately upon arriving, I began to pal around with two of my college buddies. One of them was pursuing a doctoral degree in physics at Cal Berkeley. I ended up crashing on his couch for a couple of weeks until I found a place of my own. The other got a job in import/export and moved in with her mother. They had just lost her father, a firefighter who had succumbed to cancer. Rounding out our little social group was her cousin, who lived nearby and taught preschool. We all got together so often that we began to (sarcastically) refer to ourselves as "The Unit."

The Unit's near-daily mixing came to an end when everyone got a regular job (including me), but we still got together on the weekends, often having dinner at the house my friend shared with her mother. They were Italian, and we all joined in preparing elaborate pasta dinners, arriving early to prepare vegetables, chop meat, open bottles of wine. Eventually we would be drinking the wine, eating a bit of cheese as we talked and laughed in the kitchen. Finally we sat down at the table, my friend's mother inviting me to say grace, joking that I was "the holy one," since everyone knew I was off to the seminary before the year was out. Very often the conversation turned to her husband, my friend's dad. They shared stories with us about him. Sometimes we would muse about death itself—what it was like, where he was now, what it meant to leave people behind you loved. I marveled at the two of them and their willingness to talk to us about their ongoing experience of grief. As they spoke, it seemed as if the man they loved were present with us.

More than anything, the dinners brought us all closer. Time stopped while we ate, talked, laughed. I cannot rationally explain to you the connection that occurred in that dining room, there among the pasta and wine, nor the change it worked inside me. But I know I felt comforted, less afraid. At that transitional moment in my life and in the lives of those other four people, a temporary but deep connection occurred that strengthened us as people. The anthropologist Victor Turner calls this "communitas," and he claimed that in the midst of such an experience time stops, everything seems possible, people let go of status and everyday distinctions. Remarkable transformations can take place. As we laughed and shared at those dinners—trying to make sense of the mundane, the silly, the serious, and the sacred in our lives—we did seem to forget our usual anxieties and inhibitions and were open in an extraordinarily unusual way. It was a special time, a spiritual time.

No doubt after all these years I've endowed the memory with some romance and nostalgia, but I hope not too much. I do believe that we experienced together around that table a sense of what we might call "communion"—a real connection with each other that included a divine element. After years as a priest, I still think of this experience when I think of Communion at mass. It is not so much that I expect mass to turn out like those dinner parties. Seldom does a public ritual have such an intimate character. And the circumstances of those dinners remain unique. They belong to a particular time in our lives, when the changes we underwent—some people beginning their adult lives, one woman starting hers over—lent themselves to vulnerability and openness. Yet, at the same time, I cannot but be struck by certain parallels. In the Eucharist, Christians share food (in Mediterranean fashion, bread and wine), remember someone (Jesus) who has passed from their midst and yet lives again among them. They feel God's Spirit restoring their strength and vitality. Such do we Christians believe. And also it is, at root, a community experience. Of course, there are differences between Eucharist and my dinner parties, and my friend's dad is not Jesus. Still,

I learned something crucial about faith and about the Eucharist at that table—while we ate our pasta and talked of death.

In an age of tremendous geographic mobility, of more people than ever living alone, of gated communities and hermetically sealed homes, the human hunger for experiences of communion and connection grows with our isolation. Spiritual communities— experienced in churches, synagogues, mosques, and temples, or according to more informal arrangements like my dinner-party group—respond to that hunger, and they always have. Human beings are social animals, and religious groups have understood from time immemorial that clan and kin do not always satisfy the longings of the human heart for connection. Especially the larger religious traditions have adopted the language of family and community to their own purposes, what anthropologists call "fictive kinship." Thus, Muslims address one another as brother or sister united in the *umma* ("community" or "people") of Islam; Christians similarly call each other "brother or sister in Christ" (and Catholics call the priest "Father"); and a woman who is both elder and leader in an African-American faith community is called the "Church Mother."

Forms of address aside, real bonds of affection do develop in faith communities that provide people with deep comfort. Early one summer some time back I returned to my university town for a sad occasion. Due to a shortage of personnel, the religious order of priests I belong to would no longer be serving the university parish there. The parish gave us a going-away party. Afterward I drove various old friends home, including a former staff member of the parish who just one month before had lost her husband to emphysema. She invited us all in for a drink. We pulled out the wine, and the stories began. They concluded hours later. We remembered everything from the recycling drive entitled "Bring Your Can to Church" to the priest who appeared dressed as Batman in a cloud of smoke at the bishop's fund-raiser. Beneath the funny stories and memories, though, was something more. Some of us had seen little of one another in a decade or more, yet that time we had spent together in church almost twenty years before had been formative. We were at home together.

Many Catholics remain involved in the church today at least in part because of some seminal experience of spiritual community like what I experienced in my university parish. My former coworker in Internet ministry had incredible retreat experiences in college. A civic planner from Virginia in her late twenties and a man I went to high school with in Southern California both spent a year volunteering with the Jesuit order after college, and they found it a powerful experience of spiritual community.

Yet I realize not every person's experience of community is the same, even among those who feel their experience was positive. My university parish experience was freewheeling and progressive, though with a good theological foundation and with strong pastoral leadership. When I lived in New York, I often heard about a polar opposite experience. At weddings or baptisms I would find myself standing at the back of the church talking to some young man. Usually this was a guy in his twenties, perhaps in the military or attending one of the local colleges. These men often had small children of their own, and they talked to me about the importance of faith communities as a kind of haven, a source of discipline and focus for young men and women in a time of temptation and distraction in their lives. Church bestowed the right values. Spiritual community felt to them like a still point in a chaotic universe, and that, too, was comfort.

## God for Grown-Ups

A seminary classmate came to me in the fall of 1992 and told me he had lost his faith. Regaling me with amusing stories about the dogmatic pronouncements of an ideologue philosophy professor, he suddenly turned to me and said, "Brett, I just can't buy it anymore." He meant, I realized, the whole package of faith. He was leaving the seminary—immediately. Our director had concurred in his decision. In a way, he sounded like someone backed into a corner who politely excuses himself and walks away. I listened to him, but I didn't understand what had happened. He offered no details about his questions and doubts, and I did not ask him to wait it out a bit, to see how things might turn out. I did not yet know that this scenario would be repeated in hundreds of conversations I would have over the next fifteen years with college students, young working people, and even older people going through a transition in their lives. I simply told him faith was a gift, and you either had it or you didn't. I think I imagined faith like some sort of internal organ. A licensed faith practitioner could apply a few tests and tell you whether you had it, were born without it, or perhaps it had suffered irreparable damage from some spiritually transmitted disease ("I'm sorry, but your faith is shot. There's nothing we can do."). Once you had this diagnosed lack of faith, you would have to live without it for the rest of your life.

I soon discovered how wrong I had been. Faith is more like a sport than an internal organ—like hockey or soccer or baseball. There is some gift (or talent) involved, but that turns out to be the key factor only for a choice few. For the rest of us, faith is dynamic and constantly developing. Like with sports, players grow in skill and understanding. Sometimes it changes rapidly, other times more gradually. Events on the field of play make a difference. Losing your faith is not the end of the game, any more than the awareness that a certain pitch or hitting style will no longer work means the end of a baseball career. It just means it's time to try something else. In fact, for most people, "losing your faith" is a prerequisite for significant growth. In the seminary we used to say that the first year was dedicated to destroying your faith so that it could be rebuilt in the second year. There was sarcasm involved, but it was not entirely misplaced. Life *is* a struggle, and the life of faith is no different. In a way, the idea of seminary preparation was to preempt the intellectual and spiritual struggles other people have so that we would know how to help them.

Unfortunately, for many people, the testing of faith serves simply as the end of the line. Once a college student came into my office, proclaimed her disagreement with Catholic moral teaching on premarital sex, and then concluded boldly that this meant she was no longer a Catholic. Though it may have felt that way to her, she was not the first person in the world to face this dilemma. We had a long conversation about what it meant to have the faith of an adult versus the faith of a child. We talked about the Catholic Church's teaching on sexuality. We tossed around what it meant to have a conscience and to follow it. She was shocked. No one had ever suggested to her that anything but a very simple "pray, pay, and obey" mentality was available within the Catholic Church (or any other religion for that matter).

That is why a lot of people presume that organized religion is for children, or at least for people without any interior strength. No one has ever shown them that a more nuanced, complex view of faith is both available and necessary.

Yet every major religion has both its simpler childlike versions and its complicated versions for adults. How else could it speak to the same person at different points in life? Of course, literalists and fundamentalists of various stripes—Protestant Evangelical, Catholic, Jewish, Muslim, Hindu—do not want people to know this. Their leaders maintain their influence and power by keeping people in a childlike state of fear and obedience. Sometimes even the mainstream religious authorities insist on the same—it becomes just easier to deal with folks in that way. But wise people in every age have always known the emptiness of this prospect. People have to grow up. The ecumenical retreat leader (and Franciscan priest) Richard Rohr told me that he believes all people need to start off life with a structured and conservative foundation, but then they need to question and probe and open up that foundation en route to a larger vision of the divine and the world, what he calls "the contemplative mind."

Most people find comfort in a faith that survives shifts in the spiritual ground. Several years ago a colleague and I ran spiritual retreats for young working people in the New York City area. Some of these folks had paid little attention to their spirituality since childhood, and they came away from our retreats relieved that faith did not mean checking your brain at the door. In the mid-1960s Malcolm X found peace in a broader, more orthodox Islam. Nation of Islam leader Elijah Muhammad had continually restrained him from greater political activism, and increasingly Malcolm felt tension over the gap between orthodox Islam and the racial ideologies of the Nation. This personal and political turmoil drove him to break with the Nation and go on the hajj, the pilgrimage to Mecca undertaken by all Muslims who are able. Encountering the great global diversity of Islam resolved his religious struggles, and he broadened his political activities, networking with all sorts of people in the spirit of this new and more expansive Islamic outlook. In those final days of his life, he was a man set free.

A minister, psychologist, and theologian by the name of James Fowler spent a great deal of time in the 1970s documenting how religious faith changes over the course of a person's lifetime. He called that rocky time when a person questions and doubts her way to "owning her own faith" the "Individuative-Reflective" stage in faith development. In this stage of life people take responsibility for their own critical reflection, fulfillment, and place in life. They lose faith and pick it up again. Young women and men especially ask all those existential questions because they have to know *for themselves*. Each decides his or her own faith identity. Fowler admits that this process of transition is often messy, set in motion by tensions that develop in the previous stage when conventional religious ideas begin to appear inadequate. *Discomfort* is what drives change. The security of the previous world of faith collapses, but the momentum of change lifts a person to a new and more comprehensive view of things. Old images of God are replaced by newer and more adequate visions of the Divine.

We used to call this "conversion." "I once was lost but now am found; was blind but now I see," wrote the former slave trader John Newton in the nineteenth-century hymn "Amazing Grace." The seeker finds himself or herself in darkness, afraid and confused. Discomfort bids a person reach for a new equilibrium, and it comes, almost like a gift dropped from the sky. Doesn't it sound familiar? You enter through the doorway of a crisis; everything goes crazy; then somehow life comes back together and you emerge through another doorway a different person. It sounds like adolescence. It sounds like entering college. It sounds like falling in love. It sounds like military basic training or the police academy. It sounds pretty much like any contained transformative process that a human being could go through. A sustained period of chaos is required in order to truly emerge in a different state of life.

In fact, most of the world's important religious stories involve a struggle with chaos as prelude to major growth and discovery. Thus, Jacob wrestles with God (or the angel, depending on how you read the story) in the book of Genesis (chapter 32, verses 23 through 33) and then emerges blessed and renewed. Jesus goes to the desert to fast and be tempted by the devil ("devil" means "divider," one who breaks down order into chaos) before he can be fully prepared for his mission to proclaim God's reign. The Buddha engages in a final verbal struggle with the demon Mara under the bodhi tree and emerges fully enlightened. In a more contemporary example, the chaos of systematic, government-sponsored violence and oppression turned Archbishop Oscar Romero of El Salvador from a church "company man" into a champion of human rights and a defender of the poor.

In all of these stories described above, people passed through the gauntlet of chaos and emerged wiser and more spiritual. This is how we grow up as people of faith, discovering a "God for grown-ups" in the process.

## The Rhythm of Comfort

From the dawn of time ritual has brought comfort to human beings in all kinds of predicaments. Particularly when there isn't a lot to say.

As a newly ordained priest, I was called to the bedside of a middle-aged man dying in the hospital, a Mexican man whose family spoke no English. They asked for the sacrament of anointing for the sick, what Catholics used to call "last rites." It was my first sacramental anointing, and it was to be in my adequate-but-not-stellar Spanish. Inside I panicked, but I tried to stay strong and steadfast for the family. Gathering the family members around the bedside, we entered into the ritual dialogue that the Catholic rite calls for. "*Señor, ten piedad,*" we began together. *Lord, have mercy.* After several responses I laid my hands on his head as he lay unconscious. Tracing out a cross with the oil on his forehead and hands, I desperately tried to pronounce the words invoking the Holy Spirit as reverently and correctly as I could, but I made several mistakes, messing up tenses and subject-and-verb agreement. I became self-conscious, certain I was failing this kind and vulnerable family in their hour of need. When all was finished, I hung my head and turned around. Every one of the members of the family was weeping, oblivious to my errors.

I understood there and then that the comfort that comes from ritual operates at a deep and emotional level. When there is nothing left to say, we *do* something—we pray with our hands, our heads, our tears. We anoint with oil, wash with water, ask for a touch or a kiss, eat food that speaks to us of special times and places. We do things with our bodies. In the days immediately following 9/11, as we wondered what to do with ourselves, how to keep going, the renowned preacher Reverend James Forbes of Riverside Church in New York City said in a sermon, "The body knows."

Indeed it does, though sometimes that is because we ritually train it to know. A Jewish woman from a Reform synagogue in Northern California agreed: "Participating in a ritual on a weekly or monthly or annual basis is very important in the Jewish religion. To make things come back, you can quickly go into that spiritual place because something is triggered in your body." My former yoga teacher taught me that the point of yoga postures is to prepare the body for meditation, so that it knows what to do while the mind empties itself to listen to God. Five times a day Muslim men dip their heads to the ground as a sign of submission to God, and after years of practice the conscientious and devout physically *feel* that sense of submission. A former coworker of mine watched helplessly while his mother nearly perished of intestinal perforations and complications. A devout Catholic, he nevertheless had trouble praying to God for help. Then one day he took up the rosary, something he had seldom prayed since childhood. Immediately the old rhythms kicked in. The steady rhythm of repetition between Hail Marys and Our Fathers, the feel of the beads underneath his fingers, put him in a near trance. He felt continually calmed as he watched and waited in the hospital and on the commuter trains back and forth. God was watching with him, it seemed, and as the weeks passed his mother began to recover.

The body *does* know, but the words of the mouth are not irrelevant either, as the repetition of prayers in the rosary shows. Old venerable phrases, bits of Scripture and poetry, prayers repeated from memory from childhood, all these remain lodged in our consciousness, ready to go to work when the occasion calls for it. Such words often retain actual power over us—to soothe, to inspire, to change the way we think about ourselves. At an American wedding, both guests and couple anxiously await the ritual words, "I now pronounce you husband and wife," and all sigh in comfort when they finally get uttered. People get disappointed to find the phrase generally missing from Catholic and

Jewish ceremonies. Traditionally Muslims begin every important verbal act, from a book or a public lecture to a simple letter, with the initial words of the Quran in Arabic: "In the name of God, the Beneficent, the Merciful." All who hear this know it is time to pay attention as a compassionate God watches over the human act of communication. Even the tiny announcement when someone sneezes, "God bless you," functions as a ritual word of comfort. A friend from my Catholic high school days once told me about "training" his more secular college friends to say, "Bless you," when he sneezed. It comforted him.

## Beyond Words

Yet there is a comfort beyond words, too.

A lot of talk about religion and spirituality in polite society centers on moral matters—how religion instills good family values. Generally I imagine it does. Though plenty of hypocrisy can be found among religious people, sociological evidence also suggests that people involved in religion are among those who "play well with others." Churchgoers volunteer, help others on a regular basis, and are involved and interested in their local communities. But I've also heard people say that this is *all* there is to being a person of faith, that religion really amounts to "being a good person." While I would not want to deny that living as a kind and moral person is a necessary part of being a woman or man of faith, other things matter, too—what you believe, how you worship, your faith community, the wisdom you absorb from others, your spiritual practice. There's a lot more to being spiritual than just doing the right thing. Work and love and beauty, science and art, family and friendship, personal fulfillment and peace—all these things weave their way in and out of faith. Real belief involves more than seeing God as some kind of cosmic hall monitor, or even worse, a heavenly bureaucrat entering our sins in his celestial ledger.

Surely there is something at the heart of this religion business, beyond all these other questions. What people seldom talk about amid all the old stories and the rules, the ritual practices, sacraments, philosophical debates, and holy art—what lies deep within the spiritual—may be more important than anything else.

Mystery.

Not mystery like Sherlock Holmes or *CSI* or Kay Scarpetta, and not mystery like exploring the unanswered questions of physics. This is mystery where an answer isn't the point at all.

Plumbing the depths of spiritual mystery *begins* with our experience of life beyond our understanding and control.

That happens at big threshold moments of life—death, illness, childbirth, crisis, falling in love, travel. When we hit one of those life markers, our ordinary attempts to account for things fail us. We trip some kind of boundary, pass beyond conventional ways of thinking and acting. We run out of words, stop trying to explain. Our normal categories for description don't measure up. Sometimes we grow frustrated or upset; other times this moment of surrender brings happiness or even excitement. However we feel about it, we are no longer in charge. Sometimes that serves immediately as a comfort. In early 1998 I found myself suffering terrible insomnia for weeks as I struggled with anxieties becoming a priest had thrust upon me. I wanted to remain in control while I struggled with other people's expectations and my own fears and loneliness. Then my grandfather died, and I found myself on a plane home for his funeral. Suddenly I was faced with an incontrovertible fact that I could not control; anxiety melted away to sadness, and at home with my family that night I slept in peace for the first time in many weeks.

On that occasion I was offered no choice about my fate. At other times we mightily resist our lack of control before coming to terms with it. Back in 1995 I learned a small lesson about this while working a weekend spiritual retreat for college students. Halfway through, the thing looked like a failure—team leaders were revolting against the priest in charge, logistical problems multiplied, the mood seemed anything but meditative and spiritual. I accepted that we had worked hard on this, but it had failed. I had rushed to judgment. The next morning several participants spoke of how they found themselves radically reevaluating their faith, asking new questions, passing to a whole new spiritual level. One participant was enveloped in a profound mystical experience. *Something* worked, even though I could not understand. I simply stood back in awe.

So goes mystery—where one's ability to understand ends but one's ability to appreciate picks up. When my friend Debbie died on September 11, I learned the same day that a mutual friend was pregnant. She had already told Debbie about it—despite the fact that most of us had not yet heard. Joyful new life rose in the midst of tragic death. Mystery often becomes apparent to us in these juxtapositions, in the contradictions and paradoxes. And then sometimes it's just sheer beauty. One spring back in the 1990s, I stood quietly with a group of family and friends in the Arizona desert at twilight, not far from the Grand Canyon. We were walking among the Ancient Pueblo (or Anasazi) ruins there—the remains of a people who scattered a thousand years before. The place was desolate, and a lone coyote howled. It was,

I suppose, a normal event for a desert evening, but it had an inscrutable beauty for us, and we huddled together in silence. It took hold of us, as mystery does. As with poetry and art, images and metaphors, something is evoked rather than seen or understood. Rational analysis offers little more than a clue.

Traditionally the mystics have acted as guardians of mystery. They wrote about it and cataloged it as best they could for future generations, often employing paradoxes and riddles, resorting to erotic imagery at times. While they remain the experts—the Christian mystics Meister Eckhart and Saint Teresa of Avila, the Hindu Sri Ramana Maharshi, the Muslim Sufi master and poet Hafiz—still ordinary people tap (or perhaps stumble) into mystery all the time. We experience *connections* beyond the ordinary. We find them in the midst of human encounters—every human being is a mystery no one can ever fully comprehend. I sat and had a long talk with a good friend at the top of a mountain once, and as we got up to leave he said, "I feel like this is holy ground because of the time we shared here." Many of us recognize "moments of mystery" in our deepest experiences of friendship and sexual intimacy; a lucky few perceive it even in the simplest of everyday human relations. The American monk and writer Thomas Merton was walking along a street in Louisville, Kentucky, in the middle of the afternoon when suddenly a burst of spiritual clarity made him see all the people around him in their mysterious, divine splendor. He later remarked on the moment, "There is no way of telling people that they are all walking around shining like the sun."

Perhaps the great spiritual giants, then, were not, as we sometimes think, people utterly unlike the rest of us. They were just more sensitive to the presence of divine mystery in the world. Jesus was stirred by the deep human mystery of the sick, the poor, the rejected, and even the people most foreign to him, such as the Canaanite ("pagan") woman who came to him with the report that her daughter was ill. Believing his work to be for the sake of his own people, he meant to send this foreigner away, yet her trust and persistence awed him and changed his mind (Matthew 15:22–28). Saint Francis of Assisi was struck even by mystery in his encounters with the creatures of the animal kingdom, a spirituality virtually unknown to other Christians of his time. Like Saint Francis, the Persian Sufi master Hafiz saw all creation awash in mystery.

Whatever the encounter with mystery looks like, it brings comfort, and a comfort beyond mere ease or coziness. The mystics speak of genuine joy and peace. Saint Catherine of Genoa said, "Might but one little drop of what I feel fall into Hell, Hell would be transformed into a Paradise." The intrepid nun (and adept dodger of the Inquisition) Saint Teresa of Avila commented, "This joy is greater than all the joys of earth and all its delights and all its contentments and more." Of course, this joy and delight proves so powerful that when it fades for a time, the sense of disappointment and even abandonment is palpable. This is what Saint John of the Cross called the Dark Night of the Soul. Yet great spiritual teachers tell us that spirituality nearly always remains a cycle of connection and abandonment, joy and sorrow, mystery felt close at hand and then off at a distance.

This is perhaps partially to teach us that more important than the joy we feel is the way brushes with mystery change us. I always tell people on spiritual retreats that what happens afterward matters, how the experience makes us different. One man I know had fretted all his life about being alone until one day, he told me, "I simply wasn't afraid anymore." He felt that God had touched him, taken away his fear, though he could not say how or why. Others have told me how the experience of mystery has left them more tuned into the interconnectedness of all people and all things. People of most religions know this intellectually, but it is another thing to feel it in one's bones, an experience the monk Thomas Merton likened to "waking from a dream of separateness."

Ultimately, changes worked in people touched by mystery permeate their entire lives. They find themselves "waking up" in a host of ways—knowing themselves as free beings with the divine spark within, capable of tremendous good. This, after all, was what happened to the spiritual giants of history. *Buddha* means "Awakened One." Awakened people accomplish great things, love deeply, behave justly, encourage those they know to do the same.

# CHAPTER TEN

# Practical Comfort

*Life is made up, not of great sacrifices or duties,*
*but of little things, in which smiles, and kindnesses,*
*and small obligations, given habitually, are what*
*win and preserve the heart and secure comfort.*

—HUMPHREY DAVY

## Cultivating Comfort (or the Couch Potato's Dilemma)

I confess: this journey into comfort turned out differently than I expected. Comfort was a simple matter in my estimation. I imagined an exploratory sojourn into the ever-increasing coziness of contemporary life, a metaphorical highway littered with comfort food, firm mattresses, and long warm baths. I planned to catalog the quantity rather than the quality of comfort in the world around us. After all, everywhere we go someone tries to donate, sell, or market comfort and convenience. On the other hand, I felt this would surely make clear the disaster of a world inundated with comfort. People stop reaching and dreaming.

Empathy or compassion loses out to the protection of a person's comfort zone. Everyone wants to be left alone with the Food Channel or ESPN or smartphone solitaire. The piling up of stories, I surmised, would demonstrate how a widening "comfort gap" in the world brought about a kind of mass exodus to Easy Street—the archetypal seat of affluent cushiness, boredom, and indifference to the rest of the world.

While these stereotypes contain a kernel of the truth, from this vantage point near the end of our comfort journey, I see that a bit too much black-and-white thinking crept into my initial notions. It was as if I had planned a talk-radio show on comfort rather than a book. I began with grand, opinionated generalities and forgot to nuance them. I might have titled this *The Comfort Conspiracy*, a locution not far from "the godless church of liberalism," "the gay agenda," or "the neo-con conspiracy." My initial ideas lacked what talk radio lacks—finer details, an openness to the other side, any accounting for the exceptions to the rule. Fortunately, I was urged to produce a steady course of research and feedback from real human beings. Delving into the specifics of brain science, seeking out people's stories, studying up on the psychology of grief and consolation—all these things complicated my initial sweeping generalizations. The central worry about a world of all-comfort and no-challenge did not disappear, but everything began to look different.

Comfort is a human need. Beginning with the most basic physical and emotional levels of our existence, we need recovery and relief from what ails and oppresses us. We are not machines. We need to smile; we need to feel good. As human beings of flesh and blood, heart and spirit, we long for touch and warmth, security and connection, community and meaning in our lives. The need for comfort persists from one end of our lives to the other.

The younger and more fragile we are, the more we focus our energies on elementary forms of comfort, on physical warmth, touch, and security. We know this about ourselves as small children, but we forget as adults. In a vulnerable state—a crisis, an illness—we find ourselves unexpectedly reminded. Why else should we want comfort food when we're sick, a hug when we are scared? I know smart people struggling with mental illness who know that they must have structure and security in their lives—basic comforts.

Of course, the older and more together we feel, the more we seek complex forms of comfort. We want intimacy, spirituality, and meaning. My parents spent their whole lives seeing to the foundational needs of their children, and now they clearly desire a different kind of "comfortable lifestyle." They want to see new places and learn things; they read, travel, and go to museums and the theatre; they want to spend time with their children, their grandchild, and their friends. Living with older adults, I note how it irritates them when they must attend to issues of basic comfort (such as their health) when they would prefer to be learning things and enjoying life. Yet comfort also has a building-block quality to it—the more complex forms stand upon the more basic, which we always need.

Paradoxically, the same flesh-and-blood humanity that makes us *need* comfort also sends us chasing after challenge in our lives. We have bodies and minds highly evolved to respond to a complicated and constantly changing environment. We were literally *made* to learn and grow. Many anthropologists suggest this is exactly what distinguishes human beings from other animals— we have so few instincts that we make a life out of learning. We acquire a culture, negotiate relationships with friends and enemies, recover from pain, and resolve a thousand daily practical problems. Through all of this, we become resilient and resourceful. In other words, without the challenge of navigating major difficulties we cannot become who we are, physically, emotionally, and intellectually. Without a good dose of challenge, normal cycles and phases of development get stunted. Like author Washington Irving's legendary Rip Van Winkle, we essentially go to sleep while the world moves on.

Of course, in reality, avoiding challenges remains as unrealistic as falling asleep for twenty years. Even the most ambitious attempts to protect ourselves from hardship usually fail. I used to live in a gentrified portion of New York City, where many people dwelled in luxury apartments with gorgeous views, central heating and air, and doormen guarding the entrances. Many had short walks to work. You could get almost anything delivered, from furniture to groceries. While I lived there, New York had one of the lowest crime rates in the nation. In theory, this was the good life, protected from many problems other people had to face—commuting snafus, housing trouble, joblessness, poverty, a lack of immigration papers, children in prison. Yet these affluent people could not escape from stress at work, family dysfunction, divorce, alcoholism, and the contingencies of living in the city. Just in the seven years I lived there, we had a major blackout, an anthrax scare, and a terrorist attack. Challenges have a way of penetrating even the most highly developed defenses.

Whoever you are, you will have comforts and you will have challenges. We all find both throughout our everyday lives. This places us in what you might call the "couch potato's dilemma." Like the archetypal couch potato, we all crave comfort. We love our cozy spaces though we know that a pleasant life does not give us enough. How then to "cultivate comfort" in a healthy way while also managing challenges well? These are practical matters.

We might look on them like the old Christian idea of developing good habits or virtues, or the Buddhist idea of a regular spiritual practice. Or perhaps they work more like an art or a craft, perfected in the continued development of specific skills and an aesthetic. Many insights culled from these pages could serve a person in the development of the *practice of comfort*, of "comfort habits" or "comfort skills." In this final chapter I aim only to highlight a handful of practical insights in the hope that all of us can engage the quest for comfort in daily life with greater wisdom and grace.

## The Practice of Love and Community

She poured a tiny bit from the small syrup bottle onto her waffle and then handed it to me, smiling broadly. She knew I would dump the rest on my pancakes. Apparently, after repeated breakfasts, you begin to know how a person handles his syrup.

For five of my seven years in New York City, I breakfasted every Wednesday morning at a diner on Fifty-eighth Street. A dependable group of five or six of us would gather, ranging from a theater costume designer in his early fifties to a retired nurse in her seventies. All were members of the local Catholic parish where I lived. Our conversation ranged from church gossip to political griping to discussion about vacations, jobs, and ailing parents. In effect, we were checking in with one another, keeping tabs on people's lives, creating a space where anyone could vent when necessary—about an angry boss, a wayward cat, a mother losing her memory. Initially I had joined the breakfast group thinking that a good priest appears wherever his parishioners assemble (especially if pancakes are involved). But I kept appearing, week after week. I grew fond of these people. I found that I missed them when I could not get to the diner on a Wednesday. I did not see it right away, but their consistent presence in my life had become a great comfort. In a world of uncertainties, a cadre of friendly faces every week made a great deal of difference. In a world of playing roles for people, a regular place where people expected nothing but my presence felt like a gift.

We all know that our connections to other people bring us comfort—the physical warmth of an embrace, the security of company over time, the renewing fire of sexual love, the self-esteem boosted by affection, and the deep vitality and inspiration bestowed by emotional intimacy. We find out who we are through the other people in our lives. Yet these kinds of connections can also bring us hurt and misery. And so we hesitate. After all, if we seek no embraces or affection, we cannot be rejected. If we do not look to fall in love, we cannot be used. If we do not let people into our lives in a deep way, they cannot scar us. And in our individualized, car-to-house world, it becomes easier than ever to shut other people out.

At certain times in our lives things like friendship, love, and community, they just *happen* to us, almost by surprise. In the 1996 film *The English Patient*, a booby trap kills Sergeant Hardy, the English brother-in-arms of Kip, a Sikh officer from India. Kip is deeply shaken by the man's death, even though he admits he knew nothing about him personally. They had fought side by side for months, constantly under threat. Kip finds himself speechless trying to describe the bond between them. Yet Hana, his French-Canadian lover, is unsurprised at the deep connection among these men. She seems to understand a fundamental fact of human life: in times of crisis, in moments of stress and transition, people find themselves thrown together as if by invisible forces.

But most of our lives do not work out like that. Even that intense period of crisis and transition called "youth" does not last. Life becomes structured and ordinary. We do not go quickly from high to low, and we do not bounce around the world in groups and cliques. Busy about many things, we have to make time for the people in our lives. Connection no longer just *happens.* Friends have to pick up the phone. Church members have to show up every week and sign up for their favorite activities and groups. Married couples have to arrange their schedules to talk (or sometimes even to make love). Love and community, in effect, come to those who choose it as a practice in their lives.

Legend has it that instead of in the usual manner, the Buddha was born from his mother's side next to her heart. The symbolism suggests a life marked by the practice of love and compassion even from the moment of his birth. Most of us are no Buddha or Christ, but we do have great hope for our lives. By choosing to invest ourselves in relationships and community and the good habits that go with them—communication, empathy, compromise, give-and-take, mutual respect—we hope to build a world of comfort not only for ourselves but for the whole world around us.

## The Art of Practical Detachment

A practice like *detachment* hardly sounds like a recipe for comfort. It conjures up images of quiet monks and nuns living on meager rations, walled up in a monastery far away from the rest of the world.

Except that it doesn't really work like that in the monastery. Saint Benedict, one of the founders of monasticism among

Western Christians, maintained that every visitor to a monastery should be welcomed as one would welcome Christ—hardly a formula for quiet isolation. And Buddhist monks call their religion "the Middle Way" because it rejects *both* extremes of pleasure seeking and body-negative austerity. Yet somehow these stereotypes (that *quiet* and *isolated from people* equal *more spiritual*) remain with us, appearing in odd ways. When I was young, people at our Catholic parish overlooked the engaging and opinionated pastor and talked about the quiet, shy, and frequently ill curate as the "holy priest."

But as a real monk or nun would tell you, the *practice of detachment* has less to do with ascetical stereotypes and more to do with a kind of practical simplification process that ultimately makes our lives more comfortable. When I went to Guadalajara, Mexico, to study Spanish for the summer in 1995, I faced luggage limits and had to seriously curtail what I could take with me. Unused to surviving for so long without countless means of amusing myself, I worried as I packed. I needn't have. No longer armed with my usual thousand distractions, I felt a strange sort of freedom. Time seemed more valuable. I studied, talked with my host family, and enjoyed quiet. On the weekends I explored Guadalajara. When I finished my studies, a friend and I hopped a bus to Mexico City without having to haul a thousand pounds of luggage. I did not worry about theft or loss of what little I had. I felt oddly comfortable and free. What I did not have, I did not need. This did not inspire me to get rid of every possession in my closet, but it did persuade me to be less attached to the things I had.

The generosity of others can help communicate the point. I had a classmate in the seminary who would appear in my doorway when he finished a book. "Interested?" he would say, hand-ing me the book. He never seemed to shelve and warehouse books the way I did. Each time he appeared felt like a personal message: books exist to be read, not owned. Of course, there are good reasons to collect books (or anything else for that matter). Certain books we read over and over again. Others serve as reference material. Still others feel like heirlooms, having reached all the way through the pages and into our hearts. But many of the books and possessions we hold on to have no such function at all, either practical or sentimental. We just own things. In fact, many people own so many things today they cannot fit them into their houses and apartments, and so the cities and suburbs brim with storage facilities for our extra stuff.

I admit that *owning things* does bring a certain comfortable satisfaction. You know you are surrounded by whatever you might need or want. But this approach also brings headaches. The more stuff you have (and the more attached to it you are), the more you have to think about storing, insuring, ordering, and keeping track of it. A young professor friend playfully suggested that she needed a full-time personal assistant exclusively devoted to filing, cleaning, and organizing her stuff. She claimed this would increase her productivity a hundredfold, but I told her it would probably just allow her to watch more reality television.

Then, of course, there is the issue of protecting our stuff from theft. The security industry, a business worth hundreds of billions of dollars, can provide people with gates and armed security officers, alarms and video surveillance, walling off upper-middle-class and wealthy neighborhoods from the rest of the human race. Yet the rest of the human race has a way of intruding. When I lived in our fortresslike seminary in Washington, D.C., back in the early 1990s, a particular thief broke in repeatedly to steal our VCR. We called him "Spider-Man" for his extraordinary climbing abilities. Each time we dutifully replaced it, and each time he would snatch it again. One of our priests noted that, of course, the problem would disappear if we didn't *have* a VCR to steal. We laughed nervously at this apparently ridiculous suggestion.

Detachment, however, usually does *not* mean not having things at all. Real poverty is lamentable, and strict voluntary poverty will probably remain the purview of monks, nuns, and a few hearty activists. Instead most of us recognize the benefits in not getting too caught up in too much stuff. This, again, turns out to be a surprisingly practical matter. Practical detachment calls for truly enjoying what we have instead of just collecting it. It asks us to hold on to what is actually *useful*. What if suddenly I do not have the means or the room to keep all my appliances or an extra automobile or books or kitchenware? The owning addiction says I have to find a place for everything. But why? A practical detachment wants to know, "Why not make it available to someone who might need it, either by selling it, loaning it, or giving it away?" Ancient saints and philosophers taught that hanging on to an extra coat or food that you did not need was tantamount to stealing it from the poor. The fourth-century Greek bishop Saint Basil said, "You would call a robber him who strips from the clothed his dress; but does he, who, being able, does not give to one who is in want, merit any other name?"

Practical detachment contends that people are more important than things. We all know how a razor focus on possessions makes people fade into the background. Generosity feels impossible if nothing is more precious than money or possessions. People get lost in the consumer shuffle. Computer games, reorganizing DVDs, and shopping for a new microwave all bring comfort of a certain sort, but as they demand increasing quantities of our time, they take us away from interacting with the people we love. When we have a measured attitude toward the *things* in our lives, we are able to steal ourselves away to pay proper attention to the *people*. In countless ways, this is real and practical comfort to them and to us.

## Big Picture: Comfort Cost-Benefit Analyses

My younger brother used to drive about 130 miles round-trip every day to work. On a very good day, this took him less than an hour and a half each way. An accident or construction on the freeway, however, could delay the trip significantly. My pragmatic brother nursed few illusions about all this. He bought a little car with excellent gas mileage. His wife worked forty miles in the other direction from the quiet suburb where they lived. Until he got his current job as a park ranger, he clearly looked upon this as a necessary evil, what had to be done under the circumstances.

He is certainly not alone in having done this. The Harvard public policy professor Robert Putnam coined the term *suburban triangle* to describe how more and more people live, work, and shop in three different corners that grow farther and farther apart. Putnam's chief concern has been that the triangle phenomenon destroys community involvement—exhausted and scattered people do not have the time or the will to contribute to the local civic good. And long commuting isolates people. More than three-quarters of the workforce drive to work in a car alone. Commuting times have steadily increased. By the turn of the century, Americans spent on average fifty-one minutes getting back and forth from work. A study five years later found that almost 8 percent spent two hours plus on the road every day.

When I lived in New York City, I knew a man who commuted all the way in from Pennsylvania.

My own interest is how commuting functions as a comfort contradiction. Many commuters claim to *appreciate* their hours alone in the car—some even call it "relaxing." Yet hours alone on the road inevitably disconnect people. The more you sit in the car by yourself, the less time you have to spend with your family and friends. Of course, many "realists on the road" acknowledge that commuting is a trade-off. They accept the small irritations of getting behind the wheel week after week in order to have home comforts where they want them. A long ride in a car may feel like a small price to pay in exchange for a nice (or affordable) house in one's suburb of choice. Unfortunately, the trade-off may not be as much of a deal as people think. Research shows that the farther people have to commute, the more miserable they are. Miserable commuters make for miserable families. Nor does it seem that job satisfaction and happy neighborhoods justify the trek. Long commuters tend to be more unhappy with their jobs, dissatisfied with their health, and less content with the environment in which they live. As expected, they mourn lost spare time. Richer or poorer does not matter much. Simply put, long commutes make us more uncomfortable than we think.

However, as the writer Nick Paumgarten rightly points out, not everyone has a choice in the matter. As my brother would have told you, even the choices people do have are limited by the complex calculus of work, marriage, family, and the housing market. Still, the comfort contradictions of commuting remain. Nearly everyone is doing it. The suburbanization and exurbanization of the country depend on it. Yet it does not make us as happy or comfortable as we think. Our comfort cost-benefit analysis is decidedly off.

This isn't the only area of our lives where the big picture of comfort proves elusive. For a long time, sports utility vehicles struck many people as a great experience in driving comfort. The driver sits high on the road, and the vehicles have spacious and cozy interiors. Older folk find them easier to get in and out of, and many parents like their roomy ability to accommodate children and their protective seats, strollers, soccer equipment, skateboards, etc. Fuel bills from these behemoths, however, are not so convenient, and their extra use of gasoline both increases carbon emissions (accelerating global warming) and contributes disproportionately to our ongoing "oil addiction." Their size also makes them more difficult to maneuver on the road than regular automobiles. Research also shows that people in passenger cars struck by SUVs are at greater risk of being killed. SUVs roll over in accidents more often than cars, a sometimes deadly occurrence. These last elements will certainly make the potential driver *less* comfortable getting behind the wheel of an SUV. They form part of the "big picture" of that driver's comfort. Yet admittedly that may be more difficult to keep in perspective than the cushy seats and the roomy interior.

I am not on a campaign against either commuting or SUVs. Neither one is intrinsically evil, and both provide necessary benefits under the right circumstances. My point is that, as a practical matter, we need to take a serious look at the real human costs and benefits of what we *believe* makes us comfortable. I speak not just of money or possessions but of things difficult to assess but more important to us—life, relationships, time, community, the quality of our environment, and happiness. It is not impossible to get a sense of the big picture. We just may need to take a fresh look to see it.

# The Art of Enjoying Life

Waiting for a tour company bus at a hotel in Bath, England, I met a young travel writer from California. I was traveling alone and she was with her ninety-year-old grandmother. The bus arrived late, with only one seat left for the three of us. Needless to say, her grandmother got the place on the bus, and the writer and I went off in search of the train station. Later, on the train, we talked about her travel-writing work in France. "My favorite word in French," she said, "is *parfait*—'perfect.'" In France, she said, people seem to find it easier to appreciate and enjoy the moment—things can seem perfect. In American English, however, *perfect* presents an impossible standard to live up to.

I agreed. In a restless country like the United States, we look on *perfect* as the impossible future to work toward. The present moment is beside the point. We always look ahead to the better-paying job, the bigger house, a place to live with more pleasant weather. Nothing should stay the same; it must improve. If most of us arrived at some moment that began to feel *perfect*—a beautiful day, a fantastic job, a magnificent work of art—we would probably begin to look for ways to enhance it. This does many good things for us as a culture, in terms of productivity and innovation. But, as my train companion pointed out, it makes it that much harder to really be happy in the present moment. It makes it harder than ever to just be comfortable.

We might benefit from the Buddhist spiritual practice of *mindfulness*. This means essentially a discipline of heightened awareness in whatever one does—eating, walking, talking with a friend, working, waiting for the bus. Behind this lies the assumption that much of the time we live an unexamined and automatic life. We do not really know or appreciate what we are doing. We stuff down our food, half listen to the people we encounter, mindlessly groom our amazing bodies, pass by miles of natural wonders without any of them registering on our personal radar. The beautiful and the fascinating surround us, but we do not see them. Once I attended a retreat where, as a meditation exercise, I was instructed to watch insects for half an hour. Initially I dreaded the potential boredom of the exercise, but before many minutes had passed I was captivated. That afternoon I saw butterflies, moths, ants moving large burdens, beetles I could not identify. It was like gaining unexpected entrance to a secret world. Buddhist mindfulness invites all seekers to slow down and take a look, to listen, to notice. It is an invitation to enjoy ourselves more in every moment.

The world may be imperfect and at times immensely frustrating, but it is also stunningly beautiful, interesting, humorous, and fun. As I sat working at my desk one day, a hummingbird passed by my window, beating those marvelous wings at lightning speed. That same week I had the most delicious tuna in a little Spanish restaurant on an alley in San Francisco. Later that year, in the summertime, my aunt came to visit. My sister and I got her going about her high school dating adventures back in Indiana in the 1950s. Some weeks later I met a woman at a Eugene, Oregon, craft fair who makes eccentric little night-lights out of cat-food cans. As I drove back home to Northern California from Oregon, the moon was a silver crescent over the pine-crested mountains. Back home I visited the home of an architect friend of mine. He has a huge, multiframe architectural diagram of Rome on his wall. I found it lying on the floor of his house in sections on that visit—it had slipped from its moorings during a renovation. He dubbed this the "fall of Rome." Late in the summer, I made that trip to England. En route home, I picked up a beautiful but sad British novel in which a child's misunderstanding ruins a young man's life.

All these details from a few months in my life make up a store of richness and grandeur, yet so much of the time I know I have become too busy or preoccupied to notice such things. What does it take to wake up sufficiently to pay attention? It feels easier to persist in an unconscious, uncomfortable life.

During my first year studying for the priesthood, the priest in charge of our novitiate told me he did not believe that Saint Peter would meet us at any pearly gates when we died. This did not particularly faze me—I had always pictured this as more the stuff of jokes than the literal truth. He went on: there would be no ledger of sins and good deeds, nor would there be an interrogation about doctrinal purity or personal faith in Jesus Christ. I obediently played the "straight man" in this routine. "Well then, what will happen?" He said God would simply ask, "Did you have a good time?" The idea sounded preposterous to me, an existential joke. Is life nothing more than one long frat party? I must have looked at him as if he had no sense at all. Now I wonder at what he said, and I believe that rather than advocating hedonism, he was trying to get me to think.

If God went to all the trouble of setting in evolutionary motion a remarkable world, what sort of ungrateful creature doesn't enjoy it? The early Christian theologian Saint Irenaeus once said, "The glory of God is the human person fully alive." I look around at the astonishing beauty of the world, the sheer blessing and gratuity of being alive. Who am I not to enjoy it? It does begin to feel like a commandment: "Thou shalt enjoy thy life."

# The Practice of Humility

The year before I began studying for the priesthood, I worked in Northern California as a fund-raiser for the Muscular Dystrophy Association. One beautiful day I was visiting businesses in downtown Santa Cruz, trying to get them to participate in an MDA program. A homeless man and I ended up standing at the same street corner, waiting for the light to cross. A middle-aged white man with a long gray beard, he looked a little weary but friendly enough. He asked for some change, but I had none. We struck up a conversation. "Are you a lawyer or something?" He eyed my shirt, tie, and dress slacks. Santa Cruz is a beach town, with the usual informal dress code. I replied nervously, "No, actually I'm a fund-raiser for charity." "No kidding?" And when I nodded, he smiled and added, "Me, too."

I chuckle when I think of that afternoon, which occurred in January of 1991. With a quick retort, the man had ingeniously but gently prodded himself and me with ironic humor. He drew attention to his own begging, a shameful behavior in our society, while at the same time pointing out that my "respectable trade" of fund-raising was essentially little more than professional begging. We were the same, he and I. He never treated me with deference, even as he asked me for a handout. In fact, he really set the terms for our subsequent conversation. As far as he was concerned, we were equals in dignity, even if we weren't equals in social station or appearance. I liked him for that. I thought, now here is a man who realistically knows who he is and who he is not. There is comfort in that.

. . .

So much human energy gets spent on pretense, subterfuge, competition for status and prestige. We cover over our own pettiness and weaknesses, as if every other human being did not suffer the same. We fear we will never be as beautiful or handsome or clever or talented as the other people in our lives. Our insecurities and fears lead us away from a realistic sense of the landscape of our own gifts and talents, flaws and limits.

As a priest, I have spent a fair amount of time hearing confessions. Listening to people meditate on their biggest weaknesses and worst mistakes (and obsess over their minor lapses) offers a person perspective. I can tell you that the nicely coiffed people with good manners and well-behaved children do not have perfect lives. Everyone has skeletons in the family closets. Everyone possesses embarrassing frailties. Everyone has secrets.

We all need the clarity of the homeless man, who knew *both* his frailty and his dignity. He understood himself as a citizen with rights like everyone else but also as a beggar without access to "polite society." Eschewing pretense for clarity, we might call this the "practice of humility." It inevitably brings comfort. We simply are who we are, warts and all. More often than not, that allows other people to feel they can be who they are.

## The End of Comfort

What lies at the end of this journey of comfort?

Friedrich Nietzsche famously wrote in *Twilight of the Idols*, "That which does not kill me makes me stronger." Everyone knows that surviving and learning from our challenges brings us strength. But what of comfort itself? Does it ultimately only make us weak? Or as its etymology suggests, does it also make us strong?

On the one hand, there is the couch potato side of comfort. To my knowledge, no one has ever gotten stronger through air-conditioning. No one has ever built up their internal reservoir of courage watching the weekend *Gilligan's Island* marathon on TV Land. On the other hand, other kinds of comfort—friendship, good family connections, mentoring, the reassuring presence of others in a time of crisis—without a doubt these do renew us and make us stronger. Even comforts more basic do this for us: good shoes, a firm mattress, regular coffee breaks, financial security. A strong sense of faith and a solid spirituality make people stronger. Otherwise the survivors of addiction, war, and grave illness would not claim that it was so.

Perhaps the highway of comfort does flow onto an avenue of strength.

The problems come on the detours. It is not so much that comfort itself spoils or weakens us. Rather, it is the associated temptation to run away from trials and difficulties. Once immersed in ease, we become fearful and unwilling to seek the life lessons that make us stronger. Perhaps comfort gets a bad name because a small class of creatures comforts—our electronic distractions and cushy chairs—can serve as a shelter or vehicle for escape when we want to avoid what we must inevitably face. What do we do? It is once again the "couch potato's dilemma."

Comfort is strength, the ability to struggle and go on. But really that is only half the story.

In an April 2001 *New York Times Magazine* article about the so-called lost boys of Sudan, writer Sara Corbett embarks on a supermarket shopping expedition with Peter, Riak, and Maduk, three Sudanese refugee brothers in their teens and twenties. Having survived a trek across the desert and grueling years in refugee camps, they find themselves face-to-face with a virtual cornucopia of goods they have never laid eyes on. They end up in the pet-food aisle, where Corbett tries to explain the logic of rows upon rows of dog-food cans to young men who have had nothing but rations of porridge to eat for years. Peter, the oldest, seems to understand. He turns to Corbett and asks a question that shows he assumes that dogs must perform some important job in America. Reading the article, I thought of horses and oxen. The article does not record her response. His comment reminded me once again of the vast difference in material comforts between the so-called first world (and especially the United States) and the majority of the world. But it also made me think about the point of comfort.

When we have so much comfort in our corner of the world, we might legitimately be asked by someone like Peter, "What is it for?" Then we could say that it gives us strength. But then why do we need so much strength? Some do face significant personal threats: unemployment, illness, cutthroat neighborhoods, family stress. Lots of strength means survival and success under threat. Others of us, however, might ask ourselves what good we intend to do with the strength we have accumulated from our comforts. The New Testament says, "From everyone to whom much has been given, much will be required" (Luke 12:48, NRSV). If a large tree branch fell on a car in a storm, injuring the mother and children inside, no strong person would hesitate to come, lift the branch from the car, and rescue the family. Yet problems and disasters lurk everywhere in the world all the time, and strength is more than physical. Our surplus of comfort and strength could always go to good use in a troubled world.

The funny thing is that most people find great *comfort* in using their strength to help others and do good. Both times I went with a small group to desperately poor places to help with building projects—once at an orphanage in Nicaragua, another time in a slum in Tijuana, Mexico—no person complained about the lack of "creature comforts," even though at times the food and sleeping arrangements were far below what people were accustomed to. No doubt they would have felt ashamed to complain, having seen the far humbler local living conditions. But also people got caught up in the work; they found meaning and consolation contributing to something that made other people's lives better.

What if we looked upon all the comforts in our lives as equipping us to dedicate ourselves to some greater purpose, to do some good in this world? In college I had a boss who was a confirmed atheist. We got in constant arguments; he liked and respected me, and he found it inconceivable that I could find solace in religious beliefs. But one day after yet another heated debate, he put his hand on my shoulder and said, "Brett, we don't agree on this, but we agree on something. It's not enough just to live for yourself. You need to live for something bigger than you in this world." He believed this, and it made a difference for him. After all, what comfort is it to know at the end of a life that you pleased yourself, protected your turf, or "maintained your lifestyle"? What good is that? Who would want to be remembered for that?

We have only one life. With all the comfort and strength we have been given, what will we do with it? The highway of comfort may flow onto an avenue of strength, but where it goes from there is up to us.

# NOTES

## CHAPTER ONE: The Human Story of Comfort

Statistics comparing generational mass attendance come from the Center for
Applied Research in the Apostolate at Georgetown University (2002). The
information about Abraham Lincoln's inability to sit still for a photograph
comes from "Abraham Lincoln's Fight with Depression," *Ability Magazine*
(Abraham Lincoln Issue), http://www.abilitymagazine.com/abe_story.html.

## CHAPTER TWO: The Anatomy of Comfort

*Comfort 101*: The quote from Mark Twain comes from his book *Roughing It*
(Hartford, CT: American Publishing Company, 1891), pp. 140–141. The
monkey study was reported in Harry Harlow, "The Nature of Love,"
*American Psychologist 13* (1958): pp. 573–685; and Carol Tomlinson-Keasey,
*Child Development* (Homewood, IL: Dorsey Press, 1985), pp. 276–278.

*Comfort Physiology*: For the general physiology of comfort, see Harold M. Kaplan,
Ph.D., and Lee A. Kaplan, M.D., "The Physiology of Comfort," *Transactions
of the Illinois State Academy of Science* 95:2 (2002), pp. 99–106. Information
on the physiology of emotions can be found in Daniel Goleman, *Emotional
Intelligence: Why It Can Matter More Than IQ* (New York: Bantam, 1995).
Page 6 in Goleman's book specifically discusses the impact of anger on the
body as found in this chapter. Sources for the information about emotions
and the anatomy of the brain include Goleman, *Emotional Intelligence*, pp.
13–29; and Harold M. Kaplan, Ph.D., and Lee A. Kaplan, M.D., "The Physiology of Comfort," pp. 99–106. The point about there being no definite

"comfort center" in the brain is made in Kaplan and Kaplan, "The Physiology of Comfort," p. 105.

*The Feel of Comfort*: Katharine Kolcaba's nursing theory regarding comfort can be found in Katharine Kolcaba, "Comfort Theory and Its Application to Pediatric Nursing," *Pediatric Nursing* 31:3 (May 1, 2005), pp. 187–195; in her book *Comfort Theory and Practice: A Vision for Holistic Health Care and Research* (New York: Springer, 2003), pp. 14, 34–35; and in an article she wrote with her husband, Katharine Kolcaba and Raymond J. Kolcaba, "An Analysis of the Concept of Comfort," *Journal of Advanced Nursing* 16 (1991), pp. 1301–1310.

*Comfort Food and the Mission of Meatloaf*: The "rat comfort food" study is found in Mary F. Dallman, et al, "Chronic Stress and Obesity: A New View of 'Comfort Food,'" *Proceedings of the National Academy of Sciences* 100:20 (Setpember 30, 2003), pp. 11696–11701. They make the argument about comfort food as a response to stress but overuse as causing obesity on page 11700.

*Cultured Comfort*: The story about children in mission schools comes from Louis Luzbetak, *The Church and Cultures: New Perspectives in Missiological Anthropology* (Maryknoll, NY: Orbis, 1989), p. 184. The point about "getting acquainted" questions being impolite in the Southwest comes from Guadalupe Valdés, *Con Respeto: Bridging the Distances Between Culturally Diverse Families and Schools: An Ethnographic Portrait* (New York: Teachers College Press, 1996), p. 11.

*Say the Word*: For the information on nursing studies, see Kolcaba, *Comfort Theory and Practice: A Vision for Holistic Health Care and Research*; Kolcaba, "Comfort Theory"; and Kolcaba and Kolcaba, "An Analysis of the Concept of Comfort." The information on Victorian-era comfort can be found in John R. Gillis, *A World of Their Own Making: Myth, Ritual, and the Quest for Family Values* (Cambridge, MA: Harvard University Press, 1997), p. 119.

**CHAPTER THREE: American Comfort**

I am very indebted in this chapter to social historian Merritt Ierley's excellent book *The Comforts of Home* (New York: Clarkson Potter Publishers, 1999).

*Comfort by the Numbers*: The initial information on comfort in Europe and the United States in comparison came from "Alabama, France of the

South," *Atlantic Monthly* 294:2 (September 2004), p. 50. Automobile figures come from European Commission figures for the twenty-five nations of the new European Union from 2003—figures are for passenger cars per one thousand people. Figures on per capita consumption in Europe vs. the U.S.A. come from Fredrik Bergström and Robert Gidehag, "EU Versus USA," from the Timbro economic think tank in Stockholm, Sweden, pp. 12–15. Info on central heating, household appliances, air-conditioning, and television sets are from the Residential Energy Consumption Survey of the Energy Information Administration of the Department of Energy, 2005. Statistics on house size come from the U.S. Census Bureau's "Annual Characteristics of New Housing," and from the National Association of Home Builders' report "House Facts, Figures and Trends," both the version issued in August 2005 and the one from May 2007. Add stats about household size from the U.S. Census Bureau and you get space-per-person comparisons. Juliet B. Schor did this in *The Overworked American: The Unexpected Decline of Leisure* (New York: Basic Books, 1991), pp. 109–110, but I have refigured it and updated it here. Statistics about television, computers, DVDs, and VCRs come from the 2005 Residential Energy Consumption Survey. The information on Internet use comes from *Cyberstats* by Mediamark Research and Intelligence from 2008 (and available on the U.S. Census Web site). Car and telephone statistics come from the 2009 American Community Survey of the U.S. Census Bureau. Statistics on poverty, the income gap, and reduced social mobility come from the U.S. Census Bureau's Current Population Surveys 2009 as reported in the 2010 Census report by Carmen DeNavas-Walt, Bernadette D. Proctor, and Jessica Smith, "Income, Poverty, and Health Insurance Coverage in the United States: 2009"; and in Clive Crook, "Rags to Riches, Riches to Rags," *Atlantic Monthly*, June 2007. The stats comparing U.S. financial comfort to that of Europe come from "Alabama, France of the South," p. 50.

*Before Comfort*: The information for the snapshot of Philadelphia in the 1780s comes from Gillis, *A World of Their Own Making*, p. 37; and from Merritt Ierley, *The Comforts of Home*, pp. 16–32. The post–Civil War snapshot info adds to the background from Gillis and Ierley. It was found in Gina Kolata, "So Big and Healthy Grandpa Wouldn't Even Know You," *New York Times* (July 30, 2006), p. A1. The infant mortality rate in 1850 comes from Michael Haines's article "Fertility and Mortality in the United States," posted on the Economic History Association's Web site (EH.net). The note about standard of living in 1860s comes from Ierley, *The Comforts of Home*, p. 94, as does the general background information about nineteenth-century levels of comfort. Information on historical changes in food prices comes from an article by Dr. Karen Carr (Portland State University) on "Food in North America after 1500," on the Web site Kidipedia (history forkids.org).

*A Map of the Comfortable Home*: It is Merritt Ierley who makes the argument that water and power (and also increased wages) were crucial to the progress of American homes in comfort in his book *The Comforts of Home*. Tales of Victorian homes becoming more private and of emotional importance occur in Gillis's book *A World of Their Own Making* on pp. 109–129. The story of central heating and accompanying developments comes from the U.S. Census Bureau (1940) and from Ierley's book, pp. 200–206; the story of the bathroom's transformation can be found on pp. 220–228. The point about air-conditioning becoming available after World War II is found in this book on p. 211. The information on the modernization of the kitchen comes from Ierley's section on it in *The Comforts of Home,* pp. 235–249, and the info on laundry comes from pp. 229–232. Much of the information on middle-class home ownership after World War II comes from Stephanie Coontz, *The Way We Never Were: American Families and the Nostalgia Trap* (New York: Basic Books, 1992), pp. 76–79. *Is Everybody Comfy?*: Abhijit V. Banerjee and Esther Duflo wrote about conveniences in the third world in "The Economic Lives of the Poor," MIT Department of Economics Working Paper no. 06-29, February 9, 2007. Stats about phone service are from the U.S. Census Bureau, American Community Survey, Selected Housing Characteristics, 2009. Digital-divide stats are from the National Telecommunications and Information Administration, and from a report of the National Center for Education Statistics of Institute of Education Sciences of the U.S. Department of Education: "Computer and Internet Use by Students in 2003," September 2006, and from Robert Putnam, *Bowling Alone* (Cambridge, MA: Harvard University Press, 2000), pp. 174–175. The statistic on health care comes from Carmen DeNavas-Walt, Bernadette D. Proctor, and Jessica Smith, "Income, Poverty, and Health Insurance Coverage in the United States: 2006," a U.S. Census Bureau Report, 2007, pp. 18–19. The note on mortality and lack of health insurance comes from a review of research: Institute of Medicine, *Insuring America's Health—Principles and Recommendations*

(The National Academies Press, 2004). The Institute of Medicine is part of the National Academy of Sciences. The statistics on unemployment during the Great Recession and race come from "State of the Dream 2010: Drained," United for a Fair Economy (based on Bureau of Labor Statistics data), www.faireconomy.org/dream. The information on home loans and race came from "Unfair Lending: The Effect of Race and Ethnicity on the Price of Subprime Mortgages," Center for Responsible Lending, 2006.

CHAPTER FOUR: When Comfort Goes Bad

On James Olds's experiment with rats, see "Science's Growing Fix on Addiction," *Howard Hughes Medical Institute Bulletin* 14:1 (January 2001), on the Web at http://www.hhmi.org/bulletin/addiction/addiction2.html. Regarding the Detroit newspaper's attempt to pay people to give up TV, see Putnam, *Bowling Alone*, pp. 240. Stan Cox's book *Losing Our Cool: Uncomfortable Truths about Our Air-Conditioned World* was published by the New Press in 2010. For the material on the hero's adventure, I am indebted to Joseph Campbell's famous work *The Hero with a Thousand Faces* (Cleveland: Meridian Books, 1956), especially pp. 3–25, 49–58, 97–109.

CHAPTER FIVE: Home Alone

*The Home as Comfy Castle:* The story of the family's ascendancy over village community can be found in Gillis, *A World of Their Own Making*, pp. 3–57. Coontz's work on American family privacy appears in Stephanie Coontz, *The Way We Never Were*, pp. 93–121. She goes on to write about boardinghouses and private space as a condition of welfare on pp. 133–137. Pp. 24 and 76–79 describe the rise of single-family home ownership after World War II.

*Home Alterations*: Moving and household statistics are from the 2009 American Community Survey. Divorce statistics are from the Centers for Disease Control. According to the 2000 census, 8 percent of households are people living together outside marriage and 1 percent are gay couples. The information on living alone comes from the U.S. Census Bureau, Census 2000: Table DP-1, Profile of General Demographic Characteristics; *Demographic Trends in the 20th Century*, p. 148.

*Channeling Comfort*: The stat about TV and leisure time comes from Robert Kubey and Mihaly Csikszentmihalyi, *Television and the Quality of Life* (Hillsdale, NJ: Lawrence Erlbaum Associates, 1990), p. 24; and from Putnam, *Bowling Alone*, pp. 221–223, 240. The info on the "physiology of TV" is found in Kubey and Csikszentmihalyi, *Television and the Quality of Life*, pp. 37, 139. Csikszentmihalyi writes about TV's impact on a nervous system designed for "fight or flight" in *Finding Flow* (New York: Basic Books, 1997), p. 66. In Kubey and Csikszentmihalyi, *Television and the Quality of Life*, pp. 129, 137, there is the source material I used here on the brain and TV, and pp. 158–160 discuss the impact of heavy viewing on the sadness and irritability that I mention. Steven Johnson provides the counterpoint in an article, "Watching TV Makes You Smarter," *New York Times Magazine*, April 25, 2005. Robert Putnam in *Bowling Alone*, pp. 190–191, 222–223, discusses how TV takes up people's leisure time, and Kubey and Csikszentmihalyi in *Television and the Quality of Life*, on pp. 150–151, 157–162 (and Putnam, *Bowling Alone*, on pp. 240–241) take on the question of isolation and heavy viewing.

*Virtually Connected*: Internet statistics are from the U.S. Department of Commerce, Economics and Statistics Administration, and National Telecommunications and Information Administration, *A Nation Online: Entering the Broadband Age*. The 2007 information on Internet use comes from *Cyberstats* by Mediamark Research and Intelligence from 2008 (and available on the U.S. Census Web site). Facebook statistics come from Facebook.com. The 2004 survey on what to bring to a desert island is from IPSOS Insight US Express Omnibus August 2004 and reported in "Primary Sources," in the January/February 2005 issue of the *Atlantic Monthly*. The research on the Internet bringing people together comes from Putnam's book *Bowling Alone*, pp. 172–173, but the note about missing nonverbals also comes from that book, pp. 174–178.

## CHAPTER SIX: A Comfortable Living

*Blessed Are the Poor*: Statistics on poverty and health insurance come from the 2009 American Community Survey.

*The Tyranny of Expectations*: See Juliet Schor, *The Overspent American: Why We Want What We Don't Need* (New York: HarperCollins, 1998), pp. 121–124, on these "lifestyle comparisons," including the point about TV and petty theft. Malcolm Gladwell discusses the tipping point in *The Tipping Point: How Little Things Can Make a Big Difference* (Boston: Back Bay Books, 2002), pp. 1–29. Schor continues about the consequences of comparison in making a lifestyle in *The Overspent American*, pp. 129–133. On Salman Rushdie's tale of thwarted expectations in New York, see especially p. 184 of Salman Rushdie, *Fury* (New York: Random House, 2001). Juliet Schor's discussion of a pattern of unhappiness and the work-and-spend cycle is found in another book, *The Overworked American: The Unexpected Decline of Leisure* (New York: Basic Books, 1992), pp. 115–116. The material on downshifting in Juliet Schor's work is found in *The Overspent American*, pp. 113–142.

*The Bread of Comfort*: Data on street children can be found in the United Nations International Children's Emergency Fund report, "The State of the World's Children 2006: Excluded and Invisible," available online at http://www.unicef.org. The note about families being among the fastest-growing groups among homeless people can be found in a report by the National Coalition for the Homeless, "Homeless Families with Children," June 2006. On the "Justice for Janitors" campaign, see the paper by Roger Waldinger, Chris Erickson, Ruth Milkman, Daniel J. B. Mitchell, Abel Valenzuela, Kent Wong, and Maurice Zeitlin, "Helots No More: A Case Study of the Justice for Janitors Campaign in Los Angeles," Lewis Center for Regional Policy Studies, Working Paper Series 15 (1996). The information on foreign aid comes from FAIR—Fairness and Accuracy in Reporting.

## CHAPTER SEVEN: The Comfort of Company

*It's Not Good for the Man to Be Alone*: The review of research on extreme isolation came from the July 29, 1988, issue of *Science* as reported in Daniel Goleman, *Emotional Intelligence*, pp. 178–179. Other data on isolation and on the connection between happiness and social connections also came from Goleman's book. For the research on how having loved ones in one's life helps people survive illness, see Jimmie Holland, M.D., and Sheldon Lewis, *The Human Side of Cancer: Living with Hope, Coping with Uncertainty*, pp. 34–37; and Daniel Goleman, *Emotional Intelligence*, pp. 178–181.

*Families by Any Other Name*: For more information on our world of diffuse connections, see Robert Wuthnow, *Loose Connections: Joining Together in*

*America's Fragmented Communities* (Cambridge, MA: Harvard University Press, 2002). Psychologist Mihaly Csikszentmihalyi writes about making your family a family of choice in *Finding Flow*, pp. 85–89.

*Comfortable in Common*: The note on "lifestyle enclaves" comes from Robert Bellah, et al, *Habits of the Heart: Individualism and Commitment in American Life*, updated edition (Berkeley: University of California Press, 1996), pp. 71–75. Nina Eliasoph's article about avoiding politics is "'Close to Home': The Work of Avoiding Politics," *Theory and Society* 26 (1997): pp. 605–647.

*Mentor Me Mucho*: On Jefferson and his legacy from mentoring, see David C. Whitney, *The American Presidents: Biographies of the Executives* (New York: Doubleday, 1975), pp. 26–38; Willard Sterne Randall, *Thomas Jefferson: A Life* (New York: HarperPerennial, 1993), pp. 33–88; and Merrill D. Peterson, *Thomas Jefferson and the New Nation* (New York: Oxford University Press, 1975), pp. 1–19. On Saint Clare, see Joanne Turpin, *Women in Church History* (Cincinnati: St. Anthony Messenger Press, 1989), pp. 101–109. On Confucius, see Mihaly Csikszentmihalyi, *The Evolving Self: Psychology for the Third Millennium* (New York: HarperCollins, 1993), pp. 258–260. The tales of Elijah and Elisha can be found in the Jewish and Christian Bibles in 1 Kings 19:15–21 and 2 Kings 2:1–25 (the notation is, of course, the Christian one).

CHAPTER EIGHT: Comfort in Crisis

*On Sending Angels Away*: For many of these examples of common American sayings, I am indebted to Gary M. Wederspahn's article "Avoiding the 'Ugly American' Stereotypes," *Practical Planet*, Tales from a Small Planet Literature, available on the Web at http://www.talesmag.com/tales/practical/ugly_american.shtml.

*Good Mourning*: I am, of course indebted to Elisabeth Kübler-Ross in this section, and I have made use of her book as a source to build upon with my own experience. On the possibility of hope and peace in death in Kübler-Ross's work (and the resources we have for this), see *On Death and Dying* (New York: Macmillan Publishing, 1969), pp. 122–138. Paul K. Maciejewski, Ph.D.; Baohui Zhang, MS; Susan D. Block, MD; and Holly G. Prigerson, Ph.D. wrote about a recent study reviewing Kübler-Ross's stages, "An Empirical Examination of the Stage Theory of Grief," *Journal of the American Medical Association* 297:7 (February 21, 2007), pp. 716–723. The material on yearning comes from them. On denial and isolation in Kübler-Ross, see *On Death and Dying*, pp. 34–43. On anger (and in particular anger at God—she mentions the well-known Yiddish proverb), see Kübler-Ross, *On Death and Dying*, pp. 43–71. Kübler-Ross's piece on bargaining is found in *On Death and Dying*, pp. 72–74. The parts I refer to on depression are found in Kübler-Ross, *On Death and Dying*, pp. 75–98. Kübler-Ross's writings on acceptance referred to here are in *On Death and Dying*, pp. 99–121.

## CHAPTER NINE: Spiritual Comfort and a God for Grown-Ups

*A Pastiche of Spiritual Comfort:* The information on American belief and church attendance comes from the U.S. Religious Landscape Survey, June 2008, by the Pew Forum for Religion and Public Life; the figures on the connection between volunteering, charity, and religious organizations comes from Putnam, *Bowling Alone*, pp. 65–69. The quote from the Katha Upanishad, I.iii.i14, is from p. 14 of the Upanishads as translated by Max Müller in the series *Sacred Books of the East* (New York: The Christian Literature Co., 1897). The information on Jonathan Edwards's context comes from Eugene Taylor, *Shadow Culture: Psychology and Spirituality in America* (Washington, D.C.: Counterpoint, 1999), pp. 27–33.

*The God of Comfort and the Comfortable God:* I am indebted to Sister Mary Kay Oosdyke, OP, for the story about Communion and toothpaste. Thanks to my friend Rabbi Rachel Miller for the interpretation of the *sefirot*. See also Lawrence Kushner, *Honey from the Rock: Visions of Jewish Mystical Renewal* (Woodstock, VT: Jewish Lights, 1977), pp. 124–125. The story about the Buddha and the merchant Yasa is from Karen Armstrong's biography *Buddha*, Penguin Lives (New York: Viking Penguin, 2001), pp. 116–118. Moralistic Therapeutic Deism is discussed in Christian Smith and Melinda Lundquist Denton's book, *Soul Searching: The Religious and Spiritual Lives of American Teenagers* (New York: Oxford University Press, 2005), especially pp. 118–171. For the story of the massacre at El Mozote, I am indebted to Mark Danner's now-famous account in *The New Yorker* magazine, "The Truth of El Mozote," December 6, 1993. I also read the account of the El Mozote massacre in the report of the El Salvador Truth Commission entitled, "From Madness to Hope: The Twelve-Year War in El Salvador," which presents forensic evidence to back up Danner's claims.

*God for Grown-Ups*: For the story of Malcolm X, see *The Autobiography of Malcolm X* (New York: Ballantine Books, 1965), as told to Alex Haley. Also, Hans A. Baer and Merrill Singer, *African American Religions: Varieties of Protest and Accommodations,* 2nd edition (Knoxville, TN: University of Tennessee Press, 2002), pp. 123–129, 145–151. James Fowler offers basic information about the individual decision making in the Individuative-Reflective stage of faith in *Stages of Faith: The Psychology of Human Development and the Quest for Meaning* (New York: HarperCollins, 1981), pp. 174–183. He talks about images of God in different faith stages on p. 31 of *Stages of Faith.* The story about the Buddha and the demon Mara is found in Karen Armstrong, *Buddha,* pp. 90–92.

*Beyond Words*: The statistic on churchgoing and local community involvement comes from Robert Putnam, *Bowling Alone,* pp. 66–69. The story and quote from Thomas Merton's experience in Louisville comes from Thomas Merton, *Conjectures of a Guilty Bystander* (Garden City, NY: Image Books, 1968), p. 157. The information about how unusual Saint Francis's love of animals was in his time is found in David Chidester, *Christianity: A Global History* (New York: HarperCollins, 2000), pp. 248–254. The quote from Catherine of Genoa comes from Baron von Hügel's book, *The Mystical Element of Religion,* volume 1 (London: Dent, 1909), p. 159. The quote from Saint Teresa of Avila is my translation from her original *Obras Completas.* The quote about waking from separateness comes from the same book by Merton, *Conjectures of a Guilty Bystander,* p. 156.

## CHAPTER TEN: Practical Comfort

*The Practice of Love and Community*: The story of the Buddha's birth from his mother's side is found in Karen Armstrong's biography *Buddha,* p. 95.

*The Art of Practical Detachment*: The size of the security industry came from Jasmin Persch, "Espionage for Sale at Spybase.com," *Paramus Post,* August 30, 2006. The quote from Saint Basil of Caesarea on not giving to the poor being tantamount to stealing from them comes from "Extract from Homily on Pulling Down and Building Greater," *The Post-Nicene Greek Fathers,* edited by Reverend George A. Jackson (New York: D. Appleton and Co., 1883), pp. 92–93.

*The Art of the Big Picture*: Robert Putnam writes about the suburban triangle phenomenon and its consequences in *Bowling Alone*, pages 211–214. See also Putnam's Comments in Nick Paumgarten, "There and Back Again: The Soul of the Commuter," *New Yorker*, April 16, 2007. The figures on commuting time come from the 1980 Census and 2000 Census, American Community Surveys, 2002 and 2005 (U.S. Census Bureau). For the information about commuters seeing time in their car as a bonus, I am indebted to Putnam, *Bowling Alone*, pp. 211–213; and Paumgarten, "There and Back Again: The Soul of the Commuter." Both Putnam and Paumgarten refer to the isolation as well. Paumgarten also points to an important study: Alois Stutzer and Bruno S. Fey, "Stress That Doesn't Pay: The Commuting Paradox," Discussion Paper Series (Bonn, Germany: Forschungsinstitut zur Zukunft der Arbeit/Institute for the Study of Labor, August 2004). In that study, Stutzer and Fey offer the data that I present here about how long commuters are less content. I am indebted to Nick Paumgarten, "There and Back Again: The Soul of the Commuter" for the reminder that not everyone has a choice. The deadliness and greater frequency of SUV rollovers is pointed out in National Highway Traffic and Safety Administration research.

*The End of Comfort*: The story of the lost boys supermarket expedition comes from Sara Corbett, "The Lost Boys of Sudan: The Long, Long, Long Road to Fargo," *New York Times Magazine*, April 1, 2001.

# INDEX